Editor's Note

Jonathan Wilson, Editor

It was a summer of enormous transfers that confirmed what we already knew: football has entered its third age. It has gone from being a sport to being a business to being, well, what, exactly? Some sort of game for the mega-rich? A propaganda tool for oligarchs and the commodities industry? Something, anyway, in which it's impossible for 11 men from Montevideo or Glasgow or Amsterdam or wherever to develop a style of football that multiplies their individual abilities to the point at which they can conquer the world.

Once romantics reflected gloomily on a world in which balance sheets vied in importance with league tables. Now we look back wistfully on those days. Arsenal, sitting on cash reserves of over £150 million, are openly derided. Up to a point that is understandable — fans who pay the highest season ticket prices in the world are quite right to demand that their money is spent on improving the football they watch rather than building up interest — and yet Arsenal's achievement, competing with the best while making a profit, is remarkable. Besides which, the fact is that for them spending money still has consequences. They have worked hard to build those resources and would rather not waste them. They're not like the sheikhs of Qatar or Abu Dhabi or the oligarchs of the former Soviet Union: their pockets are not bottomless.

As I wrote in *The Guardian* recently, football has become the preserve of a handful of superclubs (at times in the eighties you could look over the previous five seasons and see 17 or 18 different European Cup semi-finalists; over the past five years the total is nine). It's true, of course, that there have always been teams with more money than the others and that they have tended to prosper, but this is different because of the nature of the wealth of the present breed of owners, for whom there are, effectively, no consequences. After Nottingham Forest had won a second European Cup in 1980, they could have become a major European force; as it was, they took on significant debts to build a new stand and wasted around £2.5m on Justin Fashanu, Ian Wallace and Peter Ward. The result was that they remained another provincial side who punched above their weight for a while before reality set in. A Paris St-Germain or a Manchester City, though, can waste £250m every year if need be — it matters only in so far as Financial Fair Play has any grip.

That means a mental recalibration. Footballs tiers are more rigid than ever before and can be broken only by enormous investment where previously a clever manager and a decent crop of young players might have been enough. These days the occasional surprise team does emerge to play brilliantly for a few months but, as Athletic Bilbao, Shakhtar Donetsk and even Borussia Dortmund have found, the best players are skimmed off and they must begin again the wearying process of building. And of course Athletic, Shakhtar and Dortmund are doing exactly the same to the teams in the tier below them, and so on down the chain. That's always been the case to an extent, but the modern distribution of revenues and the investments from the incomprehensibly rich have made the process happen more quickly than ever before.

There is a benefit, in that the best teams are probably better than any teams have ever been before; the quality of football in some games in the later stages of the Champions League is extraordinary, but the cost has been to render most domestic leagues less competitive (the Premier League this season, old certainties shaken by the richest three clubs all changing coach, is a happy exception). The gap between the top two and the rest in Spain this season could be embarrassing. Nick Harris looked at 14 leagues across Europe and found that in only one, England, were more than three teams priced at 10-1 or shorter to win the title. In many there were only two — and in Scotland, only one.

That is a worrying trend and it points in only one direction: some sort of superleague in which the superclubs clash on a regular basis. It may not happen soon, but the path is clearly marked. Perhaps that will deliver even better football, perhaps, if a regionalised pyramid can be organised, it can even stimulate the game in countries in which the league is moribund, but it's hard not to feel that much of the game's soul would have been lost.

....

Finally, an apology. One of the driving forces in establishing *The Blizzard* was to treat writers with respect, so it's embarrassing and chastening to have failed in the standards we set ourselves. Owing to an authorial oversight, a couple of lines from Wayne Gamble's Leeds United blog thebeatengeneration. co.uk appeared unattributed in Anthony Clavane's piece *That Grandish Pile of Swank*. I'm happy to say that Wayne has accepted Anthony's explanation of how the slip occurred, but obviously it shouldn't have happened. Sorry.

September 2013

Stroke is the third biggest killer and the leading cause of severe adult disability in the UK.

Behind much of the Stroke Association's unique work are people just like you – people who want to do something powerful and lasting through their Will.

To find out more about leaving a gift in your Will please call us on **020 7566 1505** or email **legacy@stroke.org.uk**

stroke.org.uk

Stroke association

Contents

The Blizzard, Issue Ten

FSC
www.fsc.org
MIX
Paper from responsible sources
FSC® C008152

Forgotten

"I had an idea, but my legs could
not turn it into reality."

The Dreamers

Amid the protests of 1968, a group of journalists took French football leaders hostage

By Philippe Auclair

"What characterises our public life at the moment is boredom. The French are bored. They play no part, from close or from afar, in the great convulsions which are shaking the world. [...] Our youth is bored. Students are demonstrating and fighting in Spain, Italy, Belgium, Algeria, Japan, America, Egypt, Germany —even in Poland. They feel that they have something to conquer, a voice of protest they want to be heard, [while] French students concern themselves with questions such as whether the girls of Nanterre and Antony [universities] will be allowed to have free access to the boys' bedrooms — a somewhat limited conception of human rights."

François Viansson-Ponté of *Le Monde* wrote those words on 15 March 1968. A week later, a group of those sex-mad students, 150 of them at most, shook off their boredom and stormed the administrative quarters of the University of Nanterre and occupied its eighth floor, calling for the release of six extreme left-wing militants who'd been arrested after the sack of the American Express HQ in Paris — a violent but mostly symbolic attack on US imperialism at the height of the Vietnam War, one of several sporadic explosions of unrest which had pricked France's apathy for several months but which no one, and certainly not Viansson-

Ponté, had guessed would lead to what is now known as the 'failed revolution'('*la révolution manquée*') of 1968.

In my native Yvetot, a market town where no one had any recollection of anything ever happening since German bombers had razed most of it in 1940, by mistake it seems, the news that a few excitable admirers of Leon Trotsky and, hard as it is to believe today, Lin Biao and Mao Zedong, had made nuisances of themselves on a university campus barely created a stir. A benign sun was shining on the peaceful countryside. Teachers taught their stuff, catechism, history, geology, using books that my grandfather would have been familiar with. Farmers attended the twice-weekly market on the main square, some of them still wearing the traditional blue serge blouse which stopped just short of their knobbly knees. I was cutting out pictures of George Best from *France Football* (the organ of the establishment, not that I knew anything of it) and *Le Miroir du Football* (of which more later) after Manchester United had seen off Górnik Zabrze in the quarter-finals of the European Cup. Young as I was, I soon realised that an unusual wind had freshened in Paris, strengthened into a squall, then a hurricane we were all caught in. It started with queues at petrol stations, where pickets from the

Communist *Confédération Générale du Travail*, the most powerful and best-organised trade union at the time, made sure that the local bourgeois drove off with an empty tank, sending them on their way with a satisfied smirk. A neighbour of ours, who'd been in trickier spots before (Chad just before the decolonisation) took to placing a .22 pistol in his Citroën's glove compartment, "just in case", which at the time seemed a perfectly reasonable thing to do. My school's gates were kept locked at all times, except when we lined up mornings and afternoons to slip in and out like monks heading for the cloister, manned by an odd chap who kept surveying the soles of his shoes as if he'd trodden in the remains of last week's run-over cat. The yard where we played five-, six-, or seven-a-side echoed with cries of 'mine!', but we could sense, innocent as we were, that thunder was rumbling beyond the horse-chestnut trees that dotted the gravelly surface.

The clouds took a while to gather. More people saw Saint Étienne make a huge step towards securing the first of the four doubles in their history by beating Bordeaux 2-1 in the French Cup final, played on 12 May at the Stade de Colombes, than demonstrated in the streets of Paris that day. A crowd of 70,000 greeted the victors when they paraded the trophy in their home town on the 13th, whereas less than a third of that number responded to the call of the main left-wing parties and trade unions to march from the Place de la République to Denfert-Rochereau in the capital. The great Rachid Mekhloufi, the undisputed star of the 1958 Algerian FLN (National Liberation Front) team, who'd been forced into a brief exile — to Servette, in Switzerland — once his country had acquired the independence he'd fought for, in 1962, scored twice as he brought the curtain down on his career with *Les Verts*. The figurehead of the struggle against the French imperium was known to feel sympathy for the youth who, looking for "beaches under the cobbles" and praising Ho Chi Minh, faced the baton charges of the feared anti-riot police on a daily basis. But Mekhloufi, like all other footballers, kept his counsel. Daniel Cohn-Bendit, aka Dany the Red, the French-born German spokesman of the 22 March Movement, later to become a Green MEP and a regular on French TV sports shows, did not mention his love of the game when cameramen and reporters sought him out in the teargas mists[1]. Football was a proletarian sport in France then — and still is — but those who called for the destruction of the established order on behalf of and for the benefit of the *prolétariat* turned their noses up at the smoke rising from the people's opium pipe. As the country veered between chaos and paralysis, ending with a strange mix of both, two discourses took hold. One was the preserve of a hyperactive, militant minority, which championed a utopian 'year zero', a concept which borrowed its constituent parts from Lenin, Bakunin, Proudhon, McLuhan, rock'n'roll and

[1] *Things have changed. Cohn-Bendit, a passionate fan of Les Bleus, became the chairman of FC Gutesding, a 'self-governed' Frankfurt club, in 2012 and intends to direct a documentary on the 2014 World Cup for the Franco-German cultural channel Arte.*

the *situationnistes* alike, in no particular order; it was adhered to and fiercely debated by the romantics of May '68, some of whom chose to 'opt out' after the events and can now be found herding goats in the depths of rural France. The other, not quite knowing what to do with itself, whispered in parlours and churches until Général De Gaulle called on the *bourgeoisie* to reclaim the streets, which they did, decisively, but very late in the day, which doesn't mean that the forces of reaction won. Consumerism did. The 'failed revolution' went out with a whimper on the back of multiple covenants, mostly pay-rises and generous holiday arrangements of which public sector workers were the chief beneficiaries. At first, the Communists, who could count on the support of a quarter of the electorate, had been scared stiff by the anarchic nature of the movement. Then the Party set its apparatus in motion to channel this explosion of revolutionary feeling into the more disciplined kind of protest which they were used to managing. Some aftershocks notwithstanding, France could be bored again. Their larders and fridges replenished, the masses went back to work, the café and the stadium; it had taken a little under three months for the system to right itself.

Football — as an event or as a spectacle — had only been superficially affected by the events of May 1968. There was a simple explanation to that: the domestic season was already drawing to a close when the thousands who'd taken to the streets to the streets in March and April turned into millions. The first division title had been Saint-Étienne's to lose from the first days of spring onward and France had, not for the first time, failed to qualify for the European Nations Cup. The 1967-68 campaign was to all intents and purposes over when strikes multiplied with extraordinary speed and vehemence.[2]

True, there was frustration among the more dedicated fans at missing out on Manchester United's European Cup Wembley triumph on 29 May and, to a lesser extent, the European semi-finals that took place in Italy from 5 to 10 June. The French state broadcasting monopoly had stopped transmitting its normal output as early as 17 May, five days after Saint Étienne's victory in the Coupe de France, and would stick to a 'minimum service' until 23 June, which meant that no live sport was shown on television. But these were mere disruptions, not a revolution. What almost no one realised at the time, and almost everyone has forgotten since, is that French football — a section of it, admittedly — did stage its own insurrection and that, had it not been for some unfortunate timing and lack of decisiveness at a crucial point in the protest, might easily have changed the face of the game altogether in the country. This shouldn't come as a complete surprise. While football's rulers

---

[2] *Saint Étienne were 11 points clear of OGC Nice at the conclusion of the competition, at a time at which a win was only worth two points. Security concerns and the disruption to transport services forced the postponement of the 38th and last round of the championship to July 5. The promotion and relegation play-offs were only completed two weeks later.*

conformed to the type that was to be found in other European countries — gentlemen of a certain age who were suspicious of change and leant to the right of centre — a number of France's foremost sporting figures made no secret of their left-wing sympathies. The Saint-Étienne manager Albert Batteux, who, in the late 1950s and early 1960s, had taken Stade de Reims and *les Bleus* to a level that no French club or national side had attained before, was not nicknamed '*le rouge-gorge*' ('the robin') for nothing . He could warble like a songbird, but also, more importantly, he was *un rouge*, the author of columns which were regularly printed in the Communist press. For him, football was an instrument of social transformation, as it showed how the freedom and desires of the individual need not be stifled by the recognition that the *collectif* had to prevail; quite the opposite, in fact. Another of those *rouges* was Just Fontaine, the World Cup's record goalscorer, the former national team manager (in 1967) and the first chairman of the French players' trade union, the UNFP, which he'd set up in 1961 with the help of another *progressiste*, the Cameroon-born Eugène N'Jo Léa, in order to put an end what he called the "slave-like status" of the pros, an expression which was also used by the man then considered France's greatest-ever footballer, Raymond Kopa. The views and values of these men — who were far from the exception in a milieu in which badly-paid players called themselves workers (*travailleurs*), just as others did on the factory floor — were also those of the already-cited *Miroir du Football*. Despite being published by *Les Éditions J*, a Communist-controlled company, the *Miroir* did not tread the orthodox Party

line and promoted a 'progressive' agenda whose foundations were ethical rather than *stricto sensu* political. And it was the men behind *Le Miroir* who were to initiate one of the most remarkable coups of that troubled period: the storming of the French FA headquarters and the sequestration of some of its highest-ranking officials within it.

The idea was first floated in mid-May at a dinner party organised at the home of one of the magazine's most eloquent writers, Pierre Lameignère. His flat was located in the heart of the Latin Quarter in Paris, a stone's throw away (*le mot juste*) from the scene of some of the most brutal clashes between demonstrators and the CRS in the spring of 1968. His editor François Thébaud was among the guests that night. Meeting again a few days later, the two men, joined by a number of friends, mostly recruited from the club for which they played Sunday football, APSAP Bretonneau, resolved to take action. They were following a popular trend: the occupation of landmarks such as the Odéon Theatre, the Sorbonne university and the Renault and Citroën factories had been a recurrent tactic of protesters since the beginning of the troubles. Violence would not be resorted to. There would be no sack of the luxurious *hôtel particulier* of 60 Avenue d'Iéna. The aim was not to overthrow the current regime, despised as it may be, but to force the federation's panjandrums to listen to their demands, and, given the publicity that the occupation of the headquarters would undoubtedly generate, make it a necessity to open the national debate on the state of the game which *Le Miroir* craved. Anything and everything was possible, be it to re-invent society or to transform football. It was a heady scent that was carried by the breeze in that month of May.

A few days were spent monitoring the comings and goings in and out of the federation's head office; a small vanguard of conspirators patrolled the area on scooters and bicycles, evaluating the number of people in the building at any given time and the resistance the invaders could expect to meet. On the given day, on the morning of May 22 , sixty-odd men, divided into three groups, one per exit of the Iéna metro station, made their way to the building and waited for the agreed signal. As one of them bent over as if to tie a shoe-lace, ten others, led by an oil company engineer called Jean-Pierre Lemeaux, entered the FA's marble halls, soon followed by their accomplices. The organisers of the operation had made sure that none of the first intruders worked for *Le Miroir*. Journalists would have been recognised by the ushers, refused entry, leading to the kind of confrontation which Thébaud and Lameignière wanted to avoid. The general secretary of the FFF, Pierre Delaunay, Fernand Sastre, who was to become its chairman a year later, and George Boulogne, who would soon be named national team manager, were led to safe rooms and ordered not to leave the premises. Boulogne, in particular, was fuming, but, contrary to what he later suggested, no blows were exchanged, no insults were traded. The plan had, so far, been executed to perfection. A banner was unfurled and suspended from the first floor balcony. It read: *LE FOOTBALL AUX FOOTBALLEURS* — "football for footballers". A second one proclaimed, "The FFF, the property of 600,000 footballers", that is, of all those who held a licence, be they amateurs or professionals. Volunteers, posted outside the main entrance, handed out leaflets in which the newly-formed *Comité d'action des footballeurs* outlined its demands: abolition of the eight-month season, which made it illegal to stage games outside of the period defined by the FFF; abolition of the 'B' licence, which prevented players moving from one club to the other; abolition of the 'slave contract' which professionals had no choice but to sign if they wanted a job; abolition of automatic fixed-term contracts, to be replaced by freely agreed covenants of variable duration; integration of active footballers within football governing bodies; and a typically *soixante-huitard* call for the 'dismissal of football's profiteers and incompetent pseudo-benefactors', which made it all the more puzzling that Marcel Leclerc — the chairman of Olympique de Marseille, not one to miss an opportunity — had agreed to have his name and signature added to the application form of the *Comité d'Action*.

Leaving that last request aside, none of the demands seem particularly revolutionary in 2013. In fact, all of them, bar that for the significant representation of players within statutory bodies, carry — today, if they did not then — a distinctly liberal flavour and were eventually met, even if Jean-Marc Bosman's lawyers only won their case in 1995. But stopping at specifics would be wrong. The flamboyant rhetoric in which those demands were dressed in by the activists was in many ways more revelatory of the Committee's true intent. These men dreamt of a football in which every participant would be a valued stakeholder, a football the pyramidal top-to-bottom structure of which would be flipped over. This, and not the brief captivity of some of its most powerful employees, is why the FFF took fright and, without any discernible irony, denounced the "anti-democratic" nature of the protest. Within the building itself, the occupiers behaved impeccably, offering an apéritif to their hostages before sending them on their way as the sun was coming down. A small group of volunteers, all of them unmarried, set up camp for the night, laden with food prepared by the wives of those who'd left, uncorking what veterans of this action say was a prodigious number of bottles of wine, before repairing to the FFF's private cinema where they played spool after spool of the federation's Super-8 film archives. Some day, some night.

The operation could only truly succeed, however, if the media reported it widely enough to enable the protesters to enter the second phase of their action. The aim was to use the FFF's HQ as an agora for French football as a whole and stage discussion forums to which amateurs as well as professionals would be invited, true to the spirit of 'self-management' which had inspired almost all of Mai 68's most admirable actions. Some footballers of renown got in touch, Rachid Mekhloufi among them, as well as the former France international striker Yvon Douis, by then playing for AS Cannes, who assured the occupiers of his support. A far greater number of players from lower-division clubs of the Paris region visited the Avenue d'Iéna: it was the very first time that footballers had been allowed within the FFF's inner sanctum, as one of the federation's apparatchiks observed at the time. But whatever interest was shown within the world of football itself, far too much was happening elsewhere for newspapers and independent radio stations, the sole sources of information in those TV-free days, to devote any significant space or airtime to the Quixotes of Iéna. Those who did — *Le Figaro*, *L'Humanité*, the former Gaullist, the latter Communist — derided their deed as an empty, meaningless, slightly ludicrous gesture. It is true that the peaceful occupation of the FFF coincided with far graver events, such as the torching of the Paris Stock Exchange and the second 'night of the barricades' on May 24, one of the most violent episodes of the failed revolution.[3] The foreign media showed a modicum of curiosity, but mostly to use the event as an illustration of the more eccentric side of the tremors shaking old, crusty France. A couple of US TV crews paid a visit to the 'hostage takers', the *Times* despatched one of its reporters to meet them, as did *La Gazzetta dello Sport*. And that was all. The lack of coverage, especially at home, was one of the main factors behind the decision of the football *enragés* to leave the Avenue d'Iéna after a mere five days, to concentrate on "alternative types of action". It wasn't a lack of courage that made them stop in their tracks. They proved it by carrying on fighting within new organisations

---

[3] *Six people died in the riots, a remarkably low number given the size and frequency of the demonstrations and the clashes that almost inevitably followed.*

such as the *Association Française des Footballeurs* and the *Mouvement Football-Progrès*,[4] making themselves pariahs once the old order had been re-established, which was promptly, on the heels of the Gaullist tsunami at the June parliamentary elections. True to their ideals, they believed that dialogue was the way forward, when direct confrontation with the football authorities would — perhaps — have caused the chain reaction in the game's grassroots which they'd hoped to provoke in the first instance. Jacques Ferran, the editor of *France Football*, while recognising that the rebels had acted with the best interests of football at heart and had, indeed, come up with some genuinely interesting proposals, could dismiss their operation as "a sword slash in the water". As so often happens in fights of this kind, it was child's play for the FFF to address some points of detail in their desiderata, the abolition of the 'B' licence, for example and, by yielding a little, recover the power that might have been subverted by more forceful action.

What Lameignère, Thébaud and their friends dreamt of was a transformation of the game as a whole, not just the improvement of the working conditions enjoyed, if that's the word, by professional footballers in 1968. The real 'kidnapping' had been that of the demands they'd made in their leaflets, demands which the UNFP appropriated soon afterwards, but not from the perspective of a popular movement: as a corporation defending the interests of its members and nothing or nobody else. In 2007, Michel Platini, campaigning against Lennart Johansson in the run-up to the UEFA presidential elections, made *"le football aux footballeurs"* his slogan. Did he remember the banner which was hung over the balcony at 60 Avenue d'Iéna? Or was it not, rather, history repeating itself, first as (some sort of) tragedy, second as a farce? Like Arsenal and Chelsea playing the apocalyptic 'London Calling' at 130 decibels on their PA sound systems before kick-off? The *enragés* of '68 had believed they could write that history and ended up as one of its footnotes. Ⓑ

---

[4] *That group had first chosen 'Mouvement de libération des footballeurs'(MLF) as a name, before somebody pointed out that the French Women's Lib movement had already appropriated the initials.*

The Silenced Crowd

When Manchester United and Liverpool colluded to fix a match

By Richard Fitzpatrick

There was no fooling the 18,000 spectators at Old Trafford. "Play up, you rotters!" they screamed. The fix was on. They knew it, as Manchester United went through the motions against Liverpool on 2 April 1915, winning 2-0 in a listless performance. According to the court testimony of Fred Hargreaves, a linesman for the match, fans made their disgust known in "unmistakable Lancashire fashion". John Robson, Manchester United's manager was so appalled he left the ground before the final whistle.

During two court cases, which dragged on until 1919, it emerged players from each side had fixed it so that United would win, with a goal to be scored in each half. Bets were placed on a 2-0 score-line around England at odds of seven and eight to one. The plot was the biggest British football scandal of the first half of the twentieth century.

The match was played on Good Friday. It was a holiday weekend but over on the continent the Great War raged. The snow was so deep underfoot in the Carpathians that Russian and Austrian soldiers stood plugged in the ground shooting at each other. The Second Battle of Ypres was a few weeks away. The war, which was dragging on interminably, undoubtedly influenced the players who rigged the match. The feeling at large was that the league should be shelved until the fighting had finished, by which time many of its players would be too old or too dead to play professional football again.

In the months preceding the game, the front pages of *Athletic News*, a Manchester-based newspaper, were peppered with items exhorting players to enlist in the army and applauding the minority who had done so. A few days before Good Friday 1915, Colonel CF Grantham, a commander of the 17th Battalion, otherwise known as the Footballers' Battalion, noted bitterly that only 122 professional footballers of an estimated 1,800 available had enlisted. The historian AF Pollard wrote to the *Times* in similar disappointment: "We view with indignation and alarm the persistence of Association Football clubs in doing their best for the enemy — every club that employs a professional football player is bribing a much needed recruit to refrain from enlistment and every spectator who pays his gate money is contributing so much towards a German victory."

On the day of the match, the official programme, amid advertisements which claimed that "a bottle of Manchester Brewery Milk Stout contains more nutriment than a glass of milk", did a little bit of soothsaying on its sixth page: "The continuance of the war may prevent the opening of the season next September. In the result of the military situation taking a turn unfavourable to the Allies, football will be out of the question."

The match kicked off in heavy, showery rain, which subsided after about 15 minutes. United, decked out in their customary red jerseys, won the toss and played with the breeze; the visitors Liverpool wore black shorts and white shirts.

Liverpool's goalkeeper was Elisha Scott from Belfast. His brother Billy was Everton and Ireland's goalkeeper. Scott was only 20 years of age, but was such a promising keeper that two years earlier Liverpool had forked out £1,000 for him. He tended goal for the club until 1934, and became famous for his jousts with Everton's Dixie Dean, but never put in a more unusual shift. He was overrun in the first half. United's keeper, Bob Beale, was so redundant that he had time, apparently, to spark up a cigarette and walk up to Scott's goal and share it with his counterpart.

Shots rained down on Scott, including, according to the *Sporting Chronicle*'s reporter, "a hot shot" by 25-year-old Joe Norton, which careered off the post. Scott finally yielded five minutes before the break when United's striker George Anderson latched on to a cross-field ball and whipped a volley past him.

Liverpool's dressing room was in disarray at the break. Some of their players were so furious that they threatened not to return to the field for the second half. There were effectively two matches

being played — one by the players in on the fix, and one by the others, which included the future England captain Ephraim Longworth, who tried to get on with the game.

Midway through the second period, the home team won a penalty, according to the *Sporting Chronicle*'s correspondent, "for hands" against Liverpool defender Bob Pursell. Anderson, United's normal penalty-taker, stood aside to let the team's captain, the Irishman Patrick O'Connell, take the kick. O'Connell, or 'Don Patricio', was a picaresque character who later managed Barcelona during the Spanish Civil War. According to a *Liverpool Daily Post* correspondent, the big half-back blazed his shot "ridiculously wide".

As the ref and Hargreaves, his linesman, conferred about their suspicions after the kick, boos echoed around the ground. The match officials allowed to game to continue, however. Anderson bagged a second goal. By this stage, the match had descended into farce. Enoch James West, or "Knocker", as he was known to fans and friends, was particularly off his oats, having sent two good chances wide.

West, 29, with boyish good looks, was Manchester United's top scorer for three of his five seasons at the club, including the league-winning campaign of 1910-11. He fell back into defence, citing ankle problems, as the game progressed. "West was chiefly employed in the second half in kicking the ball as far out of play as he could," wrote 'Veteran', the *Manchester Daily Dispatch*'s match reporter. Just before play finished, Liverpool's striker Fred Pagnam crashed a shot off the bar.

He was upbraided for his efforts by some of his teammates.

Newspaper reports about the shenanigans in the match were muted, although the *Manchester Football Chronicle* quoted "one famous old player" in attendance that was aghast: "You don't need the War to stop the game, football of this sort will do it soon enough." Coverage of the war and Lord Rothschild's burial left little room for the fripperies of holiday football. The *Daily Mirror*, which, it claimed, had a "certified circulation larger than any other picture paper in the world", published the result without a match report; ditto *Sporting Life*.

The *Manchester Guardian*'s correspondent failed to register any suspicions, remarking that Manchester United had the better of proceedings; that "play was scrappy"; and that "in the closing stages both sides showed more dash, but there was not a dangerous forward on the field." Most pressmen acknowledged, in the words of *Manchester Daily Dispatch*'s reporter, that "the second half was crammed with lifeless football". The *Manchester Football Chronicle*'s roving reporter 'Wanderer' wrote that he was "surprised and disgusted at the spectacle the second half presented" but neglected to elaborate.

The unrest in the terraces went unnoticed, with the exception of an ambiguous aside from the *Sporting Chronicle* that "the crowd were very silent". They wouldn't shut up once they got back out on the streets. The football community and in particular out-of-pocket turf accountants were appalled. They cursed the footballers for their blatant charade. Newspapermen cocked their ears. "There is almost

as much about this Manchester v Liverpool match as there was about the Liverpool v Chelsea match of a year or two ago," wrote *Sporting Chronicle* a week afterwards.

The "unsavoury comments" the journalist was overhearing brought to mind a game in March 1913 when Liverpool lost 2-1 to Chelsea, a defeat which helped preserve the London club's First Division status. Henry Norris, Arsenal's chairman had gone to the match and wrote a huffy letter afterwards to a London newspaper, maintaining that "had the Liverpool team, as a whole, desired to win the match they could have done so quite readily." The FA sprung into action, but their enquiry failed to land any convictions.

Illegal betting on football was rife at the time, a vice that the country's elders tried in vain to curb. The Football League was so disturbed at how widespread it had become that in 1902, like a man wrestling with the waves, it tried to ban everyone who attended a football match from betting on its result.

In July 1913, the House of Commons debated a Ready Money Football Betting Bill. The Right Honourable W Hayes Fisher told his peers in parliament that "the FA has long been determined to endeavour to free this game from the excrescences which have grown upon it in connection with betting and gambling."

Two weeks after the game, *Sporting Chronicle*, on behalf of a betting firm, put up a £50 reward to anyone who furnished information regarding allegations that "a certain First League match played in Manchester during Easter weekend was 'squared'". The paper specified that several of those playing had put bets on a 2-0 scoreline.

On 20 April, it was announced that league football would be suspended until the war was over. A few days later, the Football League established a three-man commission to investigate the Good Friday game. It began hauling players in for questioning while billeted in hotels in Liverpool and Manchester, including the Grand Hotel in Manchester. The commission also trawled the country acquiring evidence, the ingredient which bedevils the prosecution of most football-betting scams. It wasn't until 23 December 1915 that it published its verdict. It was shocking.

It concluded that there was "a conspiracy to defraud bookmakers", but exonerated both clubs, who helped with the investigation. Eight players received life bans, as, curiously, did the Lancashire first-class cricketer Lol Cook, presumably for helping to place bets; a ninth footballer , Manchester City's Fred Howard, who was alleged to have pocketed money from bets on the match, got a 12-month suspension.

The players' expulsion extended to management in the game. They weren't even allowed to enter a football stadium again. Of the four from Liverpool, Jackie Sheldon, who was fingered as the ringleader, had won a championship medal with Manchester United in 1911, a spell in which, inevitably, he had formed friendships with the three banned Red Devils — Arthur Whalley, Sandy Turnbull and Knocker West.

Strangely, West was the only Manchester United player who took part in the actual

match. The commission stated it did not have enough evidence to convict any more of his teammates. The *Liverpool Echo* dwelt on the men who escaped the gallows: "There are some lucky fellows connected with the inquiry, that's certain. It is a fact that some fellows have scraped through the inquiry 'by the lip of their mouth'."

West took it the worst of the blacklisted bunch. Against the advice of solicitors, he launched an extraordinary crusade to clear his name. He lived in a house on Railway Road, within walking distance of Old Trafford. During a wartime regional league match between Manchester United and Liverpool, he stationed himself outside the stadium — a ground, of course, he couldn't enter — passing out handbills, printed at his own expense, promising a reward to anyone who could supply information proving he had made a bet or won money from the Good Friday match in 1915. As Simon Inglis remarks in his book *Soccer in the Dock* he must have cut a tragic figure.

He got his day in court, though. On 5 July 1917, a libel case he brought against the Football Association and several newspapers opened, in which he also hoped to overturn his ban from football. He began spiritedly enough in the witness box, maintaining he played up front in the first half of the game, but retired to defence under instructions from his captain, O'Connell, who also, as it happened, was working as his foreman in the same war supplies factory, Ford Motor Works at Trafford Park. When questioned, West conceded that it was odd that there was so much heavy betting on a 2-0 score-line in Hucknall Torkard, Nottinghamshire, the town where he was born in 1886, but added that according to reports there had been big bets laid in other districts around the country.

O'Connell was next for cross-examination. When asked about his ballooned penalty kick, he drew laughter with his response: "I have missed dozens in my time." He denied there was an attempt to "square" the match and said West had played his normal game, commenting that it was not unusual that West "hugged" the ball, as that was his playing style. It seemed the wind was travelling in West's direction. It changed with the next witness summoned by the court.

The evidence given by Sheldon, who had enlisted, was taken before an examiner, as he had to return to the front. It was forthright, influenced, perhaps, by his predicament, and a U-turn on a melodramatic letter, claiming he was "absolutely blameless", he sent from the trenches in April 1916 to *Athletic News*. In it he pleaded for understanding given "how difficult it is for me to explain while doing my bit somewhere in France."

Sheldon's old teammate, Sandy Turnbull, one of the three banned Manchester United players, was reported "missing believed wounded" during the Arras offensive. He had been part of General Haig's spring push in northern France. Turnbull's wife clung to the Army's suggestion that he might have been "picked up by the Germans". It was only in August 1918 that his commanding officer, Captain CJ Lonergan, who returned to England from his spell in a German prison, confirmed his fate to her. In a detailed letter describing the events

of 3 May 1917, he concluded that Lance-Sergeant Turnbull, his "best NCO", must have "been 'sniped' by a German lying low." The remains of his body, which have never been found, lie in the region's chalky soil.

Sheldon confessed to fixing the result with players on his own team. He said on the Monday before the match he went to Manchester and met up with three co-conspirators in the Dog and Partridge pub: Turnbull, Whalley, who was seriously wounded at Passchendaele and later became a bookmaker — of all things — in Manchester, and West. They agreed to fix the match at 2-0.

Once the goals were scored, Sheldon said West fell back into defence and started hoofing the ball into touch. It was obvious to the crowd what was going on, especially as United kept the ball away from their teammate Billy Meredith. The Welshman was the Ryan Giggs of his day — known as the "Prince of Dribblers", he used to play with a toothpick in his mouth while plaguing defenders wide on the right and played his last game, an FA Cup semi-final, at 49 years of age.

When Meredith was questioned in court, he said he felt something was amiss as no one would pass him the ball. There was a reason why he'd been kept out of the loop — he was suspended in 1905 for a year because he attempted to bribe Aston Villa's captain with £10 to lose a match, but he'd rehabilitated himself with the authorities and was a prime mover in the Association Footballers' Union.

Sheldon said several of his teammates were in on the scheme and placed their own bets. Others "jibbed" and objected. One of them was Pagnam, the Liverpool forward who hit the bar in the dying minutes of the match. During questioning, Pagnam said that Sheldon told him in a cab on the way to Old Trafford that the game was fixed — United were to win 2-0 and that he'd get £3 if he rowed in. He baulked and said he was going to "bang one in". Sheldon threatened him, saying he was "bloody well finished" at Liverpool if he did.

Anderson, who scored both of United's goals, testified that he was present at a pub near Manchester's Great Central Station on the day before the match when the conspirators met again. At the gathering, one of the players asked, "Is it still 2-0?" West answered, "Oh yes, I have written to Nottingham for £70 to £10." Anderson, who a year later was convicted of a betting conspiracy and jailed for eight months with hard labour, maintained he'd nothing to do with the swindle, but he'd keep his silence. When they were about to break up from their eve-of-match pub meeting, he told the courtroom West said, "I am not afraid. They cannot get any evidence against me."

The court had all the evidence it needed at this stage. West's case collapsed, though he ploughed on. In a Court of Appeal, he succeeded in getting another trial to examine whether the newspaper reports about the Football League commission's verdict in December 1915 were defamatory. It was heard in January 1919 and again he was unsuccessful. He'd lost 2-0, which was ironic, as Graham Sharpe pointed out in his book, *Free The Manchester United One*.

In recognition of their army service, Liverpool's four banned players, including Sheldon, were allowed to apologise for their misdemeanour and all but Thomas Fairfoul renewed their professional football careers at Anfield.

West could probably have secured a pardon also if he'd owned up to his guilt, by "tugging his forelock", as his son Eric, who played for Grimsby in the 1930s, said. His lifetime football ban was eventually lifted in October 1945, as part of a general amnesty, but he never visited Old Trafford again before dying in 1965. It remains a mystery how he funded his legal challenges.

The Reluctant Cabbie

The tragically curtailed career of the Czechoslovak great Rudolf Kučera

By Michal Petrák

His name might have been mentioned in the same breath as Cruyff, Beckenbauer or Masopust. He was probably the most talented footballer in post-war Czechoslovakia. Yet very few people have heard Rudolf Kučera. A single blow to his head ended his career when he was 23 years old.

He did taste success and recognition. In June 1961, a New York crowd, composed predominantly of Czechoslovak ex-pats, chaired him from the field and stuffed dollar bills inside his shirt. Kučera had the world at his feet: he had scored four goals in two games against Everton, games Dukla Prague had won 2-0 and 7-2, to become the hero of the city that never sleeps. Or at least of the part of its population that cared about soccer.

In 1961, Dukla broke all kinds of records in the short-lived annual US International Soccer League which that year included the likes of Crvena Zvezda, Rapid Vienna, Shamrock Rovers and Espanyol as well as Dukla and Everton. The 21-year-old forward scored 15 goals in eight group games before tormenting English opposition in a two-legged final. He was so impressive that the US press dubbed the team from Prague 'Kučera and his Boys' — and that was a squad that included Josef Masopust, Svatopluk Pluskal and Ladislav Novák, all heroes of the Czechoslovakia national team that reached the final of the 1962 World Cup.

Kučera, then several years younger than most of his teammates, outshone them all. "He was one of the finest young players in Europe at that time, the greatest talent of post-war Czechoslovak football," said Miloslav Jícha, the Dukla secretary and a font of knowledge about the army club. "The tournament in New York was his amazing display," agreed Josef Vacenovský, Kučera's teammate.

He was so dominant on the pitch that it irritated opponents beyond just the goals he scored. He relished the games and the grateful cheers of the crowd, and he fuelled them. When Dukla were 4-1 up with only a few minutes to go against Espanyol in the group stage, Kučera nutmegged a defender in the box — then he turned and nutmegged him again. "Zamora, the Espanyol head coach, was furious. He started jumping in front of the substitutes' bench and shouted to our coaches that we were making fun of them," said Josef Jelínek, who played alongside Kučera in Dukla's attacking quintet.

Kučera was a magnificent talent. People who saw him play regarded him as one of the best they'd ever seen. He was a subtle striker with a low work-rate but astonishing speed of thought and execution. He was no sprinter, but when he got the ball in the box there was no stopping him. He would dribble past three defenders in a phone-box rather than let the phone ring twice. "His movement in the first three meters was unrivalled. He would push the ball to the right, to the left and the defender was behind him. He was also a great finisher," said Jelínek. "He didn't run much but in the box he was deadly. [Jaroslav] Borovička, our teammate who was ten years older than Kučera, would tell him, 'Rudy, you can stand in the box all the time, we'll do your running for you. We know you will score the goals.'"

"When I later saw Johan Cruyff, he reminded me of Rudy very much," said Vacenovský. "And if I picked anyone from the current crop, I would point at Robin van Persie." But, according to him, Kučera could have been better than the Manchester United striker.

The fans loved Kučera. Not only because of the goals, but also for his carefree attitude — so atypical for the army club — and his ever-present smile. While the other players were afraid of Jaroslav Vejvoda, the head coach who shaped the famous Dukla in the sixties, Kučera didn't mind the strict disciplinarian's methods and anger.

He was almost a childish character: a boy among men, an open, playful and phlegmatic soul in the military environment. His blond hair only added to the youthful image. "I remember clearly the day in 1959 when he enrolled for military service," recalled Vacenovský, the day when Kučera left his home in Moravia and came to Prague to fulfil

his duties. "I was at the gate — I don't remember whether it was my turn on guard duty there or whether I was just hanging around. Suddenly, a boyish figure came with a tiny bag in which he could have carried only a toothbrush and a toothpaste. He looked shy, eyes down into the ground. I asked him what he was doing there and he said softly: 'I'm supposed to enrol here.'"

An excellent example of Kučera's attitude —and talent — was the game against Tatran Prešov in the autumn of 1960. With the score goalless in the first half, Dukla were awarded a penalty. Kučera took the ball although Vacenovský was the designated penalty taker. And Kučera missed. "Vejvoda was furious," said Vacenovský. "He screamed at us in the dressing room. He was angry." In the second half, Dukla were awarded another penalty. Vejvoda had clearly told his players at half-time to respect the order of penalty takers... "... but Rudy took the ball again!" Vacenovský remembered. "He said, 'I have to correct my error. I never was one for fights and arguments so I let him take it," Vacenovský rolled his eyes. Kučera missed again. "We all thought Vejvoda would have a heart attack," Vacenovský said. "We were scared even to look in the direction of the bench." Vacenovský put a hand to his forehead. In the end, Kučera scored two goals — and Dukla won 5-0. "Of course Vejvoda was furious — but at me! He gave me a proper hairdryer, but didn't say a word to Rudy."

Kučera's personality only underlined his enormous talent. He was a revelation in a team full of disciplined soldiers. "He was a child off the pitch as well as on it. He never took the coaches' instructions seriously," said Jícha. He could not have been more different from the ascetic Dukla captain Ladislav Novák. "When the coaches asked Novák to perform ten somersaults, he would do twenty. When they told Kučera to do five, he would roll over four times and smile," said Jícha.

On the one hand, Kučera looked out of place; on the other, he was an unpredictable match-winner. Defenders could not have dealt with him even if they had known what he was going to do. "He had a gift from God," said Jelínek. In 1960-61 Kučera was the joint top-scorer in the Czechoslovak league, hitting the target 17 times. At that time, there were only 26 games in a season. Over his career, he totalled 44 goals in 121 league games.

Off the pitch, Kučera loved life. As a young man from southern Moravia, he liked wine. However, he was not out of control; he never arrived drunk at training. "That would have been unthinkable at Dukla," said Jelínek, "but Rudy was always smiling. I shared a room with him all the time — with the club, with the Olympic team, with the senior national team; we were friends. He always liked fun, joined in the jokes..."

However, Kučera was far from happy-go-lucky. He might have become a star at the 1962 World Cup in Chile, where Czechoslovakia lost in the final, but missed the tournament because of a knee injury. "It happened in a friendly game with Jiskra Otrokovice from the lower division," said Jícha. "We won 15-1 but he tore his cartilage and had to have surgery."

Kučera had been eager to show his talents to the world and missing the

tournament came as a severe blow. The significance of loss was emphasised when Czechoslovakia played Austria in a friendly shortly after the World Cup. The team around Masopust, who won the *Ballon d'Or* that year, beat their opponents 6-0 at Praterstadion in Vienna, with both Masopust and Kučera scoring twice. "That was Kučera's best game in the national team. He was unstoppable," Jícha said, shaking his head sadly.

Things returned to normal for Kučera. Dukla were dominating the league, he was back at his best and the disappointment of missing the World Cup started to fade. There were successful runs in Europe, too. Bit it was one of the European matches that ended Kučera's prolific career.

Dukla were cruising in the return leg of the second round of the European Champions' Cup on 21 November 1963 against Górnik Zabrze. They had lost the first leg 2-0 in Poland, but in Prague they were demolishing the opposition 4-1 up with eight minutes to go, with Kučera having scored twice. The Juliska stadium was getting ready to celebrate.

A long ball was hoofed towards the Górnik box to waste some seconds and prevent the Polish side building up any pressure. Kučera, perhaps over-euphoric after his stellar 80 minutes, chased the ball. He jumped to head it, but in the air, his temple connected with the elbow of Stanislaw Oslizlo, a hard man in the centre of the Górnik defence. The stadium fell silent as Kučera was knocked unconscious in the air. His limp body fell to the frozen turf. "It was as if a bag of sand had fallen down," said Jelínek, who was standing just a few metres from the incident. Hubert Topinka, the Dukla team doctor, later claimed the fall was worse than the initial blow to the temple.

Kučera was carried off the pitch and into an ambulance. While the rest of Dukla squad were nervously relishing the victory that meant progress to the third round, he was undergoing scans in the military hospital in Střešovice. "We hardly celebrated," said Vacenovský. "We were sitting in the dressing room in grave silence. We felt something serious had happened, although I believed it would be a normal injury."

It wasn't. Kučera didn't wake up until the following morning. His long unconsciousness had had a devastating effect: bleeding into his brain had damaged his movement and coordination. That would have been a severe blow for anybody, but for a top footballer, it was the end. Kučera had treatment and underwent a programme of rehabilitation. He went to a spa town to work on recovery but it didn't help. When he returned, he was a different man. At training sessions, it was obvious to everybody that he would never return to the pitch. His tricks and dribbles were gone and he struggled to stay on his feet every time he changed direction. His left knee hurt terribly. "We saw some things that a footballer would never do," said Jelínek with sadness in his voice. "If we had built a concrete wall in front of him, he would have run into it."

"It was a terrible sight," said Vacenovský. "We were all friends; he and I came from the same region. It was incredibly cruel for him and for the team. He could have been at the top level for at least eight more years."

Kučera loved wine. He smoked. The doctors reproached him for loving such things too much. "He was given perfect care," said Jícha. "The military hospital is still state-of-the-art today. Maybe... just maybe he could have returned to the pitch."

It was always unlikely, though. "It was heavy damage to his brain," said Miloš Trubl, then Dukla's head doctor. "It was absolutely unthinkable that anyone could have returned to top-level football with such an injury."

Kučera tried his luck with the army club's reserves and then Slavia's for a short time, but within a year of his injury, it was clear that he would never kick a ball again. Even later, when his compassionate former teammates tried to get him to play for a Dukla over-35 team, it was to no avail. He only could run in a straight line, nothing else.

It was not only his tragedy, but a loss for Dukla and the national team. "If it wasn't for his injury, he would have become the best player in Europe," said Masopust. Some claim Kučera was even better than the legendary midfielder. That is hard to compare, but he definitely matured earlier. While Masopust made his debut for the national team aged 23 and fully broke into the squad at 25, Kučera pulled on the shirt with a lion on the chest for the first time at the age of 21. "Josef's peak came when he was 33," said Vacenovský. "Rudy was the finished article at 20."

The injury not only ended Kučera's career, it also changed his character. "Of course it scarred him," said Jícha. "Football was his job and to finish at such an age and in such a way... It was a catastrophe for him."

Kučera became a sad, lethargic man. Ota Pavel, a legendary sports journalist, wrote a melancholic short story about him. It is about a taxi driver who picks up a Czech-American tourist at Prague airport. The traveller talks to him euphorically about a soccer player who had beguiled New York. The taxi driver stares at the road in silence and denies any knowledge of the player. When the customer hands him two five-dollar bills, he drives away from him. Then he stops, turns on the light in the car and puts the money into a fine leather wallet with a name stamped on it: Rudolf Kučera.

The story shows in Pavel's typically lyrical manner how Kučera's life turned out after his career ended. He started a family, worked as a taxi driver and a garage keeper. For a long time, he looked after the Dukla tennis courts in the Prague quarter of Dejvice. He never played football again, but one can meet him to this day in the VIP box at the Juliska stadium, where he watches Dukla matches. He has a look in his eye, the look of what might have been.

....

When you meet Rudolf Kučera today, you still can see what his teammates mean when they jokingly grumble about his attitude. While the members of the golden generation of Dukla hold meetings regularly, their younger mate comes only when he feels like it. When they presented him with a mobile phone for his birthday, he hardly turned it on and placed it in a cupboard in his kitchen. He smiles a lot, but his smile is a sad one. He lights a cigarette and sits on a park bench quietly. When you see him like that you cannot but wonder whether he is thinking about the glory days.

◆ *How do you remember your career?*

It was a short one, but there was quite a lot of it. I like to remember those times, they were happy. We had a good team, a good collective. We played good football and were successful. I think I can be satisfied with my career.

◆ *When you came to Dukla, it already was a big club with players like Masopust and Pluskal. What was it like to come as a young boy from Moravia and meet such stars?*

It was a massive honour. They meant something in Czechoslovak and international football. They accepted me — I remember that when I came, I called everyone, "Sir." Josef Masopust told me to stop doing that, that I was now one of them, their friend.

◆ *Was getting used to military discipline difficult?*

No, it wasn't. I didn't take football so seriously in Moravia, not professionally: it was fun for us. At Dukla, we had to work harder, but I enjoyed doing that — maybe because I was pretty good at it. [Smiles] I was satisfied.

◆ *However, you were not a typical disciplined soldier, were you?*

No, I wasn't. I didn't want to feel tied, I wanted to be free. But I think the military environment and the discipline helped me grow up a bit. You started to take football, life and obligations differently.

◆ *They told me that if Ladislav Novák had been told to perform ten somersaults, he would have done twenty. If you'd been* told to do five, you would have rolled over four times. Is that right?

I would have done three. [Laughing] Such things were not enjoyable for me: I loved playing with the ball.

⊕ *And there was a game against Prešov and your penalties...*

Some of the things are myths, but this one is right. I hit the post with the first spot kick and when we were awarded another one, Vacenovský or Šafránek wanted to take it. I stopped them and said I had to redeem my previous error. But I hit the goalkeeper's hand. Vejvoda told me to stay away from the penalties, but in the end we won so there was no problem.

⊕ *How did you get on with Vejvoda? He was a strict coach: he must have had some problems with your attitude...*

I got on well with him. I never lied to him, I always told him what I thought. Yes, sometimes there were problems with me, but I was no rebel. I just needed some fun with football.

⊕ *Was the fun in football essential for you?*

It's a game, isn't it? I was satisfied when the fans enjoyed my performance. When they applauded and left the stadium in a happy mood. They liked me. I remember fondly the moments when I was leaving the stadium after a match wearing a uniform and I heard those old men talking about me: "Damn, that was his day again, he played well..."

⊕ *Did you feel that you were an extraordinarily talented player?*

I didn't think about it. It was nice when I played well and it was sad when I didn't. Those were all my feelings about football.

⊕ *How did more disciplined teammates react to your easy-going attitude?*

Borovička knew how to pass the ball. When he set up a chance for me and I did not convert it, he would shout at me, "Rudy, what's going on? We are running our socks off and you are walking around? I need you to score some goals!" He was a coach on the pitch, a strategist. Maybe sometimes I should have been more responsible, too...

⊕ *You were a star of the US International Soccer League in 1961. Were those the matches when you enjoyed football the most?*

I played quite well there, scored some goals... The fans were satisfied, only the coach wanted yet more from me. Our ex-pats were very grateful: they visited us at the hotel, walked with us through the city. I think they were proud because of us: they gained some confidence from the fact that the boys from Czechoslovakia were playing so well.

⊕ *Ricardo Zamora was not that grateful though...*

That was a good game. We scored some goals and started to enjoy the football. The lads passed the ball between each other, the Spaniards were running among us hopelessly. There was a forward in their team who looked like a bull. He was strong, extremely motivated... We took him into a triangle, he was the pig-in-the-middle. In the end, Jaroslav Borovička showed him the '*muleta*', let him run past himself and shouted '*Olé!*'. The striker stood like a confused bull, he didn't know what was going on. [Laughing] He started chasing Borovička, there was a bit of argument on the pitch.

✦ *The fans in New York carried you above their heads and dubbed Dukla "Kučera and His Boys"...*

...and the boys would throw it back at me. My teammates would say, "We played football when he was running around somewhere in Moravia. And now they call us 'His Boys'." [Laughing] I enjoyed it. We played well, we were winning, there were no problems. It was a beautiful experience.

✦ *A year later, you missed the World Cup because of a cartilage injury. How tough a blow was that? You were at the peak of your powers.*

Blow... I had to take it as it came. A defender hit me hard in a friendly game: it was unlucky. [He pauses, thinking] Unlucky, like all my career. After that point, the injuries started to come more often.

✦ *Was it just bad luck?*

The truth is, my playing style helped that. I was a player who kept the ball, dribbled... I did tricks, provoked the defenders and sometimes they were angry with me. They tackled me hard. Sometimes it was my fault.

✦ *Should the referees have protected you more?*

I don't think so. Nowadays football is harder. In my day the players were more respectful towards each other. Sometimes the tackles were unfair, but mostly they just tried to scare me off my tricks.

✦ *Did you watch the 1962 World Cup at which Czechoslovakia reached the final?*

I was at the spa after the cartilage surgery. I saw some games there. I wished my teammates all the best. At that time I was young and thought my chance would come later. If I had known... Maybe I would feel sorry for not being able to take part.

✦ *How do you remember the journeys into Europe with Dukla at that time? In the home game against Tottenham Hotspur in the European Cup in 1961-62, you showed the best form of your life.*

We had a disadvantage: the games were played in the winter, at a time when we were not able to train properly. We would go into the games directly from the physical preparation.

✦ *Do you remember anything from the game against Górnik Zabrze, in which you were injured?*

No. No details. It's all such a long time ago... We lost the first game in Poland and I can remember we played much better at home in the return leg, I scored some goals... And then it all went dark.

✦ *Do you remember the header with Stanislaw Oslizlo?*

I remember roughly where the duel took place. I recall how we jumped and then nothing. I was later told he hit me with an elbow, but I don't know. I can't even tell whether it was a foul or an accident.

I had my back turned towards him and couldn't see him coming.

✇ *Was the heading duel unnecessary? It was deep into the attacking half, you were 4-1 up and you were no keen header.*

It is fate, an accident. I jumped and thought I'd got the ball. He came from the back, but I do not know how he hit me.

✇ *What is your first memory from the moment you woke up?*

I woke up the next day. I asked about the result. I remember myself thinking it was a normal injury and that I would be back soon. I thought everything would be all right. However, I stayed in the hospital for quite a long time, then I had some rehabilitation and before the next season I tried to get back onto the pitch. However, there were complications all the time and in the end it meant my career was over.

✇ *What were the comeback attempts like? How did it feel not being able to control the ball and your legs any more?*

I can hardly judge it. I just felt it was not my old self. Suddenly, the inspiration would not come and I could not turn my ideas into action as quickly as before. There were limitations.

✇ *How did it feel?*

Strange. I had an idea, but my legs could not turn it into reality. In addition to that, my knee hurt. The cartilage surgery did its part and also, the left part of my body was partially paralysed.

✇ *You were desperate to get back onto the pitch, weren't you? You tried it in*

Dukla reserves, then Slavia reserves too...

Yes, I thought I could get a new impulse with the change of environment. Some new energy. But the complications suffocated the energy in me.

✇ *Some people say that your carefree attitude hurt you — that you should have worked harder and you might have come back.*

I don't know. Work harder, work harder... [shakes his head] When you really try, practise hard, run properly and for a while, for two or three days it is ok... And then something happens on the pitch — you slip, fall down and your leg swells... I can't say I could have done more. When you are not able to run, what can you do?

✇ *How much did it change your life?*

Hard to answer that. I didn't take it as a tragedy, that is for sure. What happened, happened; I could not do anything about it. I was not dead. I could live properly without any serious permanent damage. Life has dealt with it on its own.

✇ *What did you do?*

After I had left Dukla and Slavia, I went back to normal life. It was different... It was quite difficult to find a good job, for example. I could not do much. I'm a qualified electrician, but when you hadn't done that for years, you hadn't kept up to date with progress. I worked in an office, then I was a garage keeper, a taxi driver, then I was a caretaker at some tennis courts.

✇ *Have you read the short story that Ota Pavel wrote about you?*

Yes, I have.

⊕ *It's a very sad story. Your character is depicted as a melancholic man who turned away from football completely. Was it that way?*

Yes. It was at the time when I worked as a taxi driver. I didn't turn my back on football — I just didn't care. There was no sense in it, no reason. I could not play, just went to run a bit with my mates.

⊕ *Did you really stop watching football? Nowadays, I see you at the Dukla games occasionally.*

I had no time, either. And I understood completely that there was no way back onto the pitch for me.

⊕ *Was it hard to take?*

Time has healed it. It was a sad time, though. I had no depression, no moods when I wanted to end it all. I found the new meaning in life — I got married and I have a nice and good wife, two clever kids, a boy and a girl... I live a happy life.

⊕ *Did the injury change your character?*

Yes, definitely. I used to be very carefree, taking everything for granted. Then I suddenly got back into life. I had to take care of a family, the children...

⊕ *Do you sometimes look back on your career with regret?*

No, I would not say that. It was a short career, but even now, some people, some older people recognise me. That makes me feel proud — I think that it was not all in vain, for nothing. **Ⓑ**

The Unmarked Grave

What really happened to Andrew Watson, British football's first black star

By Tom Adams

In an unremarkable corner of an unremarkable cemetery lies an unremarkable grave. Its dull grey stone is mottled by yellow and green lichen while a scatter of brown leaves, rigid and decaying, surround it like a wreath.

One solitary word — "Resting" — constitutes the entirety of an unassuming inscription which has been weathered into partial oblivion. The expanse of grey beneath this single word is untouched, a blank slate hinting at a story untold. If this headstone were truly to capture the life and career of the footballing pioneer lying beneath, it would need to be considerably more eloquent: this is the final resting place of Andrew Watson, a true sporting trailblazer who, having been born in Georgetown, British Guiana, to a wealthy plantation owner, became the world's first black footballer and international, notably captaining Scotland in a 6-1 rout of England at the Oval in March 1881 — a result which remains the country's heaviest ever home defeat.

Watson, described by the Scottish Football Association Annual of 1880-81 as "one of the very best backs we have", represented two of the 19th century's most prestigious clubs in Queen's Park and Corinthians, forging a successful career on both sides of the border as he won multiple domestic trophies and attracted widespread admiration for his robust but proficient style of play. Yet until only recently, Watson's story had been allowed to fade into history's murky depths, obscured by supposition and inaccuracy.

Even the official record was faulty. In November 2012, a decade after researchers at the Scottish Football Museum first unearthed photos of a mysterious man who contradicted the widely held opinion that Preston's Arthur Wharton was football's first black player, Watson was inducted into the Scottish Football Hall of Fame. But even on this auspicious occasion both the dates of his birth and death were incorrect, substantially so in the case of the latter.

The unchallenged assumption was once that Watson met his demise in Australia in 1902. But this unremarkable grave for a remarkable man is not located in Richmond, South Australia, or Richmond, Victoria, but in Richmond, west London, and the date of death marked on its headstone is 8 March 1921. Only this year were the true details of Watson's later life and death established and as a consequence football's historical record has been lacking an accurate and detailed account of the life and career of one of its more impressive individuals; an epitaph that extends to more than just one little word.

Andrew Watson was born on 24 May 1856 in the Demerara region of what was once British Guiana but is now known simply as Guyana, a country Caribbean by allegiance but nestled between Venezuela and Suriname at the northern tip of the South American continent. His father, Peter Miller Watson, was a sugar planter and a wealthy middle-class Scot; his mother is believed to have been a local black woman called Anna, or Hannah, Rose.

Watson moved to England as a young child, received a scholarly education as a boarder at the Free Grammar School in Halifax, West Yorkshire, from August 1866 and then attended King's College School in London until 1874. He matriculated at the University of Glasgow in 1875 but left his studies shortly afterwards and began playing for a club named Parkgrove. It was here that football's first black player began to forge his career in the senior game.

Tactics were still at a rather rudimentary stage at the beginning of the 1880s and the formations of the time were heavily loaded towards attack — with seven or eight forwards in one team. Watson, though, was becoming known as a formidable back, a more exclusive position which, according to the Scottish Football Association Annual of 1885-86, demanded "clever tacklers, [who are] able to kick with either foot, and take the earliest opportunity of retarding the progress of a dribbler." Watson, wrote DD Bone in his Scottish Football Reminiscences and Sketches of 1890, was "famed for his fine tackling and neat

kicking. He had one fault, however, and this consisted in kicking over his own lines occasionally when hard pressed by a dashing forward."

As well as establishing a reputation as a player of promise, Watson also assisted the club's growth off the field. This apprentice mechanical engineer was a man of means thanks to his father's wealth and exercised his financial muscle to Parkgrove's benefit. Bone added, "Mr Watson did a great deal for football in the Glasgow district a dozen years ago, both with his ready purse and personal ability in the game. It was in great measure owing to his interest and energy that the young Parkgrove Club obtained proper ground, and was fairly put on its way rejoicing."

Significantly, on 6 April 1880, the 23-year-old Watson had the honour of being recruited by the great Scottish team of the age: the famous Queen's Park. Formed in 1867, Queen's Park were Scotland's first Association Football team and became innovators of an early passing game at a time when many clubs relied on the less subtle strategy of charging. Such was their superiority, and the dearth of quality opponents, that the Glasgow club went unbeaten for the first seven years of their existence, without so much as conceding a goal.

Queen's Park had already won four Scottish Cups prior to Watson's arrival and the new recruit helped to expand the club's trophy collection almost immediately. After being described by the Glasgow Herald of April 26 as "very clever when on the ball" following a Glasgow Charity Cup tie against Vale of Leven, Watson was a member of the team that defeated Rangers 2-1 in the final on May 13.

His progress at Scotland's premier club was duly noted. In the SFA Annual of 1880-81 it says of Watson that, "since joining the Queen's Park [he] has made rapid strides to the front as a player; has great speed, and tackles splendidly; powerful and sure kick; well worthy of a place in any representative team."

Indeed he was. Having represented Glasgow as a Parkgrove player in 1880, Watson was selected again at Queen's Park, turning out for the city in a 9-1 win over Lancashire and a 3-0 win over Sheffield, both in 1881. Though he was absent a year later, Watson's talent cast a shadow over proceedings. As Richard Robinson's *History of the Queen's Park Football Club, 1867-1917*, published in 1920, details: "Rather a peculiar incident occurred at the Sheffield v Glasgow match, played at Sheffield in February, 1882. Walter Arnott, then connected with Pollokshields Athletic, complained to the association that its vice, or acting, president, Mr John Wallace, had stated publicly in the smoking room of the hotel at Sheffield, where the team had their headquarters, that had Mr A Watson, of Queen's Park, been present to play at Sheffield, he [Wallace] would have drugged Arnott, thereby rendering him unable to play."

Meanwhile, Watson's club career was proceeding nicely and in 1881 he won the first of three Scottish Cups — playing "admirably", according to the *Glasgow Herald* — as Queen's Park defeated Dumbarton 3-1 in the final. Queen's Park also recorded another Glasgow Charity Cup win — beating Rangers 3-1— and the 1880-81 campaign became a rather remarkable one as the club's first, second and third teams all went unbeaten across

63 games in total, scoring 281 goals and conceding only 44.

In 1882 Queen's Park won the Scottish Cup again. A 2-2 draw against Dumbarton in the final of March 20 had been a close-run thing — "had it not been for [Watson's] steady play, the result might have been disastrous for the Queen's Park," wrote the *Glasgow Herald* — but a 4-1 win in the replay in front of a then record crowd of 15,000 at Glasgow's Cathkin Park was navigated rather more easily. In a quaint aside, as recorded by Robinson in his *History of the Queen's Park*, "The teams, it is well to add, had tea together in the Atholl Arms, where song and sentiment prevailed until train hour."

Watson had become a key player for Scotland's pre-eminent club and international recognition was unsurprisingly forthcoming. The British Guiana-born defender made history when he strolled out for Scotland against England at Kennington Oval on March 12 1881: football had its first black international player — and a captain to boot — as Scotland hammered England 6-1 to inflict a terrible defeat on football's birthplace. Intriguingly, Watson's skin colour is not a matter for contemporary comment — nor was it at any other stage of his career. A report in the *Sheffield Daily Telegraph* merely commends him for having "cleverly tackled" an opponent in a match that "proved unmistakably the superiority of the Scotsmen at the dribbling game" — a style of play pioneered by Queen's Park. Only two caps followed — a 5-1 win over Wales two days later in Wrexham and a 5-1 home win over England in 1882 — as a promising, and indeed historic international career was quickly curtailed when Watson moved south to London, with only Scotland-based players under consideration for the national team.

Watson joined London Swifts and on New Year's Day, 1883, helped his new club become the first team to defeat Queen's Park in Scotland. It was at Swifts where Watson became the first black man to play in the FA Cup, though given he was blessed with sufficient financial resources, the full-back was able to make frequent trips north of the border and was in the Queen's Park side which defeated Third Lanark by a record margin of 8-0 in the Glasgow Charity Cup final of May 1884.

Notably, Watson's exploits with London Swifts, and Queen's Park before that, had brought him to the attention of the prestigious Corinthians, who in an era of nascent professionalism were boldly and proudly clinging to their amateur status. Being from a wealthy background, Watson had no need to chase professional wages. Indeed, the very notion of being paid to play football was regarded by many at the time as a morally bankrupt enterprise. The SFA Annual of 1885-86 describes how "this [professionalism] has been the all-engrossing subject of the season, and it has engaged more time and attention than any other matter ever before required from the committee. Mr M'Killop, our esteemed president, in particular has laboured indefatigably to have this evil suppressed in England, and to prevent it getting a resting place in our midst." Though their mutual stand against professionalism ultimately ensured the two clubs would become anachronisms, sliding into obscurity as money poured

into the game, Queen's Park and Corinthians were two enthusiastic standard-bearers in this doomed moral crusade. In the 1880s at least, amateurism was a viable and noble stance. Robinson's *History of the Queen's Park* lauds Corinthians as "a brilliant galaxy of talent, all men who have gained high honours in the game, and whose sole aim and ambition were to bring out all that is good and healthy in a pastime they followed for the love of it. Similar sentiments have always actuated the Queen's Park since its very foundation, its ambition being to keep the game unsullied, and its own reputation as pure and clean as the driven snow, and with success. It here met with kindred spirits ... the name of the club is even at the present day [1920] a household word for all that is chivalrous, clean, upright, and true in the civilised world of sport."

Watson's finest achievement with this proud band of Corinthian amateurs came in the 1884-85 season when they destroyed Blackburn Rovers 8-1 in the FA Cup. But the pull of Glasgow, where his two children were living following the death of his first wife, Jessie, remained strong, and in 1886 Watson was back with Queen's Park, winning the Scottish Cup for the third time with a 3-1 defeat of Renton in February. "A great game it was," wrote the *Glasgow Herald*, "witnessed by 10,000, on a wet and disagreeable afternoon."

A new season required Watson to show an element of tactical flexibility as he slotted into an experimental formation that utilised an increased quota of three half-backs. Though the man trained as a full-back had been used in a more advanced position as early as 1880, this positional tweak was geared towards a more progressive approach from Queen's Park. Clearly it required some adjustment as they were beaten heavily when facing Preston at the start of the campaign. According to Robinson, "the result was so disastrous—a 6-1 defeat— that the Scots at once reverted to the old formation". Still, the fact Watson had been earmarked for the role spoke volumes as to his all-round ability.

The SFA Annual of 1885-86 deconstructs the half-back position: "Of all the players in the field, the half-back is, perhaps, the most relied upon. His judgement must be perfection itself, and no amount of assumed tactics by the opposing forwards should take him by surprise, or allure him to forget his position. He is, so to speak, a back and a forward combined in one ... A clever half-back is, in fine, the most dangerous man to meet on the field. The position is a most responsible one, and many of the finest players in England and Scotland have chosen that position in preference to any other."

The 1886-87 season was to prove his last in Scotland. In 1887, Watson moved to Merseyside following his second marriage, to Eliza Kate Tyler. He was recruited to play for Bootle FC and became a favourite of the local supporters. In 1888, reporting on an FA Cup fifth-round tie against the Old Carthusians, the *Liverpool Mercury* records that: "the Bootle team entered the famous enclosure amid hearty cheers, their full-back Andy Watson being recognised by many of the Surrey supporters as a once-famed Corinthian and Swift."

In further dispatches, the *Mercury* praises Watson for his "peculiarly cool

style", his "magnificent defence" and most notably, in February 1888, for "a 'Watsonian kick'", suggesting that the boy born in British Guiana had constructed a formidable identity for himself in both England and Scotland — the two countries that drove the game's development in its formative decades. He had become a player of real substance and quality, and a pioneer, if now rather obscure, for the black footballers who would follow him.

Writing in *The Story of Association Football* in 1926, JAH Catton — a renowned sports journalist who wrote under the pen name of 'Tityrus' for the *Athletic News* and was a dedicated observer of games between Scotland and England — even named Watson at full-back in his all-time Scotland team, despite the fact he won only three caps. "It would be folly to expect everyone to agree with such a choice," Catton wrote of his XI, "but I have taken men as effective players of a ball and as schemers."

A revered three-time Scottish Cup winner and international captain, Watson had carved out his place in football's history; having done so as a man of mixed race, he has a strong claim to being one of the most important figures in the early decades of the game. Yet even in his own time, his legend faded.

Following the conclusion of his playing career, Watson moved to Surrey and died there of pneumonia and cardiac arrest at his home in Kew on 8 March 1921 at the age of 64, his occupation simply stated as marine engineer. Watson's humble grave is even less voluble about the life and career of this remarkable footballer. He surely deserves a richer eulogy.

The Talent Spotters

A glimpse into the murky and unglamorous world of football scouts

By Mike Calvin

Mel Johnson took his tea, without milk or sugar, and sat with his back to the wall at the circular table closest to the door. His eyes moved quickly, constantly, as he completed his risk assessment. He was friendly and attentive, but there were 83 other scouts in the first-floor room at Staines Town. It was his business to know their business.

A wry grin. He noticed Bullshit Pete was sitting alone, chasing a piece of chicken around his plate. Buffet Billy was working his way through chips, rice and a curry which had the colour and consistency of melted caramel. The Ayatollah was in a conspiratorial huddle with his followers, whose synchronised glances offered clues about the nature and direction of their discussion.

Agents circulated, seeking the convertible currency of casual gossip and inside information. One, nondescript in appearance apart from a lilac roll-neck sweater, was identified by Johnson as Billy Jennings, a striker who helped West Ham win the FA Cup in 1975. His bottle-blond mullet, a feature of my schoolboy scrapbook, had receded to a monkish semi-circle.

Emissaries from the international game — Brian Eastick, England's Under-20 coach, and Mark Wotte, Scotland's performance director — held court. The room hummed with conjecture and cautious conversation. It had the feel of a bookmaker's on an urban side street. The men, largely middle-aged and uniformly watchful, had the pallor of too many such midwinter nights on the road.

I had invited myself into their world, a place of light and shadow. They were the Nowhere Men, ubiquitous yet anonymous, members of football's hidden tribe. The elders, like Johnson, had paid their dues at the biggest clubs. Initiates were paid 40 pence a mile and informed decisions on players worth £10 million or more. All were under threat from technology and the new religion of analytics.

Such men are central to the mythology of modern football. Scouts may be marginalised, professionally, but they possess the power of dreams. There is no textbook for them to follow, no diploma they can receive for their appreciation of the alchemy involved in the creation of a successful player. Their scrutiny is intimate, intense and highly individual. They must balance nuances of character with aspects of pre-programmed ability and fit them to the profile and culture of the clubs they represent.

Everyone knows what scouts do, but no one truly understands why they do it and no one knows who they are. Their anonymity is anathema to the modern game, a gaudy global carousel which invites examination on its own, highly lucrative terms. Scouts supply the star system, but remain resistant to it. At best, they are indistinct figures, judged on false impressions like old-school golf caddies, who were assumed to drink heavily and sleep in hedges. They are an enclosed order, by circumstance rather than philosophy.

Anyone who has ever stood shivering on a touchline or sat shouting from the back of a stand thinks they can do their job. Whether the average football fan would want to commit to such a disconnected lifestyle is another matter entirely. Being paid for watching up to ten games a week might be the sort of fantasy which sustains a fourth former during an afternoon of algebra, but the hours are long and family-unfriendly. Scouts eat on the run, live on their nerves and receive a relative pittance.

This may seem counterintuitive, but I resolved to study them and to share their experiences, because I believed in the essential romanticism of their role. Over the course of more than a year on the road, I was seduced by the process of discovery. I saw boys whose precocity caused time to freeze, and young men, in straitened circumstances, who seized a second chance to shine. I was there when the seeds of natural talent began to germinate; this may occur in a park, or on a non-league gluepot. It may be destined to flower in one of the cathedrals of the game, but it beckons only those who comprehend its potential.

Scouts are nowhere, and everywhere. They are rivals, but mix closely.

They offered me an insight into the idiosyncrasies and insecurities of an incestuous community. Their judgements are severe, occasionally unkind, but they must be judged in the context of a game which has an unerring habit of brutalising its participants. What makes scouts different? Time and again Paul Newman's line, delivered in his role as Butch Cassidy, in the film *Butch Cassidy and the Sundance Kid*, came to mind: "I got vision, and the rest of the world wears bifocals."

On this particular Wednesday night, 15 February 2012, Chelsea were playing West Ham in the third round of the FA Youth Cup. Teenagers, courted and cosseted from adolescence, were accustomed to indulgences, such as being transported to Wheatsheaf Road in the first team's luxury coach. They filed, with studied indifference, through the tiny car park, past the picture window of a gymnasium which framed suburban wage slaves purging themselves on treadmills.

It was a big night for the Conference South club, even if its patron, the TV astrologer Russell Grant, could not attend due to unforeseen circumstances. The surrounding streets were clogged with traffic, and the Staines Massive, the club's inevitably entitled support base, swelled beyond 1500. The following night's fund-raising quiz would struggle to make a quorum.

Chelsea were under pressure to justify an academy which had consumed in excess of £60 million without producing a first-team regular in its first eight years. The annual operational budget, £8 million, dwarfed that of many Football League clubs. A single youth-team player, the

Brazilian striker Lucas Piazon, represented a £10 million investment. West Ham were quietly confident of nurturing a new golden generation, attuned to cherished principles and philosophies, but there were no guarantees.

For some, this Youth Cup run would be a career highlight. Around 10,000 boys are in the academy system. In the region of 1% will make a living out of the game. Two-thirds of those given a professional contract at 18 are out of professional football by the time they are 21. The scouts were there to scavenge; it was their job to be in a position to take advantage of a coach's lack of foresight or a club's lack of patience. They were looking for signs, hints of undervalued talent that others might miss.

Johnson, Liverpool's principal scout in the South of England, was reassessing players with development potential. His son Jamie, Millwall's chief scout, was one of many representatives of Football League clubs looking at long-term loan targets. Dean Austin, newly employed on a part-time basis by Bolton Wanderers, sought youngsters with resale value.

Austin, the former Spurs full-back, was working through his angst at the interruption to his coaching career, which had surprisingly stalled. He managed in the Conference and combined coaching with player recruitment at Southend before becoming Brendan Rodgers's assistant manager at Watford and Reading. He had been seeking a manager's role since leaving Crystal Palace in May 2011 and was prepared to keep head-butting a glass ceiling. "He's my angry young man," said Johnson, affectionately.

"I just love getting out there, on that training field' said Austin, with convincing force.

Mark Anderson arrived from another dawn shift as a senior site manager for a construction company. Football was his release, the Liver Bird on his quilted jacket a badge of honour, even if wearing it on duty defied convention. He was proud of his association with a club of Liverpool's stature, as a youth scout, and radiated unfulfilled ambition. He, too, was determined to get back into the game on a full-time basis.

Steve Gritt was in his first year as Bournemouth's chief scout. While Alan Curbishley, his former managerial partner, endured the purgatory of punditry, he was sustaining a career defined by spells in charge at Charlton, Brighton and Millwall. His most recent post, as director of Charlton's Academy, had relevance, but he remained in culture shock.

"When I first started in management with Curbs, 20 years ago, the managers went out scouting," he said, tightening the drawstrings on the fur-lined hood of his quilted coat. 'That's not the case these days. So many rely on the judgements of their scouts. Funny, that, because they are the ones who pay if those judgements are wrong. This job is a bit of an eye-opener, to be honest. Even managers don't really realise what scouts do, how hard they work. They are out in all weathers, at all hours. They don't get the credit they deserve."

The scouts sat where they could, in a 300-seater main stand. They didn't share the laughter as balls disappeared into adjoining gardens. They were blind to the idiosyncrasies of the setting. Closely planted leylandii, evergreen symbols of Middle England, stood guard behind one goal. Newly built houses, as neat and symmetrical as loaves of bread on a baker's shelf, were vulnerable to stray shots at the other end.

During lulls in play, Anderson delivered despatches from football's dirty war. Scouts were having their car tyres slashed on suspicion of poaching young players from smaller clubs, who were aggrieved by what was perceived to be the institutionalised greed of the Premier League's Elite Player Performance Plan. "There's a lot of aggro out there," he reported. "It's getting naughty. A lot of clubs won't have us on the premises."

Representatives of six Premier League teams, including Arsenal, Manchester United and Chelsea, drafted the plan, which created four categories of academy. It was, essentially, a self-selecting process since those in the top category were required to underwrite an annual budget of £2.3m and employ at least 18 full-time staff. Wealthier clubs were freed from the need to recruit young players within a 90-minute radius, in terms of travel time, from their bases.

Naked self-interest is excused when an outstanding 14-year-old has a bounty of up to £2 million on his head. EP3, as the plan is known in the trade, was reportedly forced through when the Premier League threatened to withdraw £5.4 million in so-called Solidarity Funding from Football League clubs if they did not sanction its adoption. Their resistance, understandable because it gave an open invitation for scouts to pilfer boys as young as nine for small change, was futile.

Young footballers are on the menu and the price list is set. Instead of paying seven-figure sums, the biggest clubs need only to pay £3,000 for every year a newly recruited boy has spent at another club's academy between the ages of 9 and 11. As little as £12,000 compensation is required for every year he has been nurtured — elsewhere — between the ages of 12 and 16. Premier League clubs, who had accumulated debts of £361 million from a collective income of £2.3 billion, had a vested interest in portraying anarchy as opportunity.

Johnson, a man of ritual and restraint, busied himself with his paperwork. He had folded a sheet of A4 into quarters and recorded the players' names and numbers, in formation, in blue and red ink. It would be stored, like thousands of others, in a series of suitcases in his garage. Occasionally, in shorthand designed to offer a mental image, he wrote "looks like" next to a name. Thus Taylor Miles, scorer of West Ham's 43rd-minute equaliser, was linked in perpetuity to Craig Bellamy. He lacked the Liverpool player's default mode of an enraged ferret, but shared his energy and eye for goal.

Whenever Johnson spoke, he instinctively held the official team sheet over his mouth with his right hand, to prevent strangers overhearing. His voice was soft, yet insistent. "You're very much on your own in this job," he said. "It can be very lonely. You don't really have friends, you have your fellow scout acquaintances, but they're not really friends. It's a bit of a secret world. We try not to tell each other who we're watching, but most of the time it's quite obvious."

Two young men behind us, one apparently preoccupied with his iPad, another saucer-eyed from texting on his smart phone, caught his attention. "You can tell the agents," he said, with a barely decipherable flick of the head. "They're the ones who are on the phone all the time. They don't watch the game at all. They're here to work the rooms, to see and be seen."

Jamie was initially impressed by John Swift, Chelsea's elegant, straight-backed central midfield player. He made good angles, picked clever passes and was sufficiently technically adept to be comfortable on the ball in tight areas. "A young one, a Gary Gardner type, Dad," he said, referring to another midfield tyro, at Aston Villa. "Good footballer but an academy player," came the reply. "Ask yourself the question: will he keep me in a job if I take him for a Championship or League One club? No. He'll get you the sack." Swift duly faded into insignificance.

The older man was examining body shape, the probabilities of genetic inheritance. "Look at Elliot Lee — Rob's son. Chip off the old block, isn't he? But a big arse. Not an athlete." Few words were wasted and judgements were harsh: "Look at the goalkeepers. One's a great size, but a coward. The other's a great shot stopper but too small. Their mistakes prey on your mind."

I was struck by Chelsea's Todd Kane, a full-back in the modern idiom. He was strong, adventurous and aggressive and his delivery from wide areas caused problems. "He could have a career, him. My first thought is Brentford. He's a Nicky Shorey type. He does what it says on the tin. Problem is his size — can't see him

defending at the far post at top level. He'll be a proper pro, though."

There was logic to Johnson's caution, borne out of 27 years' experience. "The window of opportunity isn't open for long, and they're out there flicking and farting around. It is a cruel world. They have only one chance to impress. There are too many games, too many players, to spend long on them. When you are working for Liverpool, a lot of the time you are crossing names off your list."

Islam Feruz, a small support striker blessed with extreme pace, earned a reprieve by scoring a goal of sublime quality. He picked up the ball midway in the opposition half, surged past four challenges into the heart of the penalty area and dinked a shot over the advancing West Ham goalkeeper. "Blimey!" exclaimed Johnson. "Didn't see that coming. That was Diego Maradona."

Feruz was a child of his times. The only son in a family of Somalian refugees that relocated to Glasgow after fleeing to London from Tanzania, he was saved from deportation at the age of 12 by the advocacy of Celtic's youth coach, the late Tommy Burns. He made his first-team debut at the age of 14, in a memorial match for Burns, a man of immense integrity in a game of shallow expedience.

Within 18 months, Chelsea had taken advantage of a loophole in the system to spirit him south. Conscious of competition from Manchester City, they installed the family in a flat near their Cobham training ground. The boy was reportedly being paid £10,000 a month and had his own website, which proclaimed, "Islam Feruz will be famous." Wotte, who might have been expected to be a little more circumspect, promptly compared him to Romario.

With five minutes remaining and the scores level at 2–2, most of the scouts had seen enough. Only Anderson stayed to witness Chelsea's win, on penalties, after the game had ended 3–3 after extra time. "What have I got to go home to?" he said with a mischievous smile. "I'll be here helping them sweep up." He would make himself busy, networking with agents, parents and coaches. He could talk for England, but, crucially, he was a good listener. He also worked a room, like a bee collecting pollen.

Johnson scurried to his car in the company of Steve McCall, Ipswich's chief scout. His small talk — "that Nat Chalobah, he's got Chelsea-itis. Got all the tools, but a laid-back Larry" — was tellingly deceptive. It was several months before he revealed he had logged the defender's speed of thought, intelligent movement and ease on the ball. He recommended him as the holding midfield player Liverpool were seeking.

Johnson had been taken to Anfield by Damien Comolli, with whom he worked as chief scout for Tottenham. He recruited Gareth Bale from Southampton, but was a victim of regime change under Harry Redknapp. It was the first time he had been "moved on" since he began scouting, as a self-confessed "football fanatic", in 1985. The following year, on Good Friday, he recommended Norwich City sign an 11-year-old midfield player he had spotted playing for Ridgeway Rovers in the Canaries Cup.

David Beckham was duly invited for trials at Carrow Road, but joined Tottenham's

School of Excellence before Manchester United and corporate canonisation beckoned. Since Leyton Orient, the boy's local club, were also unfulfilled suitors at that time, there was an appropriate symmetry to Johnson's next tutorial, an Under-19 international between England and the Czech Republic at Brisbane Road.

Johnson parked in the terraced streets surrounding the ground and popped into a newsagent to buy a local paper. "Everyone canes me for it, even Damien," he said, with a self-deprecating chuckle. "But I always buy one for the titbits. You never know what you'll find out." He returned to his car and studied the Czech squad on his iPad for an hour before he entered the Olympic Suite, 35 minutes from kick-off.

The scouts were devouring ham and mustard sandwiches, with the obligatory chips, as they retold tall tales of ducking and diving. My favourite revealed the ingenuity and duplicity of one solid citizen who monitored youth football for Portsmouth, did first-team match assessments for Newcastle United and covered non-League football for Wolverhampton Wanderers. All three clubs were ignorant of his involvement with the others.

Johnson preferred the company of the Tottenham coach Clive Allen. "He was good to me at Spurs," he explained. "He kept phoning to see how I was after they outed me. You don't forget things like that." They discussed the striker Harry Kane. He was excelling on loan at Millwall, whose manager Kenny Jackett had worked with Johnson at Watford and QPR. The one doubt, about his pace at the highest level, was neutralised by memories of Teddy Sheringham, a player whose game intelligence compensated for a slight lack of speed.

"I love this place," Johnson reflected, as we looked out on to a museum piece, the deserted old main stand. "The fans are the funniest around. I was here once when they started chanting, 'We can see you washing up,' at the inhabitants of the flats in the corner. It's a proper club, with some great people." Memories of the old John Chiedozie tea-bar and the fabled eccentricity of the former manager John Sitton, stirred a smile.

Stuart Pearce, who was to make a cameo appearance as England's caretaker manager against Holland at Wembley the following night, nodded as he bustled past with his retinue. Johnson had talked football with him the previous week, in Jackett's office at the Den, but his perspective shifted suddenly, as the teams and his sheet of A4 came out. "We know the England boys so well," he said, "this is my chance to look at the Czechs. They've beaten some top sides." He quickly concentrated on the goalkeeper Lukas Zima, a tall, slightly built fashion victim in tangerine kit and predominantly orange boots. All that remained was for him to address the error of my ways.

"Don't look at the game, look at the man," Johnson instructed. "You are following play just like the coaches who come out with me. Scouts study their man. I blank the other players out, although if the ball is at the other end of the pitch I'll watch out of the corner of my eye, just in case I get asked for an opinion. You cannot follow the ball in this job."

I felt self-conscious at first, but it was simple and startlingly effective. Watching Zima so intensely had a strange intimacy. He morphed from an unknown name on a team sheet to a definable human being. His mannerisms became familiar and the complexities of his character emerged. He unwittingly evoked sympathy and understanding. Johnson was enthused: "Look at him. Good concentration. Keeps communicating. Attention to detail. He's alert, thinking. A good size. I like him. I like his bravery. He's been out at people's feet a couple of times. I know he punches, but all the foreign ones do, especially at youth level."

As he spoke, England broke quickly from an ill-judged Czech attack. Harry Kane chested the ball down inside his own half, fed Ross Barkley on the right and sprinted to receive a return ball on the edge of the penalty area before scoring with a low shot into the corner. Johnson spoke with proprietorial authority and concern: "There was nothing the keeper could do. He's got nothing in front of him. That Celtic boy, the left-sided centre-half, is struggling for his life. It's not the keeper's fault they keep getting caught out by balls over the top."

The consensus at half-time was that the Czechs were "crap". Lil Fuccillo, Luton's technical director, was telling anyone who would listen, "It's Barça this, Barça that. I'm getting sick of it. We've got to play to our strengths in this country." Rather than enlist in the Bedfordshire branch of the Flat Earth Society, Johnson gravitated towards Dave Holden, the veteran Arsenal scout, who was instrumental in the recruitment of Alex Oxlade-Chamberlain.

There was an easy rapport between the pair — "not a lot out there, is there?" – and each knew not to read too much into the small talk. They strayed beyond the immediacy of the match to engage in a discussion about the best culture to instil in young players. Holden, a former school teacher who had retained a broad Geordie accent, insisted, "Players recognise the best players. They'll have a young one in the group if they see something in him. Players also challenge coaches. They know if the coach isn't good enough, the outstanding player in the group will regress to the level of the others."

The gossip was global. Jaap Stam was making a positive impact as Manchester United's Brazilian scout and was pushing hard for Dedé, the Vasco da Gama central defender. Barcelona had taken out first options on 39 young players at Boca Juniors. Glenn Roeder, the former Newcastle manager, had been added to Aston Villa's scouting staff. By the time the litany of opportunity was complete, the second half was underway.

We were joined by Anderson, Liverpool's youth scout, who exclaimed, "There's our boy again!" when Todd Kane delivered a cross on the run that enabled Chelsea colleague Patrick Bamford to extend England's lead with a stooping header. Johnson's other duty involved monitoring winger Nathan Redmond, who was introduced as a substitute midway through the half. "Watch him," he counselled. "He won't really be trying. He'll be more worried about playing for Birmingham on Saturday and in the Cup replay against Chelsea next week." Sure enough, Redmond was measured, to the point of indolence. He contributed little, apart from a languid flick and brief bursts of pace in insignificant areas. Another early departure was entirely excusable.

Again, Johnson had rationed his intelligence. No one had detected his interest in the goalkeeper. "The trick in this game is never to let people know what you are thinking or how you are working. There are plenty out there happy to feed off your knowledge." His report on Zima, who had been signed by Genoa from Slavia Prague, was on the Anfield system by 2 am, with a recommendation that he be watched by Liverpool's Italian scout.

It was one of 200 such reports submitted that week. Whether it would receive the attention it deserved was another matter entirely.

This is an edited extract from Mike Calvin's book The Nowhere Men, *published by Century in September.*

44

Interview

"Was it is a risk? Yes. Life is a risk."

Fatih Terim

The Emperor on the rise of Turkish football and breaking the glass ceiling with Galatasaray

By Andy Brassell

Waiting for Fatih Terim in the palatial gardens of Galatasaray's Florya training complex, you look around, you look at everything, for clues to how the coach thinks. Everything here is decided by him, they say; from the menu in the canteen to the colour of the gazebo on the main lawn that borders the players' quarters. Now 59, Terim lives the job to the extent that the club are building living quarters here for him — he often sleeps in his office after working late into the night.

He meets us here on the afternoon before Galatasaray's final game of the season, at home to Trabzonspor ("the first time I've ever done an interview before a match," he says), an occasion which should have been one of joyous celebration but has been scaled down to a more low-key affair, after the terrorist attacks in Reyhanlı and the murder of teenage Fenerbahçe fan Burak Yıldırım in the aftermath of the previous weekend's derby.

The man they call *imparator* ('The Emperor') in Turkey has that on his mind and more as he looks back on how far he's taken Galatasaray — with whom he's now in a third spell as coach — and Turkey, as well as his career's English roots.

⚽ *Tell us a bit about how you first discovered football. What are your first memories of the game as a child and how did you first begin to get involved in the game?*

I almost don't remember anything else from when I was a child apart from football. I was just focused on playing in the streets with my friends. Football was my priority ahead of anything else.

⚽ *When you joined Galatasaray in 1974, you were a forward, weren't you?*

I was an attacking player, but I was generally in midfield. By the time I quit playing, I was a *libero*. One of my coaches was Big Mal — Malcolm Allison, you remember? He made a change to the way I played, though it was Don Howe who first made me play as a *libero*, in a European Cup game against Rapid Vienna. When I was a player, I was always working with English coaches at Galatasaray... Arthur Cox [Allison's assistant at the club] was another one.

⚽ *How long did it take to adapt when you moved back to defence?*

Right away. I was quick, I had good technique and I was adaptable so it was OK. I started playing as a defender when I was at Galatasaray, but I started to play in that position for the national team as well and continued doing that for Turkey after I left Galatasaray.

◈ Galatasaray have the TT Arena now, but when you were a player, they played in a few different places. What sort of a difference does it make to have a dedicated home stadium?

It's a big advantage and it's a source of great happiness for us too. You are saying that "It's mine." Before, we were sometimes sharing with other teams and the capacity wasn't that big. It's about the facilities off the pitch as well, the other stuff. The teams that want to be in the top 20 or the top 10 in the world have to have stadiums like this. It's important economically, financially, socially... Of course the stadium has an effect on us [the staff], but the most important aspect is the economic one. It's like in London, the difference between Craven Cottage and the Emirates. The fans are different, the pressure in the stadiums is different. We respect the memories we have [of the old Ali Sami Yen], but we have to adapt to the modern structure of football.

◈ If we're talking about adapting over time, let's briefly go back to when you were a player for Turkey. When you played for Turkey it was still far from established as a world or European power. It's a very different situation to yours now, where you're used to winning all the time. How did the difficult times as a player shape your outlook when you took charge of Turkey?

It was drastically different. My mentality was very simple when I became a coach; I was only 32. In '93, when I became national team coach for the first time, my philosophy... I saw that in the past 70 years, we had done nothing. In my first press conference, the very first thing that I said was, "There's only one word that I won't say — patience. This country already had too much patience. If I do badly, you won't let me continue anyway, so I'm not going to tell you 'patience'." I told my players — don't be scared to lose, as you already lost plenty. The Turkey team was set out in a 9-0-1, with nine in defence. We were already losing playing in a defensive way. I said, why not lose in an attacking way? And then, one by one, we started to beat teams that we hadn't been able to beat for 40 years, 50 years. Being a coach and being a player for Turkey is very different, even if I used my experiences, as I was a leader on the pitch anyway.

◈ So you always planned to be a coach?

When I was playing, I always said to myself: when I stop playing, that's it for me and football. I'm done with it. My first daughter had just been born... Jupp Derwall asked me not to quit football, but I told him, "The path is too long. I won't be able to see my daughter. I'm going to quit." And I did. In the six months that followed, with my wife, I found other things to do with my life. I wasn't interested in football at all. I was offered good money to write for newspapers, to go on television as a pundit and I always said, "It's not my business." Then I was invited to go Mexico and watch the World Cup in '86. I went... and then I decided to go back to football. I couldn't escape anymore. Everybody wanted me to go back to football and that's how my journey as a coach started.

◈ Derwall, after arriving at Galatasaray in 1984, was obviously a big influence on you, along with Sepp Piontek (who made Terim Turkey's Under-21 coach in 1991).

How did he change Turkish football and Galatasaray in terms of professionalism?

The main thing was our training pitch. It was soil before. He did so much for Turkish football. He brought modern ideas and had a professional understanding of how to apply them. Piontek, as well, is a very honest guy. Very fair, very direct. I've been lucky to know them both and Piontek... I see him as family.

⚡ *You yourself took the Turkish game to another level, getting the national team to their first major finals — Euro 96. After a tough start to the qualifiers, was it the win over Sweden that really kicked it off for you and made you believe it was possible?*

100%, because if we'd lost against Sweden, it would have been all over. We did something else though — beating Switzerland away. That was the moment we took leadership of the group, and we went on from there. It was a very tough group. Sweden were semi-finalists in America in '94 and Switzerland, coached by Roy Hodgson, a very good friend of mine — please say hello — were in the last 16. Putting Sweden out of contention was very important. I made a declaration at the start of the press conference, before the game. "We, the Turkish national team, aren't going alone. All of us — the players, you the journalists, the Turkish people — if we go to the Euros, we all go together." I didn't just coach, I motivated the public. After league games, the Turkish media were harsh, absolutely killing the players, and I put a stop to it.

⚡ *That's the key to international management, in your opinion, then — getting the whole country behind the national team? It's something that Luiz Felipe Scolari, for example, did really well with Brazil and Portugal....*

Of course. It's incredibly important. You have to bring everyone together. It's inside the team as well. If the players from the different clubs continue their rivalry within the national team, you can't be successful. If, for example, Manchester United say, "Why aren't you taking this player from my team?" or Chelsea say, "Take this player from my team," it's very dangerous. You can't have a homogenised national team then. This is why you need a group of fans who really support that national team. It's like Ireland — all green. Holland — all orange. Behind the team all the time: win, lose, whatever. It's something very powerful.

⚡ *What did the finals of Euro 96 mean to you, emotionally, and how much did it tell you that Turkey still had a way to go to be competitive?*

I said in my press conference at the start of the tournament that "because it's the first time, it's a magnificent achievement for us to be there. We're not expecting anything from it. That doesn't mean we're giving up." In terms of the championships to come in the years following, it was very important. The country's belief and the players' belief increased. They started to think, "The coach was right — we can do it." It was like a dream [he breaks into English] — *"we're in England! Nottingham, Liverpool..."* and we started against a very good team in Croatia. I just told my players — play your game and enjoy being here. And we could have beaten Croatia and Portugal. I knew that after '96 the success would come; the third place in 2002 [at the World Cup], the Euro 2008 semi-final, as well as the successes for our club sides. England was like a starting point.

⊕ *Next, you joined Galatasaray as coach for the first time. Having won the cup three times as a player but never the Süper Lig, did you always have an idea about how you wanted to mould the team — and the club?*

As a footballer, I won a good variety of cups without ever winning the league. I don't pay as much attention to this as other people do. It's like in my coaching career — I have lots of trophies, but not the Champions League. I don't get hung up on that. I'll give you an important example. When I was at Fiorentina, we got to the Coppa Italia final, beating Milan after we beat Brescia. We got there undefeated but before the final, because my principles are more important to me [than anything], I resigned. They offered me a three-year deal, and if I'd have thought, "a Turkish coach is going to play this major final," I wouldn't have gone. As my conscience was clear, I felt in my heart — I knew — God would give me the opportunity to win more as a coach.

Between 1996 and 2000 at Galatasaray, we won everything. Was it is a risk? Yes. [In English again] *"Life is a risk."* Making progress is the most important thing. In 1996, we were mediocre. In 1997, we were better. In '98 we were much better, in '99 very good and in 2000 we crowned our success by winning the Uefa Cup. I always used 22, 23 players, with three goalkeepers, and made sure everyone played, and got the maximum performance out of all of them.

⊕ *Some key players joined in 1996. Ümit Davala, Gheorghe Hagi. How important were these two, and others, in getting Galatasaray playing the sort of football that you wanted to?*

First of all, I laid down a football philosophy. Anywhere around the world where we play — Milan, Leeds, Mallorca, Dortmund, wherever — we play high pressure, and in the other team's half. I took Ümit Davala from the second division. When I was coaching Turkey's under-21s, I took him into the team from the third division. Earlier in '96, there was Vedat İnceefe, whom I took from Karabükspor in the second division into the Turkish national team. Before us, Hagi hadn't been as good as he was for us, but we brought them together and became a family.

We were playing with three, maximum four foreign players at the time. When we played Arsenal [in the 2000 Uefa Cup final], they had 17. Because we had this continuous philosophy, we made fewer transfers after the second year — just occasional important ones like [Gheorghe] Popescu, Taffarel, a few domestically.

In the first game against Leeds (in the 2000 Uefa Cup semi-final), when we won 2-0 in Istanbul, we played with three forwards; Arif [Erdem], Hakan (Şükür) and Hagi. At Elland Road we played with the same confidence, the same emphasis on pressure, the same possession. The only thing I feel sad about, 13 years later, is something that was said to me when we recently had a lunch here at Florya, with the team that won the cup in 2000. What Popescu said to me that day is still ringing in my ears. He told me, "If you hadn't gone to Fiorentina, this team would have won the Champions League." Other players have told me that too. We became very strong together, in every way. When you don't call a closed training camp before the game, there's always a lot of criticism in the press here. For the whole year, in 99-00, I didn't call a camp. We'd all meet an hour and a half before the game, in Ali Semi Yen. I wrote the team on the board in the dressing room, and they got on with it.

❋ *Because everyone knew absolutely what they were doing?*

Yes. Automatic. The training, the game... they knew me. And I knew who they were.

❋ *The start of your European adventures with the club had been tough, though, hadn't it? In 1997, you had your first go at the Champions League and were drawn in a group with Borussia Dortmund, the holders. Did it eventually prove an advantage to come in at such a high level?*

It took us time to get used to the level. What's interesting for me is the qualifiers [for the group stage]. You can't sleep before them. You have to play these two games and you can [brushes hands against one another] lose everything. It's too much stress. I played in them four times — eight games — and qualified all four times for the Champions League. You play Grasshoppers, or a team from Bulgaria, and all of a sudden you're in the groups with Dortmund or Parma. It's not easy.

In Istanbul, we matched all of them. Away from home, we suffered because of our inexperience. That's normal. When our players see players like [Matthias] Sammer, [Andreas] Möller that they're used to seeing on TV and then they're actually playing them, it's tough, but very important for getting on the path that took us to where we went in the

following years. We did video analyses and shared them with the players. There are very few faults in my teaching system and they did far more right than they did wrong. Every year, we improved, made fewer mistakes and we kept showing them how they improved, until '99, when we got to the peak.

Since then [1997], I have had a principle. In every team that I've managed, after the training camp, I always want to play big teams in friendly games. The year that we won the Uefa Cup, we played Barcelona and Málaga in a [pre-season] tournament at the Giants Stadium in New York. I tried to make them get rid of any complex they had about these big teams and show them, "You are no less than them." I made every player an individual video cassette, of their good moments, their mistakes, everything. Self-analysis is very important.

❋ *And by the time we get to 1999-2000, when you won the Uefa Cup, you played Dortmund in the 4th round....*

We finished it out there, at the Westfalen. We were always an offensive side, dominating, but we played a little more tactically here in Istanbul in the second leg. Going on from the Milan game, that we won 3-2 in the Champions League group stages, against Bologna, Dortmund, Mallorca, Leeds and Arsenal, we were undefeated in 13 games. We were coming from a strong Champions League group, with Hertha Berlin, Chelsea... Hertha were unbeaten at home and we went to Berlin and beat them 4-1. No tight margins — we were always trying to score.

❋ *And it was only really the home game against Chelsea, the 5-0 loss, that had stopped you going through that group.*

In the first game in London, we had a ball go 80cm over the line and the referee didn't give it – Glenn Hoddle said it was a goal on the commentary, actually — and then we got a red card [for Taffarel]. After, we played an hour with ten players but we were hammering them. I have the video of the 5-0 game in my office here. 5-0! If you watch it, it's unbelievable. When I was going to the press conference, I bumped into [the Chelsea manager Gianluca] Vialli in the hall. He just shrugged and said, "It's football. What can I say?" I called my players here [to Florya] after the game. We got on the bus. I made a speech to them.

Next up, we had a really difficult game at Bursa — a hard pitch, and I took the decision to leave nine of them out. [Animatedly breaking into English] Everybody was against me after the game — radio, television, everybody. After all these criticisms from the media, members of the board and all, we went to Berlin. We were one down at half-time, we made a few little changes and came out with the 4-1 win and, from that point, nobody could stop us. But all of these experiences — the good, the bad — improved us, and added to our European culture. Then, we started to talk louder. In January, I said, "Champions League is tough, but we can win the Uefa Cup." People said, "He's crazy, he's dreaming," but... they all apologised at the end.

⚽ *Then there was the semi-final with a strong Leeds team. Of course, there were some tragic incidents in Istanbul before the game — how difficult was it to focus on the match, knowing everything that was going on outside?*

Even though it's been a long time now, I still feel a lot of sadness about that. After the game, even though we won, it was a very strange atmosphere. Honestly, from the bottom of my heart, I'd rather have been knocked out of the competition and that these two English fans were not murdered. With what happened, Uefa banned fans from travelling and said that we could only take a party of 80 to Leeds [for the return leg]. It was tense.

Even though we won the first game 2-0, I went to see the game before the second leg, when Leeds played Arsenal, by myself. There were 41,000 there. I didn't know the people I was sitting with, but three people around me in my box stood up when Arsenal scored. They were Arsenal directors. The people around looked at us and started shouting, "Fuck off! Fuck you!" I went there to give my players a message. To say that there's nothing to be scared of at Elland Road. I know English people very well, from way back in my career. At an English ground, you can easily give up four or five goals. 2-0 isn't a big lead [switches into English for emphasis] — especially if you are scared. With the crowd, you're always in the game.

There is a cinema room in our youth academy. I made my players watch a recording of a [Leeds] game in there before we left, with the volume turned right up high, like we were in the stadium. In 18 hours, we prepared an all-black strip — just for the warm-up, as Uefa wouldn't let us wear it in the game — and laid flowers [at the stadium]. We scored twice in the first twenty minutes and that sewed it up. In my opinion, that Leeds team... very good. Harry Kewell, (Michael) Bridges, (Nigel) Martyn, (Ian) Harte, Lee Bowyer. Young, very good players. But it was more a case of managing the tension.

⟳ You then faced another English team in the final. Both Galatasaray and Arsenal are known for pretty football, but that game was a battle, wasn't it?

Like a war. A tactical war. In my opinion, that was one of the best Arsenal teams, one of the best teams of the last 20 years. A few weeks after we knocked out Leeds, Arsenal were playing Chelsea. I took my wife to London and we went to Highbury watch the game. It was a lovely, sunny day. While we were watching the game, she didn't say a word to me. After, she asked me, "Fatih, what are you thinking about?" I said, "They are too good! How are we going to do it? How are we going to mark them? Everyone needs marking."

We only had one choice. Play the game. I came to Florya, I made my tactical plan and I decided on ten of the players to start. A day before the game, I was undecided. On the morning of the game, I was still undecided. Either I could play a flat 4-4-2 with Hasan Şaş, or the classic three forwards — Hagi, Arif and Hakan Şükür. We had a training pitch next to the hotel in Copenhagen and I set up a tactical training session at 2pm on the day of the game, so 11 versus 11, where we said to our other set of players [pointing], "OK, you're Henry, you're Bergkamp." Believe me, I was still undecided. Then, I called the forwards and I thought, "I'm going to play my game. Let's call Arif up as a third forward." Realistically, they were stronger than us. But football is something else and you have to do it on the pitch.

The first 90 minutes was a very balanced game. Arif had a one-on-one and if

he'd scored that or Arsenal had scored, I think there would have been a lot of goals in the game. In my opinion, Hagi shouldn't have been sent off on his own, [Tony] Adams should have gone with him. But, OK, we kept playing offensively. It was when Taffarel made that unbelievable save from Henry that I thought we were really going to win. The list of penalty-takers — I made it in thirty seconds. It was something amazing for Turkish football.

⟳ It's hard to ignore the fact that your current coaching staff contains some important personalities from that side that won the 2000 Uefa Cup — Hasan Şaş, Ümit Davala, Taffarel ...what did that side have that made it so special and that you still want to have around you today?

Before I became coach of Galatasaray [again] officially, I called 10 of the players [from that side] to my house. Hakan said, "I'm going into politics," a few said other things, and at the end, I chose these three. Well, Taffarel wanted to come straight from Brazil, but I told him, "Check with your wife first! That's very important!" I trust the three of them completely. I believe in them and I'm trying to give them some of my experience, so in the coming years, they will become great coaches. I chose them because they know Galatasaray very well, they know Turkish football very well, they are young, they still have the desire and they have the aim of becoming something big in coaching. The most important thing is I don't have to explain everything to them — they already know me very well.

⟳ You decided to make the leap to Serie A after Copenhagen and to Fiorentina.

When you arrived there, it's said that you took your first training session with your shirt off, in the rain, smoking a cigar... is this right? What was the idea behind this?

No. [Looks a bit perplexed]. I was smoking... I quit five years ago though and feel much better for it! I took off my coat, because I was sweating, but... anyway, it's a very special place for me, Florence. The place, the people. If you ever go there, just say "Terim" and see what people say. In Adana, the city where I was born, I wouldn't say the same.

We beat all the big teams and, most importantly, we played unbelievable football. I wrote the system down for the players on the first day and said, "Right, we're going to play like this." Intense, attacking. And the players [mimes aghast faces and raised eyebrows]... the Italian mentality, you know. After the meeting, [Moreno] Torricelli and [Angelo] Di Livio, as the experienced players in the team, came to see me and said, "Mister, don't worry. We'll do it in one month." After one month, we were playing unbelievably.

They [the media] criticised me for never concentrating on defence. Generally, when you go 1-0 up, you take a forward off and put a defender on. Nuno Gomes, Rui Costa, [Enrico] Chiesa and Leandro. With these players, we had to play 4-3-1-2, with the full-backs always [starts to wave both arms forward insistently]. And people started to love this game. They were 10,000 coming to the Artemio Franchi at first, then 20, 30 and eventually 40,000.

I didn't live there like a Turk, but as an Italian, my whole lifestyle, me and my family. My daughter went everywhere on a Vespa. We're still great friends with all the Italian families we used to eat with and live with there. In the eight, nine months I was there, I was so happy there. And, of course, I was given the second highest state honour there [Commendatore, an Italian knighthood]. I never met or negotiated with Milan while I was at Fiorentina. I only left because I couldn't get along with [the president] Vittorio Cecchi Gori.

You built your side around Rui Costa, who talked recently about how much you did for his career, and took him with you. Given that you made profound changes to the way Milan played, was it a surprise they didn't give you longer to make it work? Or is that just part of Italy's football culture that you accept?

He was an incredible player. I gave him the captaincy and so much responsibility. I put all my trust in him. There were a few options for that position at Milan — Gaizka Mendieta was one — but we chose him and he did some very good things there. He was tough, intelligent, a great personality and of course very technically gifted. At Fiorentina he was out on his own as a leader but, at Milan, there were other leaders.

And the frustration of leaving, without having the chance to finish a job you started?

It happens. I would have changed many more things in time if I'd had the chance. I still have very good friends there and it's one of the greatest clubs in the world. I'm proud I was their coach, even for a short time, and I know that in that time, I found a place in the fans' hearts.

It's said that after Euro 2008, Sir Bobby Robson recommended you to be the manager of Newcastle United. Did you know about this at the time? Could you have seen yourself in England?

No, I didn't. Sir Bobby? A legend. That makes me feel very proud. England is a place where... you play the game for the whole 90 minutes. There's a genuine struggle. It's undoubtedly the number one league in the world. The excitement, the feeling, is always there. It would have made me very proud to go there.

If we talk about passion, we should talk about the derby here in Istanbul, between Galatasaray and Fenerbahçe. Away fans are banned at the moment and there's a lot of violence around these matches. How has the atmosphere of the derby changed since you were a player?

It [the trouble] is not just between these two football teams. It's everywhere — between the basketball teams, for example. In my time, the fans were watching the games together. After the games, we used to go to dinner together. In the national teams, we were mixed, no divisions, sharing rooms. We urgently need to go back to those times. I believe Turkey will go back to that.

You had a great first season back at Galatasaray, so how did you keep the spirit from that while adding players like Didier Drogba, Wesley Sneijder, to raise the team's profile and level?

It would be a bit megalomaniac of me if I were to explain that... maybe you should tell me. It's a work-in-progress. Next season, we will be even tougher. Sneijder arrived having not played for six months, Drogba had been in China. But each day,

we know each other a little better. By the time they finish pre-season with us, I believe both of them will be more ready.

How was reacquainting yourself with the Champions League?

Against Real Madrid [in the quarter-finals], my team didn't do what they were supposed to do until after the first game, when we got them back to Istanbul. We could have had a couple of penalties out there, but I don't believe in luck. You should be able to self-criticise when you need to and not make excuses. They were a better team than us. I am happy that we went out in this kind of way, but we'll strive to do better next season.

People seem cowed by the best teams these days — Barcelona, Bayern Munich, Real Madrid — but you always went into Champions League games to attack. Will you ever change?

Wouldn't you lose against these teams anyway if you put ten men behind the ball? If you're going to lose, lose playing the game. At Old Trafford, we played three forwards. At the Veltins-Arena, three forwards. Bernabéu, three forwards. After that first game Sir Alex Ferguson told me, "Yes, absolutely, you should have had a penalty," in the first minute of that game. If we keep getting into the Champions League, these sort of mistakes won't happen as much. The referees will subconsciously start to respect us more. This year, we put the seeds in the ground for the years to come.

Many thanks to Emre Utkucan for his help and translation.

54

Nationalisms

"To make sure that the tournament
definitely did not go ahead, all local
schools had the goalposts removed
from their pitches."

Anyone But China

Football plays a vital role in establishing a sense of identity for the Uyghur people

By Henryk Szadziewski

Some time in the 1920s — accounts vary — students from the small village of Artush in what is now China's far west played a game of football against a team put together by the staff of the British Consulate in the nearby Silk Road city of Kashgar. At the time, Kashgar was strategically important to the competing ambitions of the British, Russians and Chinese in Central Asia. On a hard and dusty pitch, the students, ethnic Uyghurs [pronounced 'wee-gors'], ran out easy winners by two goals to nil. After the full-time whistle, the British Consul left in such a cloud of fury that he reneged on a promise to award the winning team the prize of a horse and saddle. The Russian Consul, enjoying every minute, stepped in to congratulate the students and gave them a football instead. The Uyghur students went on to beat a team of Swedish Christian missionaries based in Kashgar, while the Russian Consulate wisely did not offer them a game.

Kashgar, an oasis pressed into the land between the Taklamakan Desert and Pamir Mountains, is part of a vast territory which, depending on your politics, is either called East Turkestan or the Xinjiang Uyghur Autonomous Region. The Uyghur people, who live in Kashgar and throughout the region, are a Turkic Muslim people culturally distinct from their current Chinese rulers. I worked in Kashgar as a teacher at the local college for three years in the mid-1990s.

Football is entrenched in Uyghur life and like fans anywhere Uyghurs enjoy giving their mates a tough time when results go awry. As the only person from Britain living in Kashgar, Uyghur friends and acquaintances never missed an opportunity to remind me of the two-nil hammering by the students. England fans are known for living in the past, always harking back to 1966, but a loss from 70 years ago was one I was willing to concede without too much argument.

The Uyghurs ended up in modern China after the People's Liberation Army entered their homeland in 1949. In the decades leading up to Chinese Communist Party control, Uyghurs experienced two separate periods of independence as the East Turkestan Republic. The government in Beijing, having consolidated its rule, renamed the territory in 1955. With autonomy existing only in name, the arrangement did little to quell the long-held Uyghur yearning for self-determination.

In over 60 years of Chinese rule, the struggle for Uyghur sovereignty has been replaced with one for cultural survival that has been likened to the situation of the Tibetans. Faced with a steady influx of Chinese migrants to their homeland that has seen the proportion of Uyghurs shrink from 80% of the total population in 1941 to 46% in 2010, the Uyghurs are at a crucial point in maintaining their identity.

The gradual loss of cultural identity is not only a result of demographics, but is also a consequence of government 'modernisation' policies that have undermined Uyghur society. Uyghur has been replaced with Chinese as the language of instruction in schools and universities. The authorities defend the policy as a way of increasing Uyghur children's economic opportunities in the modern Chinese job market, but the shift to the Chinese language in schools seems slow in achieving that aim, as unemployment rates among Uyghurs remain high due to discriminatory hiring practices.

The modernising narrative of the Chinese government has taken root in a number of other policies that have put Uyghur culture in a vulnerable position. For many Uyghurs, Islam is both their faith and a statement of their distinctiveness from the Chinese. Government restrictions on following the basic practices of Islam are therefore a challenge to the Uyghur's sense of ethnic identity. In addition, the government-led demolition of traditional Uyghur housing across the region, most notably in Kashgar, has torn the foundations of contemporary Uyghur identification with the people who have lived among these unique buildings for centuries.

The clash between modernisation and preservation is not uncommon in a globalising world but many Uyghurs see the process as a struggle to uphold their existence as a distinct people against assimilation into Chinese culture. With so much unrequited nationalism and ethnic pride, it is no surprise that a stray teacher from Britain has to put up with the odd comment about a lost football game from 70 years ago.

The future direction of the Uyghur people is not just being played out in the classroom or the mosque, but also on the football pitch, in the stands and at home in front of televised games. Whether the Chinese state succeeds in securing Uyghur affinities for the Chinese state's version of modernity through youth football programs, or whether Uyghurs can maintain a sense of their ethnic identity by resisting China's national teams and developing grassroots football organisation in exile, football is an important part of the fight to win Uyghur hearts and minds. This is the story of the role of football in the struggle for the Uyghur identity.

Fans

In December 1996, about eight Uyghurs and I crowded into my flat in Kashgar to watch the Asian Cup quarter-final between Saudi Arabia and China in the UAE on TV. Before kick-off, while crunching sunflower seeds, my Uyghur friends were clear in their dislike of the Chinese national team. They wanted Saudi Arabia to win the quarter-final and agreed that they would be happy to see any country beat China in any game.

The Chinese took a two-goal lead inside the first 16 minutes with goals from the former Grimsby Town player Zhang Enhua and Peng Weigua. The effect was immediate in Kashgar; the Uyghurs in my flat turned their anger on the Saudi team, with some of them calling the Saudis the 'dogs of America' for having let Uyghurs down. By half-time, though, the Saudi had gone 3-2 up and the Uyghurs in Kashgar were firmly back on the side of their co-religionists. Twenty minutes into an open second half the Saudis extended their lead with a second goal from Yousuf Al-Thunayan.

Then an earthquake hit Kashgar. There had been strong earthquakes throughout the year, one in March measuring 6.9 on the Richter scale. Everyone in my flat bolted down the three flights of steps to the ground floor. Waiting outside the building for the all clear proved difficult for everyone who had been following the match. Despite warnings from some neighbours not to go back inside, we returned to my flat to see out the rest of the game. For the Uyghurs it was worth it. Although Zhang Enhua scored his second, China were eliminated.

The swing in support for the Saudis during the game and the 'anyone but China' sentiment made me wonder whether the way that Uyghurs identify

I put together a quick survey early in 2012 to establish whether Uyghurs broadly did not identify with the China national team and to see if there was some kind of pattern to those international teams they did like to see win. I posted the survey on three online forums used by Uyghurs worldwide and collected 95 responses. The first question asked:

If the below teams were in a hypothetical World Cup qualifying group, who would you prefer to win each game (not who you think will win on ability, but who would you like to win)?

Teams: East Turkestan, Uzbekistan, Saudi Arabia, China

Uzbekistan was included in the group to see if Turkic identity was important to Uyghurs, as Uzbeks and Uyghurs have a cultural and linguistic affinity. The addition of Saudi Arabia was to determine if any allegiances were attributable to shared faith. The results I got back left no doubt about the Uyghur antipathy to the Chinese national team:

Game	To win	%	To win	%
East Turkestan v China	East Turkestan	99	China	1
Saudi Arabia v Uzbekistan	Saudi Arabia	19	Uzbekistan	81
East Turkestan v Saudi Arabia	East Turkestan	97	Saudi Arabia	3
Uzbekistan v China	Uzbekistan	97	China	3
East Turkestan v Uzbekistan	East Turkestan	99	Uzbekistan	1
Saudi Arabia v China	Saudi Arabia	97	China	3

against the Chinese majority translates into affinities for international teams that are viewed as 'more like us'.

To get at why Uyghurs chose one international team over another in the games that did not involve the notional

East Turkestan, I asked whether their choice was down to similar ethnicity, shared religion or another reason. Overwhelmingly, Uyghurs said they based their choice to win first on similar ethnicity, then on shared religion. Either way, both the identification with Turkic ethnicity and Islam put the Uyghurs at odds with the dominant Han Chinese culture of China.

China's involvement in the 2002 World Cup is a good example of what the survey demonstrated. As the first World Cup to be held in Asia, the event had special resonance for teams from the continent and China qualified for the first time. In the first round of group games, they were drawn in a group with Turkey, a country with which many Uyghur identify through ethnic ties, its sizeable Uyghur diaspora and its role in hosting exiled Uyghur groups. The game between Turkey and China was held in Seoul on June 13 and clearly visible behind one goal was the blue and white crescent moon and star flag of East Turkestan, which is banned in China. Enver Tohti, a Uyghur activist now living in London, coordinated the action. "We knew that there would be a live broadcast of the game in China," he told me. "If we unfurled the East Turkestan flag during the game, CCTV [China Central Television] would be unable to conceal it on screen. It was also possible that CCTV may not even know what the flag signified. Such a display of our national flag in millions of Chinese homes and public spaces was an opportunity that we could not afford to miss. Flying the East Turkestan flag in China is impossible, so our action would show our people inside China the spirit of the Uyghurs is still alive. In East Turkestan many Uyghurs

suddenly expressed a new interest in football and called their friends and family to tell them to watch the game on TV. What they were really watching was our national flag! In Turkey, when some Uyghurs who had gathered to watch the game saw the flag, the atmosphere in the room turned upside down."

In *The Uyghurs: Strangers in Their Own Land*, Gardner Bovingdon writes about how the display of the East Turkestan flag at the game and China's 3-0 defeat by Turkey was greeted with glee. A contact described to Bovingdon how he had watched the match with both Uyghurs and Hans. "Uyghurs showed their delight each time Turkey surged ahead and the Hans became increasingly angry. My contact recalled with amusement that one Han had chastised the Uyghurs in the room, saying, 'Since you're Chinese citizens, you should cheer for China. Aren't you loyal to China?'"

Showing this kind of support during the game had serious repercussions for some Uyghurs in China. According to one unconfirmed report, 20 Uyghur students at Xinjiang University, who were watching the game with Han Chinese, were arrested on charges of "promoting spiritual separatism" for their support of Turkey. Another unconfirmed report said three students at another university had been expelled and arrested for the same offence.

In politically repressive societies, dissent against the government can express itself in ways that are indirect: sport is one of those outlets. While watching football on TV in Kashgar, Uyghur friends would make fun of the Chinese commentators, often by mimicking Communist Party propaganda to describe the game. In a recent video that went viral in the exile community, the Mandarin language commentary of a Chinese game was replaced with a Uyghur voiceover. Throughout the video the Uyghur 'commentator' makes continuous reference to how honourably the Chinese team play to serve the people and the Party despite showing clips of obvious bad sportsmanship.

None of this antagonism seems to suggest football fans will be the catalyst for greater understanding between Chinese and Uyghurs. Yet bars and city squares that show televised games live are often filled with a mix of Uyghur and Han Chinese. This intermingling may happen only when China are not playing, but it does show how football can create a forum for a shared experience.

Uyghurs are passionate fans of football at levels other than the international. The game has permeated popular culture — the Uyghur rappers Six City used the popular Uyghur football chant "Hurra, Hurra" in one of their songs — while the one-time local league team, Xinjiang Haitang, attracted an average crowd of 29,000 during the 2012 season. This statistic might not seem high to some, but this was in the Chinese third tier, where attendances range from 100 to 5,000. In China's top tier, the Super League, only Beijing Guoan and Guizhou Renhe had an attendance larger than Xinjiang's highest of 45,000 in 2012. The Shanghai Shenhua that featured Didider Drogba and Nicolas Anelka regularly played in front of only 16,000 at home.

The popularity of Xinjiang Haitang, based in the regional capital Ürümqi, might offer a glimpse into a less ethnically polarised future. Fans at the home games, held at the 50,000-capacity Xinjiang Sports Centre, were a healthy mix of Uyghur and Chinese. A string of blogs and forums focused on the team and football in general, and showing postings by both ethnicities, were extremely popular. However, the Chinese authorities get nervous when large groups of Uyghurs gather, especially since an outbreak of unrest between the Uyghur and Chinese communities in Ürümqi in 2009. There was usually a large police presence at the ground on match days and reports emerged that local universities forbade Uyghur students from attending some games. The fact that Xinjiang's supporters took to wearing T-shirts in the same shade of blue as the East Turkestan flag will not have been lost on the authorities.

Players

The manipulation of football for political ends is nothing new. Among the Uyghurs, the winning of hearts and minds through football is happening at the grassroots and largely among players. For the Chinese government it's all about stemming anti-state sentiment to promote a 'pan-People's Republic of China' identity that theoretically holds a place for ethnic minorities. On the other hand, for Uyghurs in exile, football is being used as a means to educate young Uyghurs about their history and culture, and to inspire a new generation of Uyghur activists.

The Chinese government has been accused of funding only elite athletes in order to gain success at international competition. However, China's lack of success in international football has been invariably explained as a lack of interest in developing the game at the grassroots. Among the Uyghur, though, informal kickarounds and local leagues based around places of work and study are common. During my time at Kashgar Teachers College, I played in an annual tournament between the various university departments that reminded me why bone-dry pitches are so dangerous, and I was often roped into street games with kids. This level of participation is nothing new under Chinese rule with Uyghur teams, especially at Xinjiang University, active since the 1950s.

Even so, the organisation of Uyghur football outside the auspices of the Chinese state is a different matter. In the mid-1990s, Ghulja, a city in the western part of the region next to the Kazakh border, experienced an increase in drug and alcohol use among Uyghur youth. In order to combat growing social problems, Uyghurs in Ghulja revived a traditional gathering called a *meshrep* that functions as an important social forum for discussing and resolving community affairs. Despite the success of the Ghulja *meshrep*, nervous city authorities banned the gatherings in July 1995.

No more than a month later, the Ghulja *meshrep* leader Abdulhelil and others organised a 16-team football league that continued to work to promote healthy alternatives among unemployed Uyghur youth. Just when the football was about to kick off, on 12 August 1995, the local government cancelled all games and parked tanks on the football pitches. They claimed the space was needed for military exercises and broadcast regular announcements over the radio that

the games would have constituted an "illegal gathering". To make sure that the tournament definitely did not go ahead, all local schools had the goalposts removed from their pitches.

The banning of the *meshrep* was among the grievances cited by Uyghurs who participated in a bloody demonstration in Ghulja in February 1997. Salam Kari, one of the organisers of the Ghulja football league, was arrested in May 1997 in connection with the February unrest. A few days after his arrest, he was dead. According to Amnesty International, his body showed signs of torture despite the police claim that he had committed suicide.

If organising independent football tournaments can loosen the grip of state control, then conversely, state-backed football programs can be a means of reasserting authority. The Chinese Football Association (CFA), unlike the majority of its counterparts worldwide, does not operate free of government control, which is a fact that Fifa are happy to overlook for the time being. The CFA has been criticized for its small number of youth football initiatives, but in the Uyghur region, there appears to be a concerted push to launch elite and recreational youth football programs.

Local and regional governments in the Uyghur region, with the blessing of the CFA and in cooperation with the Soong Ching Ling Foundation[1], have been active in promoting elite football among young Uyghur. In 2002, the foundation spent US$7.9 million to establish a new academy in Ürümqi, in conjunction with a $15.9 million contribution from city authorities. In 2008, the Xinjiang regional government built a new training ground in Ürümqi, and in 2010, the cornerstone was laid for an expanded football academy with new funds from the Soong Ching Ling Foundation and the state. The new facility will provide training for 300 13- to 19-year-old students. Local authorities across the region are also using state funds to promote recreational football among the youth in schools and universities. Furthermore, in February 2012, the Xinjiang Football Association announced overwhelming interest in registration for its 12-year-old amateur league for the coming season.

The state's involvement in promoting sport as a healthy activity is not unusual. What is different are hints at a relationship between all the football investment and the winning of Uyghur hearts and minds. At a ceremony to launch a Youth Soccer Development Fund for students at the Ürümqi academy, the CFA president Wei Di said that in addition to sharpening their football skills, new students would also "learn how to be... a good citizen." Moreover, at the President's Cup, an international youth tournament held in the Kazakh capital of Astana in 2010, a Kashgar-born Uyghur, Hirali, was clearly enthusiastic about his participation as a representative of the Under-15 China team. Describing his feelings at scoring a goal at the tournament, Hirali said, "Some Chinese people... were waving the national flag and celebrating my goal... I felt so great at that moment." Hirali has since been selected to play for the China Under-17 team.

The two most famous graduates from the Ürümqi academy are Bali Maimaitiyili and Mirahmetjan Muzepper, who were members of China's Olympic qualifying team. In 2010, Muzepper became the first Uyghur player to be selected for the senior national squad after the China head coach Gao Hongbo called him up for several training sessions in preparation for the 2010 East Asian Football Championship. Muzepper has been held up as an example of the national team's multiculturalism, as well as Uyghur success in Chinese society. The 21-year-old defensive midfielder from Kashgar plays for Shandong Luneng in eastern China and has represented both the China Under-20 and Under-23 teams. He has also featured in a number of prominent international tournaments, appearing in the Asian Football Confederation Under-19 championship in 2010 and for the Under-23 team in the 2010 Asian Games held in Guangzhou.

As much as the Chinese state uses football as a way to integrate Uyghurs into Chinese society, Uyghur exiles have made use of the game for political mobilisation and nurturing a nationalistic Uyghur identity among the diaspora. As far as I was able to discover, organised Uyghur exile football exists in Sweden, Norway, the Netherlands, Belgium, France, the United States, Germany, Canada, Egypt, Kazakhstan, Turkey and Australia, which represents only a sample of where Uyghurs can be found worldwide. With the increasing ease

---

[1] *The Soong Ching Ling Foundation was established in commemoration of the Honorary President of the People's Republic of China in May 1982 and seeks "to promote friendly international relations and safeguard world peace; to strengthen exchanges across Taiwan Straits and advance reunification of Motherland; to show concerns for the future of the nation and develop children's work."*

of communication and the growing sophistication of Uyghur exile groups, Uyghurs have taken football as a means to bring together Uyghurs within their local communities, across their host countries and on a transnational basis.

Uyghur United, a team based in Fairfax, Virginia, in the United States, is a good example of a local community club. According to Mustafa Rouzi, a team member, the team was established in 2002 to congregate the Uyghur community concentrated around the Washington, DC area (the largest in the United States) and to have some fun. Since 2004, the team has played in local leagues, mostly against opposition from other immigrant communities, such as FC Kurdistan, as well as teams from Turkish, Latin American, Afghan and Vietnamese communities.

Rouzi added that the team supports Americanised Uyghur youth in maintaining their Uyghur identity. Team members are encouraged to speak in the Uyghur language, and Rouzi commented that many Uyghur-Americans had improved their language skills simply by being on the team. On the team's travels to tournaments and in social gatherings to watch European football on TV, hanging out with other Uyghurs had been important in solidifying Uyghur identity among the players.

The East Turkistan[2] Football Club in Australia has taken a nationwide approach to Uyghur mobilisation and organises an annual tournament contested by different Uyghur teams from across Australia. The fifth edition of the East Turkistan Football Tournament was held in December 2011 and involved teams from the host city Adelaide, Sydney, Melbourne and Perth. At the opening ceremony, the vice president of the Melbourne Uyghur Association reminded participants and spectators of the tournament's significance in unifying and bringing together the Uyghur-Australian community. Furthermore, one of the players at the tournament told Radio Free Asia that, "The reason to come to Adelaide is not just for the football. East Turkistanis have gathered here... because our youth, the future generation of East Turkistan, will learn about the great history of the Uyghurs, discuss our current difficulties and how to solve these problems. We hope in the future the tournament will attract more people, even from overseas... and will become an educational venue for protecting our identity."

The dream of transnational competition was realised in July 2011 at the three-day long International Uyghur Youth Freedom Cup held in the Netherlands. The Youth Committee of the World Uyghur Congress (a transnational Uyghur organisation in exile) organised the tournament and teams from Germany, Belgium, the Netherlands, Norway, Sweden, France and the United States participated, with a total of 500 people attending the games. Uyghur teams from Kazakhstan, Turkey, Australia and Canada were invited but were unable to attend due to funding constraints.

Gheyyur Qurban, the head of the tournament organising committee,

---

[2] *This is how it is spelt, even though the more usual spelling is with an 'e'*

outlined the broader objectives of the competition as "motivating Uyghur youth, giving them an opportunity to identify as Uyghurs and learning about Uyghur history and culture." Qurban added a further objective of "finding and training the best young Uyghur minds, so that they can become politically engaged in gaining the freedom of the Uyghur people." He explained that the motivation behind these objectives came from a sense that the current generation of Uyghurs in exile was not as engaged in political activity as the preceding ones, a situation that he labeled a "dangerous development for the Uyghur movement". Qurban continued, "The generation from the 1990s were educated in Chinese schools and may be unaware of Uyghur history, but have a desire to self-identify as a Uyghur. By coming together as a people, not only in the small communities of our home countries, but also in a global context, we can build a foundation towards securing a future for the Uyghur identity. Football is an effective way to bring people together, educate them and have them identify as a nation."

The venue in the Netherlands was decorated in the symbols of nationalism, with East Turkestan flags displayed, political slogans on show and the national anthem played before games. As part of the opening ceremony, the well-known Uyghur human rights activist Rebiya Kadeer sent a message of support and Uyghur singers and dancers performed. Qurban commented that the national symbols were important in order "to give the feeling to everyone that 'we are Uyghurs, we are strong.'"

Playing for the United States team, Rouzi said, "When I heard the national anthem I felt very emotional and proud. I also felt freedom for the first time in my life. I could never have had this feeling in China. For me, it felt like victory over Chinese injustices. The tournament taught me the importance of unity and the football helped me understand leadership, communication and responsibility."

One of the coaches added, "the most emotional thing we got... is not playing the game and competing; it was seeing each other, being one unified team and showing strength." For the record, the Dutch team won the tournament, Sweden came second and Germany third. On the back of the tournament's success, Qurban said that a second is in the planning stages.

An issue that arose at the tournament was the possible establishment of an East Turkestan national team. The desire to achieve this appears strong among some exiles. A quick look through YouTube brings up simulated games between East Turkestan and China using gaming software. Fifa membership is a coveted part of international recognition for new states and is sometimes sought before membership of other international bodies. This kind of recognition for any East Turkestan team would be out of the question under current Fifa rules, but competitive football for any 'national' team is still possible. Games have been played between territories such as Tibet, Northern Cyprus, Kurdistan, Somaliland, West Papua and Darfur under the auspices of entities like the Non-Fifa Board.

The Tibetan team may provide a good template for Uyghur exiles seeking to make a political statement to the Chinese government while utilising football as a way of keeping a distinct Uyghur identity. According to the Tibetan prime minister in exile, Lobsang Tenzin, "For the exiled Tibetan, sports would be a medium to establish international relations, make political declarations and to exhibit the skills and aspirations of the Tibetan people." The Tibetans have successfully drawn Chinese government ire, with Chinese officials requesting teams turn down Tibetan requests for games. When Greenland agreed to play Tibet in a friendly in Denmark in 2001, the Chinese Embassy in Copenhagen was adamant that none of the symbols of Tibetan independence be present at the game. While the next possible step for Uyghurs in exile is the establishment of a 'national' team that would provide a larger platform for national identification, while being a thorn in the side of the Chinese government, the main impediment is funding. This has been a problem dogging many unrecognised 'national' sides, including the Tibetans.

The future of the Uyghur people will not be determined only the football pitch. Uyghurs face an array of cultural pressures that will be contested in schools, homes and mosques across their homeland while the Uyghur plight in China is presented with an additional challenge in the form of the state. Given the curbs on freedom of speech and the political restrictions, as well as the dire consequences for opposing the Chinese authorities, Uyghurs in China have little choice other than to absorb the state-imposed version of their identity. Much in the same way that jokes and poetry played an important role in relieving the tensions of repression

among people living in the Soviet Union, Uyghurs express their opposition to their predicament through furtive singing of subversive songs and whispered telling of seditious stories. Sport, and particularly football, is another one of those outlets for the Uyghurs. However, it may, through support of local teams, also present an opportunity to build community with Han Chinese through a shared experience that offers a different version of 'us and them' and allows Uyghurs occasional space to assert the value of their own identity.

In exile, Uyghurs hold the torch for their culture in a different way, insomuch as many of the Uyghur youth have become disconnected with the homeland of their parents and are becoming assimilated into their host cultures. As a second-generation immigrant myself, I can attest to the difficulties in resisting those pressures. For the Uyghurs however, this identification of the youth with the culture of their parents may in the long run be the best chance of survival for a non-Chinese state version of their complex society. Football has proved a successful way to connect young people to ensure this survival and to develop a generation of advocates willing to one day reassert Uyghur culture free of the Chinese state back into their homeland. Despite the political overlay, the game among the Uyghur, as elsewhere, is still largely played or watched for recreation. While Uyghurs in China or in the diaspora may have to resist the assimilative policies of the Chinese government or the forces of a homogenising world, it might just be that their love of football will serve as a powerful means of holding onto their distinct and storied culture. Ⓑ

The Hamburg Factor

The Euro 88 semi-final marked the peak of the Dutch-German football rivalry

By Simon Kuper

The terrible Romanian referee Ioan Igna blows the final whistle and races to the touchline to grab the ball. The Dutch coach Rinus Michels jumps off his bench, raises both arms, embraces an assistant — and that's the end of Michels's celebrations. Ten seconds later, his face is impassive again. As he walks past the stands he bites his lip, just to make sure he doesn't show any human emotion. He gives only a little half-wave to the celebrating Dutch fans, with their ironic Gullit-dreadlock hats and their non-ironic eighties' moustaches.

It's 21 June 1988 and Holland have beaten West Germany in the semi-finals of the European Championship in Hamburg. Twenty-five years later, this remains the emotional peak of Dutch football history, the match that Dutch people think about when they want to cheer themselves up, even better than victory over the USSR in the final four days later. Watching the Dutch TV broadcast of the game again, your memories of that night — and of the anti-German feelings of the time — come rushing back.

The moment Igna ends the game, people in the Netherlands begin running out of their houses onto the street. This will develop into the biggest Dutch public gathering since Liberation in 1945. There are celebrations too in the Kuper home in North London. I had moved here from the Dutch town of Leiden in 1986. In 1988 I was eighteen years old. The match was on the Tuesday of my last A-level exam week, the climax of secondary school. I didn't really have time to watch, I was gambling with my future, but there we all were on the sofa. When my mother said that Erwin Koeman was such a handsome boy, I glowed with pride, as if her nine years of alienation as an immigrant mother in the Netherlands had suddenly become worth it. In our British-South African family, I was the only spiritual Dutchman.

On Dutch TV Ruud Gullit is raising Michels onto his shoulders. Normally that's supposed to be a collective endeavour, but even though Gullit hasn't been at his best this month, aged 25 he is still about as strong as the average team.

The German midfielder Olaf Thon sits on the ground and symbolically takes off his boots: he doesn't want anything more to do with football. At least he's sportsmanlike enough to swap shirts with his conqueror, Ronald Koeman.

Meanwhile Lothar Matthäus has entered into a debate with Igna. The West German captain points meaningfully at his own eye. The Dutch TV commentator

Evert ten Napel puts him in his place: "Played off the park."

Dutch TV shows Van Basten's winning goal one last time. Twenty-five years later you realise how lucky it was. Softly, the ball rolls under the outstretched arm of the diving Eike Immel: not good goalkeeping.

Van Basten's not bothered about that. Nor about the blood on his face (apparently the souvenir of a smack from his marker, Jürgen Kohler). The Dutch striker jogs with his teammates to the corner flag to party with the fans. The moment you see his fragile supermodel's legs, you understand why his career would end just four years later, when he was only 27. In fact most of the Dutch players, with their shirts off in celebration, look like weedy teenagers compared with today's leading footballers. Even the Dutch right-back Berry van Aerle, famed at the time for his power, turns out to have almost no upper body. He probably went on to develop more arm muscles in his second career as a postman. The Germans, similarly shirtless, look a fair bit heftier.

"Holland are going to Munich again and are playing a final again," enthuses Ten Napel on TV — no need for him to remind viewers which previous final he means. "How well the Dutch team played tonight," he gloats. And, "Boy, oh boy, oh boy, what a football party." And, "The Dutch team played a fantastic match here in Hamburg, and take revenge for the defeat." (Ten Napel is referring to the defeat of 1974, although many watching Dutch people that evening will think first of 1940.)

Watching the footage again today, these are surprising words: a Dutch

commentator eulogising a Dutch football team. You rarely see Dutch footballers celebrating these days. From 1970 to 1995 the Dutch won six European Cups as well as this European Championship, but Dutch fans under the age of about 23 have experienced no greater triumph than Feyenoord's victory in the Uefa Cup in 2002.

On TV, the Dutch players in the Volkspark are now topless (with the exception of Ronald Koeman, who for some reason has donned Thon's German shirt) and yet their celebrations are considerably less sexual than the ones we are used to nowadays. The Dutch of 1988 aren't lying in a heap and they don't seem to be kissing, just hugging. The Germans too stay manly: a real old-fashioned pre-metrosexual northern European team. There's barely a tear in sight. They just stare a bit numbly into the distance. Half of them would be world champions two years later anyway. Thon and Pierre Littbarski walk off the field together, already engaged in a post-match analysis. After a remark by Thon, Littbarski glares straight into his eyes.

Uli Borowka, who would become an alcoholic, pours a sports drink down his throat. In my memory the German players were uglier than the Dutch ones, but when you see the stocky machismo of Borowka and Matthäus, and the Rudi Völler moustaches sported by several of the Dutch, you do begin to doubt. Gullit in particular has become better-looking in middle age.

The TV cameras don't register everything. They miss Ronald Koeman, who is amusing himself beside one of the goals. He has taken off Thon's shirt and is pulling it back and forth between his legs: the famous bottom-wiping that he would boast about for years. Terrible guys, those Germans, real Nazis. No wonder that a group of Dutch fans, sitting on one of the security fences around the field, is making provocative hand gestures at the German fans. True soldiers of Orange, those lads, just like when we battled the Germans in the Second World War. Or to paraphrase the old joke about Holland: after 1945, the whole country joined the Resistance.

It's 1988, so the Germans still make their public announcements in German rather than in English. The scoreboard thanks the spectators for their visit and wishes them a happy journey home. The Dutch fans will probably manage. "It's probably going to be a long, hot night, here in the port city on the Elbe in northern Germany," says Ten Napel on TV, in a mixture of diligent homework and fresh emotion. He refers to "eight or ten thousand" Dutch spectators, but on TV there seem to be far more. Since it wasn't a special match for the Germans, a lot of Dutch fans had managed to buy German tickets on the black market. Moreover, in 1988 liberal Hamburg wasn't exactly a hotbed of German nationalism. In the words of the German striker Frank Mill, "It might have been better to have played the match in Germany."

Dutch TV is about to change programmes. We get one more long shot of the cheerless Volkspark with its running track. Then, in the studio back in the Netherlands, an anchorman appears on screen. He blows out his cheeks and then bursts out laughing.

But in Hamburg the night is still young. Van Basten, who in his moment of glory

dares to smoke a cigarette in public, asks some Dutch journalists, "Kohler, who was that?" Everyone laughs. How witty the Dutch players were, we thought then, not like the humourless Germans.

One of the themes of the impromptu Dutch people's party that evening was that all Dutch citizens, from the prime minister to the footballers to the viewers back home, were equal. We didn't do German hierarchies. That's why the Dutch players danced the conga as if they were fans, and sang supporters' songs like, "We're going to Munich" and "We're not going home yet." Later on, in Hamburg's Intercontinental Hotel, even the young Prince Johan-Friso joins the players in a rendition of "Can you hear the Germans sing?" (Today Johan-Friso lies in a London hospital after a skiing acccident, in a coma from which he will probably never awaken.)

Something else that wasn't shown on Dutch TV: in Holland's team bus just outside the stadium, the midfielder Aron Winter is behaving like a drunken teenage fan. The reserve, who didn't play a single minute all tournament, is standing by the open door of the bus, and while Matthäus gives an interview to a TV camera a few metres away, Winter jeers in schoolboy German, "Lothar! You lost, Lothar! A pity, Lothar!" Other Dutch players sitting in the bus find this hilarious. But then suddenly the German coach Franz Beckenbauer arrives. He climbs aboard the Dutch bus, shakes every player's hand, and congratulates everyone. This display of civilisation silences even Aron Winter.

When Michels walks into the press conference, the assembled European press gives him a standing ovation. It turns out that Holland hadn't just buried its own German trauma; apparently the whole continent had had the same trauma. Everyone wanted to beat Germany most of all.

The period from 1954 to 1996 was the German era in European football and European economics. The British writer David Winner says that in those years, Germany was the "Darth Vader of European football", the villain whom everyone wanted to beat, and therefore the most thrilling figure in the football drama. Hamburg '88 was one of the few important matches that Germany lost to a European opponent in those decades. For once, Good had defeated Evil. That night resonated far beyond the Netherlands.

But in Muswell Hill in London, only one fan ran celebrating onto the street that evening. I needed this victory. When I had arrived in London two years before, I discovered that nobody there had the slightest bit of interest in the country where I had spent most of my childhood. A big chunk of my life was being thrown away. I had had friends in the Netherlands, but not in London. And now here at last was official proof that Holland was the best country on earth!

So there I was, alone on an empty street in a London suburb with my bottle of Heineken. In the Netherlands, millions of people were outside. But in Muswell Hill, the local Cypriots and Indians were sitting at home on the sofa, watching something else on TV. Where could I take my emotions and my Heineken? Of course: to the German neighbours.

We lived at number 16. Lukas and Karin (names changed) lived at number 18.

Lukas was a historian. He liked football, although curiously enough he didn't support Germany. But surely he would have watched the match? For several seconds I pressed on the bell of number 18. Lukas congratulated me on the Dutch victory, which was a little irritating. Then he invited me up for a beer.

Upstairs, Karin was happy for me too.

"Holland were better," said Lukas. "Your penalty wasn't a penalty, but ours wasn't either."

"The German players were much uglier," said Karin.

We asked her, as an expert, who had been the most handsome player. "Rijkaard," said Karin. "He was the one who looked most like a human being."

I stuck around drinking for another hour. This was in part because I had an above-average interest in Germans. After the summer, I was to go to university to study German and history. I'd chosen German partly because I barely spoke a word of French and partly because in 1988 any idiot could see that West Germany was going to be a global superpower. In my generation, knowledge of German would be much more useful than knowledge of English.

In those days I cribbed football news from the Dutch press for *World Soccer* magazine. I had never met the editor of *World Soccer* and he didn't know I was a teenager writing the articles in my bedroom. But late that evening, I reached him in his hotel room in Germany. Could he get me a ticket for the final on Saturday?

A day later he called me back. He had the ticket. My final exams were on Friday, and my parents agreed to pay for a flight to Munich as a school-leaving present. Soon after landing, I was fined 40 Deutschmarks on the bus and ended up having to sleep two nights penniless in the train station, but that's another story. The point is that I took part in the symbolic Dutch invasion of Germany. Hours before kick-off I was sitting in the stands of the Munich Olympiastadion, soaking it all up, when a silver-haired German spectator tapped me on the shoulder. "Are you a Dutchman?" he asked.

That was a good question.

"Ja," I answered.

"Then I want to congratulate you on your brilliant team."

Don't you just hate the Germans?

In September 1990 I moved to Berlin to study at the Technical University. A few days later, on the evening of October 3, I wandered by myself down Unter den Linden to witness the birth of the mighty new Germany. The Germans were already world champions, and as Beckenbauer had said, when the East Germans joined the team they would be unbeatable. Unter den Linden was full that night, but apart from a few easterners scarfing champagne, most people were wandering around quietly too. Like me, they seemed to be just looking. Walking down the most pompous boulevard of an empire on the night of its greatest glory, you seldom realise that this is the moment that the empire starts to collapse.

Later I became a real football journalist, the kind who sometimes goes to interview footballers. In 1998 I went to Dortmund to interview Jürgen Kohler about his encounters with Van Basten. It was a freezing Tuesday afternoon and Borussia Dortmund were training in front of 17 spectators. They were doing a peculiar exercise. Two players stood in a little goal, one of them threw a ball into the air, and a third came diving in and tried to head it in the goal. Good practice for diving headers. Kohler liked it. "Ja!" he cheered when he scored.

Thomas Hässler — another villain of '88 — was there too, also having fun. "Hihi," he said as he jogged around the field after practice with a ball under his arm. Passing the heap of balls after each lap, he would take one with him for a dribble.

After the other players went in to shower, Hässler and Kohler stayed on to juggle a ball together. Every time Kohler managed to bounce the ball on his heel, he whistled triumphantly, though I don't think it impressed Hässler. Whenever Kohler dropped the ball, he laughed and rolled over the ground like a cat.

Later Kohler and I settled in a nearby hut. He rarely gave interviews anymore, because he didn't like fuss, but when Dortmund's press officer had told him that a journalist from Holland wanted to ask him about Van Basten, Kohler had said yes at once. "Because Jürgen Kohler respects Marco van Basten above everything..." began the fax I got from the press officer.

And Kohler told me, "There's one more beautiful story, which I won't forget my entire life, and I think it shows that over the years he respected me as a player. It was Milan against Juve and at one point Marco came up to me and asked if we could swap shirts."

I waited for the punchline, but it seemed the story was already over. "That he did that was the greatest recognition for me," explained Kohler. He still had Marco's shirt at home. I realised that Kohler in 1988 had not regarded himself as a member of the forces of Evil fighting the forces of Good. In fact, he didn't seem like such a bad guy.

In 2000 Holland played a friendly against Germany in Amsterdam. It was Matthäus's 144th international, a world record if you didn't count certain African players, which Fifa didn't. Before the match, Matthäus was confronted on the pitch with a bouquet of flowers — which on closer inspection turned out to be concealing the Dutch captain Edgar Davids. Matthäus looked startled, perhaps to see that the socially dysfunctional Davids had been made captain and

perhaps because when he waved the bouquet at the Dutch crowd, here and there you could hear the sound of clapping. This was the biggest possible insult: the Dutch had accepted the Ur-German because they no longer feared him. Germany had stopped winning prizes and wasn't Darth Vader anymore.

I also interviewed Völler and Klinsmann, two of the other villains of '88. They turned out to be nice guys too. Klinsmann kept grinning at me as if I was his favourite person. I can now see that Rijkaard really did trip him for the penalty. Our interview took place in Lisbon, at the end of Euro 2004. I asked Klinsmann whether he would now become manager of Germany, but he said definitely not.

We'll never again experience a Holland-Germany game as emotionally freighted as the one in 1988. In fact, if Holland isn't occupied by another country soon, we'll never again experience such an emotionally freighted football match.

No Man's Land

Siniša Mihajlović, Vukovar and the compromises of war

By Jonathan Wilson

The rain comes in bursts, hurled by a gusting wind across the pitch. The grass is clumpy and the goalframes are angled back, as though trying to turn away from the desolation. A solitary stand offers little respite. This is the home of Borovo, who once proudly took their place in the Yugoslav second division and each year hosted the most important youth tournament in the country. It was here that Siniša Mihajlović played his first competitive football. Now, like the rest of Vukovar, it stands as an awful reminder of the legacy of the war.

The physical scars are obvious. Although construction work is going on, numerous buildings are still dotted with the holes left by mortars and shrapnel and others live on only in rubble and the outlines they left on the building next door. The Borovo factory, which had been the major employer since it was founded in 1932 by the Czech industrialist Tomaš Bata to make shoes and rubber products, lies empty. There is a sense of decay, from the potholed streets to the bedraggled bushes.

Not far from the stadium, on a nondescript street, stands a house of orange-red brick. It seems incongruously bright, clearly newer than those of the buildings around it, while a small notice in the window reveals that it's for sale. It was in an apartment block there, in the village of Borovo Naselje, just north of Vukovar, that Mihajlović grew up, there that he battered free-kicks against the garage door so hard and so often that his father had to replace it every few weeks. "I soon realised," he said, "that the ball didn't want me to dribble it. So I just kicked it."

It's hard to imagine now that Vukovar was once one of the most prosperous places in Yugoslavia. In fact, it was more than that: it was almost a model for the federal ideal and there is still great pride in what the town used to be. "Before the war there were 22 different nationalities in this area," said Nebojša Šerbić, Mihajlović's old history teacher, a studious man with horn-rimmed glasses and a swept-back mass of white hair. "There was only one place with more — a village in Vojvodina that had 23. This was a hugely multi-ethnic community and it was always like that. In sport it was always like that and nobody cared. It was also a very rich area and people were hard-working here. In the 1980s only Maribor had more cars per person than Vukovar — that's an indication of how developed it was."

Mihajlović's mother worked in the shoe factory; his father was a truck-driver. Mihajlović never had any doubt what he wanted to be. "Eventually he got to a stage where he was much better at football than everybody else, but I want to emphasise that he was a hard worker and it was that that got him that far," said Siniša Lazić, who first played with Mihalović when he was 12 and went on to become a professional himself with Hajduk Kula. "There was one thing that always set him apart from everybody else and that was his shot. He always had that, even as a kid, and he worked hard on everything else." He remembers going swimming with other friends, messing about in the pool and seeing through the window Mihajlović practising alone outside. "He was very competitive in other spheres as well, especially at school," Lazić said. "He was an excellent pupil. He started going to a technical college, a very good school, but the classes were in the afternoons and that meant he couldn't train in the afternoons. So he quit that school and enrolled in the worst school in town — for people who produce shoes. That was very risky because nobody knew if he would become a footballer. Other kids wouldn't have been allowed to do that by their parents but he was so determined to become a footballer that he even quit school for it."

Mihajlović was utterly single-minded. "I always wanted to be a footballer," he said. "In Borovo there was a local newspaper that gave information about the factory and other things that were happening in the village. Once they did a survey and asked pupils at the school what they wanted to do when they grew up. I was only seven or eight, but even then I wrote 'professional footballer'."

Šerbić remembers Mihajlović as a diligent pupil, although he knew him as a footballer before he ever taught him.

He ran the school football team for boys aged between 11 and 14. "I used to work with a player who played for the national team — in 1939 he scored from a corner kick against England — Nikola Perlić. I worked with him when I was high school, mostly on passing and controlling the ball. The kids found the drills boring. We would much rather have played football but if we said that we had to run laps. Perlić said that if you tried to play football without knowing how to pass it was like studying for exams without knowing all the letters. I wasn't a real coach but I focused on that when working with kids."

When Mihajlović was nine, "a female teacher" — as Šerbić put it — "told me he was good enough to play with my boys and that he supported Zvezda which was even better. He was very well-developed, and when he shot from 10 or 11m from goal, nobody could save it. When we played games in school, I had to make sure the other teams man-marked him because he was already so sharp that if you didn't he would destroy you. I worked with other kids with talent, but they didn't have the character. Even if he hadn't made it as a footballer, he would have made it in something else because he was very persistent."

Mihajlović joined the Borovo club and in 1986, when he was 17, started playing for the first team. His coach there was Zvonko Popović, who had played for Borovo between 1964 and 1976. "You could immediately see how talented he was but nobody expected him to attain such heights," Popović said. "He couldn't let anybody beat him or be better than him, whether it was opponents or teammates. He committed a lot of fouls and got a lot of cards."

Asked about Mihajlović's personality, Lazić laughed. "He was very temperamental, really feisty," he said. "He would always protect himself and the others on the pitch. There was one game when we played this team that had a huge guy, like 2m tall, and Siniša went up to him, close to him, and said something to his face. Everybody was afraid what he was going to do but the guy backed down. That was Siniša imposing himself. He'd spit on you and abuse you to win in the heat of the action, but that's the culture here."

He soon emerged as an outstanding player. "Some games we played him in midfield, sometimes at centre-back because he was very good in the air," said Popović. "People didn't like that because he was perceived as a very talented creative player and they didn't understand why we used him in defence. It gradually became apparent he was best on the left. When it came to set-pieces he was a key player: corner kicks, free-kicks... Free-kicks from a long way out he would drop just in front of the goal."

Mihajlović's temper remained such an issue that Popović decided he had to take radical action. "We had a player who had played in the first division for Osijek, who was older than all the others," he said. "We discussed how to calm down Siniša and we concluded it would be best to make him captain. The captain was more experienced than the others but we told him we wanted to give Siniša responsibility and stop him getting into trouble with the refs. That gave him new confidence."

What everybody agrees is that Mihajlović had a classic case of white-line fever: "Siniša on the pitch and Siniša off the pitch are two different personalities,"

said Lazić. Sven-Göran Eriksson's agent Athole Still, who acted for Mihajlović for a number of years, describes him as "a Jekyll and Hyde character".

"Off the pitch he was no trouble at all," said Popović. "On the pitch he was trouble as soon as the whistle blew. He didn't respect anyone. It didn't matter how big a player was or what his reputation was. He didn't care."

"In class, he was very serious," Šerbić agreed. "There were no problems. But when he played it was something else. In the game, people get carried away."

Yet Mihajlović himself admits that it wasn't quite as simple as having an on-pitch and an off-pitch personality. "As a kid I got into a lot of fights," he said. "I got beaten up and I beat people up. I fought with older children. I didn't get frightened. I remember there was a teacher who lived on our street who didn't want me in her class because she thought I would cause trouble. However, I was always an excellent student, one of the best. Later, that teacher told me she regretted not having me in her class because I was a very different person in school to how I was on the street."

Friends and teachers remember him as a very driven figure. "He wanted to win at all sports and especially at school," said another school friend, Siniša Čučkovic. "He was very good at Serbo-Croatian language and literature. He was very confident and, if he hadn't succeeded in sport, he would have done in some other area. And the girls loved him."

Mihajlović himself seems to have been beset by doubts, not least about girls.

"I remember my friend Zlatko had a birthday party," he told *Tempo* magazine. "I went behind the curtain in the living room with a girl called Ančica. We looked through the window and then we kissed. It was my first kiss, but I wasn't uninformed. I had watched movies to see how it was done. I was afraid I might get it wrong, but everything happened spontaneously." There is at times a surprising vulnerability to him. He had only been at Crvena Zvezda a couple of months when he faced Dynamo Dresden in the Champions League quarter-final. In the tunnel before the game at the Marakana, he placed his hands on the wall to stretch and felt the concrete vibrating with the noise of the crowd. "Oh, Siniša," he said to himself. "What have you done? Why didn't you stay in Novi Sad and lead a quiet life?"

A quiet life, though, was never for him. "Dinamo [Zagreb] showed some interest when he was 14," said Popović. "They scouted him at the tournament in Borovo and also when he played in a selection for Slavonia [a region of eastern Croatia]. But I don't think they were ever serious about it. Borovo were more oriented towards Novi Sad and Belgrade so more players went to play there." In his autobiography, Mihajlović claimed he turned Dinamo down in 1987 in a bout of stubbornness after Mirko Jozić, the Croatian coach of the Yugoslavia Under-20 side, told him he would be picked for the World Youth Cup in Chile (which Yugoslavia, having gone with little hope, ended up winning) only if he joined. Instead, a year later, aged 19, he signed for Vojvodina.

"There were maybe bigger talents here before," Popović said, "but Siniša had

luck — the luck to go to Vojvodina in that season when they became champions [they only ever won the title twice]. He played very well during that season and people from Zvezda saw him and liked him." It wasn't until December 1990, though, that Mihajlović moved to Belgrade. It was then that he first came into contact with Arkan, the notorious warlord whose Tigers, many of them recruited from the Delije, the Zvezda Ultras group Arkan headed, were responsible for numerous atrocities during the war. Mihajlović's mother was a Croat and, in the febrile atmosphere of the time, that could make things difficult. Arkan protected him.

Mihajlović played in 14 league games in that first season, but it was what happened in the European Cup that made his reputation. Zvezda won 2-1 away to Bayern Munich in the semi-final and when a Mihajlović free-kick was deflected past Raimond Aumann midway through the first half of the second leg, Zvezda's progress seemed assured. But Bayern hit back with two goals in quick succession to set up a breathtaking final 20 minutes. Either side could have won it, but it was Zvezda who did, Mihajlović's cross being scooped over his own goalkeeper by Klaus Augenthaler. In the celebrations that followed, fans invaded the pitch and the turf was dug up. The jubilation had a manic edge.

Keep going along the road from the centre of Vukovar through Borovo Nasleje and you come to Borovo Selo. It was there, in April 1991, between the two legs of the semi-final, that the first ordnance of the war was fired. Vukovar stands in the far east of Croatia. When the war began, there was a slight Croat majority in the town, but Borovo Selo was predominantly Serb. As tensions increased, militias were established on both sides and Serbs under Vojislav Šešelj set up barricades in Borovo, supposedly to keep the Croat militia out, although given they also excluded Croatian police and administrators, what was effectively established was a Serbian enclave. The local police chief, Josip Reihl-Kir, who was later assassinated by a Croatian police reserve, negotiated a settlement whereby the barricades came down in return for a voluntary agreement on the part of the Croatian police not to enter the village, but attempts at finding a peaceful solution were undermined by hard-line Croatian nationalists. Three Ambrust anti-tank missiles were fired into the village by members of Croatia's ruling HDZ party, which was used by Serbian media as an example of unprovoked hostility from Croatians.

Worse followed on May 1, as four Croatian policemen, seemingly acting spontaneously — perhaps even as a dare — towards the end of a national holiday, entered Borovo Selo and attempted to change the Yugoslav flag for a Croatian one. Local armed Serbs intervened, a gun-battle followed and although two of the Croatians escaped, the other two were wounded and taken prisoner. The following day, Croatian authorities in Osijek bussed 150 policemen to the village to try to secure the captives' release. Another firefight ensued, in which 12 Croatians and somewhere between three and 20 Serbs were killed. The Serbian militia then mutilated the bodies of their enemies, further inflaming tensions. In *The Death of Yugoslavia*,

Allan Little and Laura Silber argue that the incident marked "a sea change" in attitudes in the build-up to the war, as Croatians began to regard Serbs in the republic as "the enemy within", while the Serb-dominated Yugoslav National Army (JNA) was deployed supposedly to try to keep the peace between the militias (although it has subsequently become clear that the Yugoslav leader in Belgrade, Slobodan Milosević, and the Croatian leader in Zagreb, Franjo Tuđman, were both set on the course of war).

Šerbić felt the full effect of the rising tensions. "My wife was a professor and she was sacked for being Serbian," he said. "I wouldn't let my daughter go to school any more because she felt threatened. At that time I moved to a village on the other side of the border and I travelled every day to work in Croatia. Then one day I couldn't go back any more."

On May 8, Mihajlović lined up for Zvezda against Hajduk Split at the JNA Stadium (now the Partizan Stadium) in Belgrade. Alen Bokšić got the only goal to give Hajduk victory, but the game is better remembered now for the clashes between Mihajlović and the Hajduk captain Igor Štimac. At one point they stood eyeball to eyeball. Mihajlović subsequently claimed that Štimac had said that he hoped his whole family in Borovo were murdered — a particularly sensitive subject given he hadn't heard from his parents for over a week because the phone lines had been cut. He admitted he spent the rest of the game targeting the defender, until both were sent off in the 70th minute.

Three weeks later, Mihajlović scored one of the penalties as Zvezda beat Marseille in a shoot-out in the European Cup final. Almost with its dying breath, Yugoslav football had, at last, won a major honour. As the attacks on Serbs intensified, Mihajlović's closest friend visited his family in Borovo Naselje and warned them to leave for their own safety. They did, fleeing with Siniša's brother, who was studying in Zagreb at the time. A few days later, the same friend was brought back to the Mihajlović house by two men who demanded that he shoot the family photographs on the walls, including one showing the Crvena Zvezda team before the European Cup final.

By the July, Vukovar was surrounded by the JNA. For four months they bombarded the town, reducing the 15,000 (mainly but not exclusively Croat) inhabitants who remained to living in cellars without water or electricity. Those who tried to flee were picked off by snipers. Vukovar fell on November 19. Around 260 men were massacred on a farm to the south of the town and buried in a mass grave, while hundreds of others — Croats and Serbs —were rounded up and sent to camps in Serbia. One of them was Popović. "I stayed in one of the camps for a month before they let me go," he said. "The reason they let me go was because I was a footballer. One of the people who interrogated me was a general who used to work at Partizan Belgrade. He asked me that if I was a footballer, did I know a player called Mile Stamenković. Stamenković was the best man at my wedding. So the general said it would be OK and they let me go."

By then Mihajlović had added the Intercontinental Cup, as Zvezda beat Colo Colo of Chile 3-0 in Tokyo. The following year, he was sold to Roma

and so began a 14-year stint in Serie A in which he also played for Sampdoria, Lazio and Internazionale, scoring a record 29 goals direct from free-kicks. Controversy and turmoil, though, were never far away.

Mihajlović dreams of snakes and has been told by psychologists that they represent his enemies. There are plenty of them. Mihajlović has become a hate figure, for Croatians riled by his obvious pro-Serbian sympathies and for those everywhere disgusted by his misbehaviour on the pitch. The most notorious incident came in a Champions League game in 2000 when he called Patrick Vieira a "black shit", something that earned him a two-game ban. It is the moment that defines discussion of his personality — at least in Britain — and of course it is a deplorable thing to say. Mihajlović's explanation was that he was responding to Vieira calling him a *"zingaro"*, a word meaning gypsy and often used in Italy as a term of abuse for those from the southern Slavic nations. That is also racist, but was never investigated. None of which diminishes the seriousness of Mihajlović's offence, but it does give some insight why he committed it. "Vieira provoked me from the first minute," he said. "I'm not going let somebody treat me like that. I am who I am and I would have reacted the same way even on the street. I've played football since I was 15 years old and in that time I have been kicked, spat upon and insulted. In football these things happen. What made me really angry is that off the pitch, back home, Vieira gave a press conference to talk about incidents that occurred during the match and must be kept on the field. If I am a racist, so is Vieira."

Lashing out at supposed slights to your honour, of course, is an easy excuse, but when a group of far-right Lazio ultras hailed him as somebody of similar political persuasion, Mihajlović took a microphone onto the pitch at the Stadio Olimpico before a game and addressed the crowd, admitting he had been wrong, stressing he regretted the insult and insisting that he did not hold racist beliefs.

But that wasn't the only incident. He once spat in Adrian Mutu's ear — again, he said, in response to an insult: "I was provoked in a dishonourable way and I reacted" — and there is a whole catalogue of other instances of petulance and pointless red cards. Against Slovenia at Euro 2000, he played in such a fog of fury that Yugoslavia trailed 3-0 when he was sent off for a second yellow card in four minutes but came back to draw. Still, he's hardly the only player to have let his temper get the better of him. "There are many worse incidents on a football pitch than those that are mentioned about Mihajlović," said Lazić.

And then there is the ethnic issue, something Mihajlović hasn't necessarily helped with some inflammatory comments, although Lazić insists many of them have been taken out of context. "If he'd gone to Dinamo and played for Croatia," Popović said, "it would have been the Serbs who hated him. It's like a kind of jealousy."

His divided heritage means any act is open to misinterpretation. When Yugoslavia played Croatia in a Euro 2000

qualifier in Zagreb in 1999, a huge banner commemorated "Vukovar 91"; Mihajlović knelt before it and crossed himself, a gesture that was understandable in that he wanted to commemorate the fallen on both sides but one that was also hugely provocative, drawing a torrent of abuse from home fans.

His reputation means many simply assume the worst. As Serbia manager, he was determined to stamp out the cliques that had undermined the squad — and Yugoslavia's before it — almost since international football began to be played. He introduced a code of conduct, which included singing the national anthem. The Fiorentina forward Adem Ljajić, whose parents are Bosnian Muslims, signed up to the contract but then refused to sing the anthem, saying he found the references in it to a Christian god unacceptable. Mihajlović's critics immediately took that as evidence of his nationalistic stance. "When we played as Yugoslavia our fans booed our national anthem as it was the symbol of a unification that wasn't really felt," he said. "Our opponents would absolutely bust their guts to sing theirs and, to me, that always seemed a disadvantage even before the game had started. As coach I expect that every player and member of the coaching staff sings the Serbian national anthem. That's the rule: Ljajić agreed to it. And he immediately ignored it. I don't only look at talent, but at the man as a whole. I need to be able to rely on the man."

The wounds in Vukovar are beginning to heal. Many Serbs have returned, including Popović and Šerbić. "As a historian I can tell you that in the late 17th century Croatia was freed from the Turks but Serbia wasn't," Šerbić said. "And that was a time of great movement of Serbs out of Serbia. My ancestors came with that great movement of people here so my ancestors lived here for three centuries. I kept going away to Belgrade but I came back here because this is my home. After the war I also decided to do the same. I was born here. It's normal. All my relatives and family live here. I bought my house here. It was normal."

Mihajlović last visited in 1991. "Up until the war, everybody here loved him," said Čučković. "He was a star. People would be very angry if anybody made a tackle on him — stuff like that. Only after '91 did people start to be divided in their opinion. He didn't have to do anything to be divisive: it was just the circumstances of the time. It was just because of his nationality. He didn't have to do or say anything."

His house was completely destroyed in the war, although whether it was targeted is difficult to say. What is known is that when his parents fled Vukovar during the siege, Arkan helped them cross the border and settle in Serbia. Mihajlovic's uncle, his mother's brother, was a senior officer in the Croatian army and was taken prisoner after the fall of the town. Arkan called Mihajlović and asked him to come and pick the uncle up before his men murdered him. When Arkan was assassinated in a Belgrade hotel in January 2000, Mihajlović wrote

an obituary for him, something that for many in western Europe confirmed his image as the snarling face of Serb nationalism. "It was easy from the outside, sat in an armchair, to point the finger," Mihajlović said in an interview in *Gazzetta dello Sport*. "But Arkan had been a friend of mine from the time when, as a youngster, I used to play for Zvezda and he was one of the leaders of the fans. And Arkan defended the Serbs in Croatia as they were about to be massacred. Arkan was a hero to these Serbs. I don't deny writing the obituary, but I didn't defend his war crimes. They will never go away. They were terrible. And I condemn them. As I do all war crimes ever committed, by one side or another. During civil wars there are no good guys or bad guys. There is no black and no white. The colour that dominates in the end is always red. The blood spilt by the innocent. The war in Yugoslavia had many culprits. Too many."

Even as many return, Vukovar remains a divided city. "There was a guy from a village near here, Milutin Milanković, and a few years ago Nasa voted him one of the 10 greatest physicists who ever lived but people here don't even know about him — because he's Serbian," said Lazić. "Normally, if people saw a footballer in the street — [Nemanja] Vidić, [Edin] Džeko, whoever — they'd shake their hand and wish them good luck," he said. "Not Siniša. His father died a few years ago but his mother and brother came here because of the house. But Siniša doesn't come here any more."

80

"I didn't care if I was good or
bad, I just wanted to play."

Golden Vision

The Olympic dream that fires the world's greatest blind footballer

By Felix Lill and Javier Sauras

Silvio Velo plays football every day but he has never seen a ball. He is the leader of a team that has never seen him either. Fans idolise him, although nobody chants his name during the games. He appreciates their love and wears his leadership as naturally as someone who has achieved everything. Velo is the unknown star of Argentinian football: he has won two World Cups, two Copas América and countless trophies with his club, River Plate.

His last adventure, however, left a bitter taste. Velo arrived in London one year ago, captain of the Argentinian five-a-side Paralympic blind football team, the Bats. The Argentinian side was one of the favourites to take the gold medal, but destiny matched them with Brazil in semi-finals and the battle of the South Americans ended with Argentina losing on penalties. The bronze-medal match against Spain brought a similar defeat. Velo took a penalty in both shoot-outs; he failed twice.

"At that moment, I felt my body falling apart," he said. The players went into the changing room and hugged each other for a long time. The captain wasn't criticised, at least not directly. Breaking the silence, Velo cleared his throat and told everybody that winning or losing was just part of the same road.

"Today's defeat is going to nurture us and increase the mystique around the Bats," he said. "Let's think for a moment about the championships we have won. We enjoyed the instant when we lifted the trophy, maybe even the days after it, but when weeks go by, joy fades away and then we focus on our next goal. This defeat is not going to be different."

The Paralympic gold medal is the only award that Velo hasn't yet won. He took silver in Athens 2004 and bronze in Beijing. "It's going to be one more battle, that's all," he said. "The gold medal is a dream that is going to come true when I turn 46. I only have to wait three more years." Climbing to the highest level of the podium in London would have been the culmination of a career that began four decades ago in San Pedro municipality, on the right bank of Paraná river, 180km from Buenos Aires.

The Maradona of the Bats was born on 29 May 1971 to a family of little means, open-eyed but unable to appreciate light. When he was a kid, Silvio wanted to do the same things that his brothers were doing: play football, ride a bike... "I played hide-and-seek with my friends, but I never found anyone," he joked. "When I was young I didn't know about blind football. I played with my friends and my brothers on the neighbourhood pitch, without jingling bell balls. I didn't care if I was good or bad, I just wanted to play. Then, when I stumbled upon an audible ball, when I found out that there were other blind people playing football too... Try to imagine it. I saw the ball when I heard it."

Velo's life changed when he heard the ball with bells for the first time. Nowadays, he trains three hours a day, splitting his time between the gym and the 20mx40m pitch where he plays. The 5-a-side blind football pitch is surrounded by kickboards from which the clinking ball rebounds. The sound is so important in this game that spectators are asked to remain quiet while the ball is in play. For this reason, there are no chants, nobody shouts and the fans' support is something that the players have to assume exists.

However, there is constant yelling from the goals and the sidelines. They are orders, either from the goalkeepers, the only players who are sighted, or from the guides, who call the plays and try to orientate their footballers. There are many collisions and risky situations; it's a tough game, in which injuries are common and it's difficult to restrain from shouting or clapping.

The referee often has to ask the team assistants to calm down and the videoscreens in the stands insist that the crowd should be "silent please." The assumption is that the spectators are not blind, which is one of the paradoxes of the game: those watching will never be able to appreciate fully what it takes to be good at it. All the sighted spectators can do is try to imagine a player's situation, the fear they must

have of running into an opponent and how pointless it would be to yell that one of your teammates should open his eyes. More than anything else, following blind football demands a great deal of empathy; otherwise, a spectator might just joke about how often the success of an attack seems to depend on chance.

But a recent analysis indicates that viewers do tend to understand how the game is played. During the 2010 World Cup, staged in Hereford, researchers at the Hogeschool van Amsterdam found that about two thirds of the spectators found watching a game made them understand blindness and blind football better. More than a third also thought it was "very likely" they would visit a similar event in the future. What's more, the analysis showed that most spectators had had no prior experience of blind football, contradicting the predominant view that only the players' friends and relatives would show up. In the future, the lead researcher Donna De Haan summarised in her paper, blind football is likely to "manifest itself locally, with the view to global extension."

If this is ever to happen, the sport already has a shining star. In Argentina, Silvio Velo is such a celebrity that he will soon have his own TV show, *Velo Bien*, which can either mean "look at it closely", or something like "well done, Velo." "We picked the name because it hints at something beyond the visible, something of the mind," said his manager Nicolás Halac. The programme will be screened from September 2013 and, unusually for a TV show, Velo says the visible is not all that important: "We want to get the viewers to another level. The show will consist of conversations with personalities who have faced obstacles in their lives and I will discuss how they overcame these."

Two such interviews have already been produced. The well-known Argentinian hockey coach and former player Sergio 'Cachito' Vigil spoke with Velo about his life and career. The other is Marcos de Palma, another of Argentina's icons, who was the first person known to be born in Antarctica. Velo insists he isn't nervous about this new era of media exposure. "You know, I actually like cameras because they don't do anything to me. And if they did, how would I tell?" Indeed, he is looking forward to much more than the first screening of the show. One of the subjects he dreams of interviewing is the basketball legend Michael Jordan. If he could get Jordan to tell viewers what makes him afraid or explain if he ever lacks self-esteem, Velo believes, that would mark the success of *Velo Bien*.

Another obvious choice for the programme would be Lionel Messi, his big idol, although, Velo is keen we should "not forget about Diego." Velo has already met Messi. "It was only very brief and we did not have a deep conversation," Velo said. "But I know he is not only a great footballer but also a great guy. You just feel these things, you know." Velo believes Messi is "the best player in the world" and imagines Barcelona's number ten to be agile, technically skilful and fast. "And with excellent scoring abilities," he adds, which sounds like what anybody else would say but Velo insists he has a very specific image of his idol. "It must be beautiful to see him play," he said. "I

guess he really caresses the ball, rather than just kicking it."

This is the ideal Silvio Velo himself has always been striving to achieve. And it is one that is becoming more and more prevalent in blind football generally. Last year's Paralympics saw an improved level of technical skills and, surprisingly, a lot of dribbling. David Beckham was impressed by the quality and so, to their surprise, was the Argentinian side. "We knew that the other teams were strong," said Velo's teammate Federico Acardi after losing the bronze-medal match. "But we were still hoping to be better than them."

Could Silvio Velo be Messi's idol? "I wish," Velo admits. What is certain is that Velo devotes himself to explaining what football has given him through inspirational speeches, given in schools, offices and jails. "It is always good to find people who can take advantage of your experience," said Velo. "I was born blind and I talk particularly about diversity, about not falling behind, taking advantage of one's abilities and not complaining about what you lack. It would have been impossible for me to complain about my sight, since I never had it. I had to enhance my other skills in order to pull through."

Perhaps it is a positive sign for the sport that Velo, the most decorated athlete of the discipline, still has not managed to win Paralympic gold. Blind football has been growing at an impressive pace in recent decades. Starting off as a playground game for children in schools for the visually impaired, blind football has long been played in a number of countries, but always according to local rules that varied from one place to another. Brazil and Spain were the first countries to set up championships in the 1980s, but the sport only joined the International Blind Sports Federation (IBSA) in 1996. With a unified framework of rules, blind football made its Paralympic debut at Athens 2004. Today, athletes in more than 35 countries play it and, at London 2012, blind football was one of the biggest disciplines by participating athletes.

Especially in rapidly evolving sports such as this, there are always athletes whose successes do not reflect their significance but Velo, who has twice been the Paralympic flagbearer for Argentina, hopes not to be among them. "I am already now preparing for 2016," he said. "Physically and technically, I am working on it now and I also follow a specific diet to get ready." The Games of Rio will be his last chance to win gold, in an environment in which the younger players could in theory be his children. "That's why I have to work even harder," he said, adding that he wants

"to continue to be the best player in the world for as long as possible."

Velo believes in his qualities and is not shy of talking about them. He admits that football has always been the most important thing in his life and is sure there is nothing else he could have done. "If I hadn't become a footballer," he said, "I would have been a goalkeeper." But he knows he could never be one, as in blind football the keepers are the only players who are sighted. "In that case, I would just have been a footballer anyway. I was born blind, but I always had the desire to play with the ball. Football is not something you see, you feel it."

So given his yearning for the medal, would he ever follow the example of the original Diego and use the hand of God? "The hand is never part of our game, unfortunately," Velo said with a smile. "When the ball is up in the air, we can't hear the bell in it ringing. We really prefer to keep it on the ground. But would it be tempting... yes, it would be. Very much." **B**

SPIRIT, STYLE AND QUALITY FROM THE BIRTHPLACE OF THE BEAUTIFUL GAME

AVAILABLE NOW FROM **GOALSOUL ONLINE** OR FROM OUR UNIQUE, FOOTBALL-INSPIRED BOUTIQUE IN SHEFFIELD.

RECENT SIGNINGS

1 **CHILE VS ITALY 1962** THE BATTLE OF SANTIAGO 2 **RUUD GULLIT** THE BLACK TULIP
3 **GABRIEL BATISTUTA** RENAISSANCE SIGHTS 4 **JURGEN KLINSMANN** KLINSMANN'S DIVING ACADEMY
5 **BRUCE GROBBELAAR** A MAN AMONGST MEN 6 **MICHEL PLATINI'S MAGIC SQUARE** CARRE MAGIQUE

1

2

3

4

5

6

CROWD FAVOURITES

1 **MARCO VAN BASTEN** THE SWAN OF UTRECHT 2 **BARESI/MALDINI** THE MILAN WALL
3 **ALEX FERGUSON** HAIRDRYER TREATMENT 4 **ANDONI GOIKOETXEA** THE BUTCHER OF BILBAO
5 **PAUL MCGRATH** NEW YORK GIANT 6 **CLUB ATLETICO BOCA JUNIORS** LA BOCA TANGO

1

2

3

4

5

6

THE SHEFFIELD COLLECTION
CELEBRATING FOOTBALL'S FIRST CITY

1 **SHEFFIELD** FOOTBALL'S FIRST CITY 2 **SHEFFIELD FC** BIRTHPLACE OF THE BEAUTIFUL GAME
3 **SHEFFIELD FC** ORIGINAL RULES AND INNOVATIONS 4 **SHEFFIELD FC/REAL MADRID CF** THE TREE OF MERIT
5 **SHEFFIELD WEDNESDAY** PARLIAMENT OF OWLERTON 6 **SHEFFIELD UNITED** DIAMOND-TIPPED BLADES

1

2

3

4

5

6

KEEPING THE GAME BEAUTIFUL

ONLINE | WWW.GOALSOUL.NET
INSTORE | GOALSOUL, 283 SHARROW VALE ROAD, SHEFFIELD, S11 8ZF, +44 (0)114 266 3374

94

Theory

"He had another drink, then stepped out on the street and hailed a cab. 'Saudi Arabia,' he told the cabbie and on he went to the Kingdom, only 3000 miles away, to finish off his career."

Notes on Street Football

What kickabouts reveal about the tortured artists of neoromantic myth

By Aleksandar Hemon

(1) **If I should have to venture a guess, pick-up football is the primary way of practising the sport in the world. All you need for a pick-up game is a reasonably flat surface, a sufficiently round object and someone to show up. The rules are thus flexible enough to accommodate the reality of the players' lives and surroundings.**

Pick-up football is not exactly the best name for that particular mode of playing. I prefer to think of it as street football, a variation — or, arguably, a foundation — of the sport as exercised by the majority of humans, who have no means or will to join leagues, be coached, or leave their neighbourhood. Obviously, it doesn't necessarily have to be played on the actual street: any game with no particular gain in sight other than pleasure, consensually arranged by unprofessional players, would come under street football. It is to professional football what dance is to ballet.

(2) I've played street football pretty much exclusively all of my life — no leagues, no coaches, no training sessions, no fans, no appreciation or rewards other than an occasional experience of bliss. As a kid, I played on the gravel in the playground between the two apartment buildings where my friends and I all lived in Sarajevo.

What can only generously be called a pitch included, in addition to the flesh-shredding gravel, a sandbox, seesaws, slide, merry-go-round and a metal frame on which rugs would be hung to beat dirt out of them. After the game, which, for all intents and purposes, we played inside a cloud of black dust, my mother would not let me in the apartment until I fully undressed, as all of my clothes and shoes, as well as my skin and the inside of my mouth, would be black.

Sometimes, if our numbers were low and/or odd, the rug-beating frame would serve as the only goal, and we'd play what we called *viktorija*. The single goalie would throw the ball up with his back turned to both teams (two or three players each) and the team that got the ball would attack, while the other one would defend until the situation reversed. The sand box was right in front of the frame, so the only way to score was by way of long-distance shots or from tight angles.

Most of the time, the goals were the benches at the far ends of the playground. The slide was right in front of one of the benches — effectively playing the role of the centre-back — and if you were running (imagining yourself to be, say, Ian Rush) in anticipation of a wing pass, you had to duck under to get into a scoring position.

(A late duck would've surely led to a cracked skull, but that, miraculously, never happened.) You also had to slalom among the seesaws, the merry-go-round and the swings, while making sure that your rare pass made it past the sandbox. The playground conditioned our skills and tactical decisions — our ball control developed within this physical context, as did positioning and spatial awareness, all far less useful for winning than for mere survival in the jungle of injurious objects. Even if the games mattered enough for us to risk our limbs, few somehow ever got seriously injured. The only corporal damage I can recall was sustained by one of the clumsiest players — nicknamed Bear, behind his back — who once turned into the metal frame and crashed into it with his forehead, which then bled profusely.

Now, when I see my daughter in her football class, moving the ball between orange cones on artificial turf, part of me wishes that she had to slalom among playground equipment in a cloud of black dust, as if those harsh conditions would make her a better player. It is the aging, grumpy, immigrant part of me that tends to believe that the young ones today have it too easy, which makes them less tough, less skilful and less motivated. But I'm fully aware, of course, that's bullshit: no kid from my playground has become a great, let alone professional, player. And it's fair to say that we would've happily settled for an obstacle-free grassy pitch, even if artificial.

(3) We sometimes played on the neighbourhood parking lot as well, conveniently located across the street from an emergency room. Usually, the parking lot was devoid of obstacles,

except that, when it was full, the rows of cars would be side lines. Getting the ball from under a car required rolling in a puddle of machine oil; when the ball bounced off to the busy street we ran between zooming cars to fetch it. The goals would be marked by two bricks, which allowed us to dispute and argue over any goal that was not self-evident.

Thinking about the game in tactical terms meant nothing more than that we bothered to defend at all. Passing was not something that was valued, the skills were really dribbling or ball-hogging. Stuck in my room doing homework and unable to play, I knew the game was on because I could hear the shouts: "Dodaj!" ("Pass!"), followed, with boyish regularity, by a stream of curses.

The hardest thing to learn in football is passing. It is perfectly unnatural. Children do not pass, because they're fascinated by the ball at their feet, by their nascent ability, however limited, to control the ball. So many times in my daughter's football class (she's six now), I've watched a cluster of kids in Brownian motion at the centre of which was one kid who couldn't give up the ball if his or her life depended on it. During the time the ball moves through the space between two players, it belongs to nobody — it is nowhere. To pass is to relinquish control, to give up the certainty of the ball at your feet for the uncertain outcome of a pass. To pass is to anticipate and imagine a future, while to keep the ball and dribble is to stay in the moment for as long as possible.

A forest of playground equipment or even a parking lot were certainly not conducive to creative ball sharing. Even if the ball was relinquished and kicked over to another player, he would always have to spend some time alone with it. I have no way of proving it, but my guess is that, even now, no kids involved in street games the world over play like the Barcelona the grown-up writers and tacticians admire. The Barcelona the kids like would be embodied in Messi, the runt who runs solo past the defence, with the ball seemingly strung to his feet, which is how he's been doing it since he was a kid, as evidenced by the YouTube footage that purports to be of him at the age of six.

④ Obviously, there are no managers or coaches in street football, which is to say that everyone is equally qualified to be coach or manager. The street democracy necessarily results in frequent mouthing off, as everyone believes that they know best. The neighbourhood game I play in every week requires lengthy and not always friendly negotiation during the divvying of the pool players, while nearly everyone coaches in the game, constantly talking at and even insulting other players. Professional football always has an audience — the paying, judging fans — while street players essentially perform for one another, always mutually subject to harsh momentary judgment.

A street team is always unbalanced, because not everyone is at the same skill level. The general approach to addressing the imbalance (apart from yelling) is a ruthless division of labour: the best players are in the attack and midfield (which in a small compressed field is the same thing), the less skilful and/or more aged ones defend, while the weakest one is in the goal. The

problem is often that there are too many self-declared good players up front — there is no coach or any authority to establish a hierarchy or positioning within the team. Moreover, street football often features small, six-foot-wide goals. There is no box, no offside, no penalties; defensive formations are fluid to say the least — more often than not, no one sticks to their position. This commonly leads to more unpleasant imbalance and, eventually, to fractious chaos and apocalyptic yelling. Also, a lot of goals.

⑤ A view of the game — indeed an aesthetic and an ideology — arises from the culture of street football, even after the kids grow up. It all boils down to this: 1) those who can do it alone are the best; 2) the best ones grow up on the street, where they acquire their skills by avoiding various obstacles, be they social (poverty) or physical (the roughness of the concrete pitch). Which is why the Brazilians are considered to be the best — their sumptuous skills always imply a street, a *favela* or, at least, a beach. Not only are, say, defensive midfielders unappreciated by the street kids imagining themselves as Messi or Ronaldo, they're also invisible and incomprehensible. Childish adults are not enamoured with the unspectacular diligence either: recall Florentino Pérez getting rid of Makélélé, from whose departure Real Madrid have never fully recovered.

A useful, hardworking player possessing no glamour or spectacular skills was referred to in the Yugoslavia of my childhood as "water carrier" (*vodonoša*), someone, I used to imagine, who ran around faithfully providing water for the street-bred artist who could turn the game with one fancy move. Such an artist, however, was not necessarily thirsty, as part of the artistic aura was the proudly exhibited absence of interest in running and defending. Tactical and any other indiscipline was seen as a mark of untamable genius, an expression of his artistic nature and recalcitrance, which would've been nurtured — the neo-romantic stereotype required — in some poor, obstacle-riddled neighbourhood. The artist-player, presumably merely expressing his unpredictable, exuberant nature, is essential for what might be called a neo-romantic football aesthetics. Such artistic nature deplores pseudo-rationalist tactical schemes, while being entirely dependent on inspiration and perceivable only in moments of greatness. The street-artist is by definition an underdog and is particularly valued if playing for an underdog club. This underdogness is necessarily nostalgic, a way of longing for inspired innocence, and therefore crucial. The artists who learned their ball magic on the street and scoffed at tactics and discipline could always easily be absorbed into the urban mythology customarily featuring all kinds of rebels. Hence part of that street aesthetics is always hating the rational, realist football, which was exemplified when I was growing up by all teams German, who relied on tactical discipline and hard work, and, very unromantically, always won.

A study of neo-romantic football would feature such players as Garrincha, Best, Hagi, Stoichkov, Gascoigne, Le Tissier, Riquelme, Adriano, who have left a trail of greatness and related (public) drama. Some of them earned far fewer trophies than clips with fancy footwork presently available on YouTube. Some ended up on the heart-breaking path of self-destruction, while others carried their soloist unpredictability off the pitch. In their indelible love of pleasure (for that is what is really behind all their exuberance, the neo-romantic thinking goes), many of them acquired, along with drinking and/or drug problems, more weight than property. Few of the great football artists become successful managers: inspiration is not teachable, or even expressible, outside the moment in which it exists. Their talent is an entrancing, eternal mystery, creating an image — even in their addled retirement — of a suffering, romantic loner.

(6) I've played with so many self-perceived artists that I can now identify them from their first touch, at which they always give off an air of self-importance. Having long grown out of my romantic phase, however, I cannot stand the players who do not defend, who do not retain positional discipline, who exude belief that the rest of their team ought to be grateful for their presence, who always choose a fancy move over a simple Makélélian pass in order to bamboozle the opponent just for the fuck of it, who take it upon themselves to elect — all this while hogging the ball insufferably — the teammate worthy of the masterpiece pass.

I hate watching such players just as I hate being on the team with them. Much too often, the romantics can think of themselves only within the contest of some hierarchy of greatness (even if the game is played on the street — *particularly* on the street) rather than within the game itself. They don't care about winning in collaboration with their team, ever invested in finding ways to express their tortured genius, their drama always more gripping than the game they're playing. And yet — and *yet* — as a writer and a professional story teller, I'm still attracted to and fascinated by the romantics precisely for that heroic drama, which is, needless to say, never limited to the stadium. Such players induce stories, their lives always spilling over.

(7) One of the greatest Yugoslav/ Bosnian players of all time was Safet Sušić, who in the seventies and eighties played for FC Sarajevo and the Yugoslav national team and then went to PSG. Until Ibrahimović and his class arrived, Sušić had been widely considered the best player who ever wore the shirt of the Parisian club. He was fancy-footed all right. He scored hat-tricks in friendlies against Argentina and Italy which involved quite a bit of dribbling past the opponent's defence. But in addition to all the memorable moves, he indeed had a distinguished, responsible career, largely devoid of self-destruction. Presently, he's the manager of the Bosnia national team, very much on the verge of taking them to Brazil next year. In short, a remarkable player — last year *France Football* voted him the best foreign player in Ligue 1 of all time — far more than an artist and therefore of limited narrative interest.

His older brother Sead, however, is an entirely different story. As fancy-footed as Safet, if not more so, he was believed to have been the greatest talent of his generation. He started at the FK Sarajevo youth team but was signed as a teenager, in 1970, by Belgrade's Crvena Zvezda, the biggest and the most powerful Yugoslav club, managed at the time by Miljan Miljanić. (One of the great characters of eastern European football, he also

managed Real Madrid and the Yugoslavia national team and is still fondly remembered as having an uncanny ability to avoid giving a straight answer.) Sead had a middling career at Zvezda, went on to Belgium by way of the USA, until his career fizzled out on his way to Saudi Arabia or some such place. He played for the Yugoslavia national team exactly once and retired at the age of 28. While I can without effort recall Safet's goals and the way he tiptoed past the Argentinian defence like a ballerina, my mind contains no visual memory of Sead's play, even if I remember admiring whatever it was he was doing on the pitch.

But my head is full of the stories of Sead! We in Sarajevo believed that he was (possibly to this day) the only player of Muslim background whose name was chanted by the Crvena Zvezda fans, long invested in Serbian nationalism and notoriously prone to casual racism. In Belgium, the story went, he once dribbled past an entire defence and, with unnecessary fakes, toyed with the goalie who threw himself desperately from one side to another, only for the ball to be poked in the goal when Sead got bored with his helpless victim. Infuriated by the humiliation, the goalie charged at Sead, who offered him his middle finger for consideration, whereupon he bit into it. Another time, Sead received a yellow card, which he ripped out of the ref's hand and tore to shreds. The ref then pulled out the red card, which Sead ripped out of his hand and tore to shreds. And then there was the story — my favourite — in which Sead was in Sarajevo, on his way to Saudi Arabia where he had signed his latest contract. The night before he was to report to his new club, he was drinking with his buddies at the Sarajevo cafe called Stari Sat (The Old Clock — somehow, even the name of the cafe pertains) when he noticed that he had missed his plane. He had another drink, then stepped out on the street and hailed a cab. "Saudi Arabia," he told the cabbie and on he went to the Kingdom, only 3000 miles away, to finish off his career.

Let me make it clear that none of those stories were reported in the press. The stories were produced by the perpetual myth-mill of Sarajevo's streets, which somehow made them more believable. The myth-mill also inducted him in the gambling-and-drinking hall of local fame, also featuring the singer known for the song entitled "Sarajevo, My Love" along with the greatest Bosnian basketball player of all time. Sead was thus part of Sarajevo's neo-romantic pantheon, important for the maintenance of our urban mythological system. I would've hated playing with him, but I could never have enough stories about him.

I met Sead only once. I worked at a Sarajevo radio station in the late eighties, and there I managed to accompany a colleague to an interview with him. Already comfortable in his retirement, he was a quiet, pudgy guy, not so much exuberant as projecting a melancholic kindness and modesty. My colleague and I were eager to check the veracity of the stories his legend rested upon, so we outright asked him. Yes, he confirmed, a goalie did bite his middle finger. (I recall him now as showing me the little scar on his middle finger, but that could well be an embellishment perpetuated by the narrative machinery in my head). No, he did not tear the red and yellow cards to shreds: he grabbed the yellow one from the ref's hand and threw it to the ground, for which he received a red one and then simply left the pitch without further drama. No, he did not take a cab to Saudi Arabia. He was indeed at the Stari Sat, drinking, and decided that he missed Safet, who was playing for PSG at the time. Sead was burning to see him, so he hailed a cab and told the cabbie to take him to Paris, but then came to his senses before the cab left the city and went home instead.

It was one of the most enjoyable interviews I've ever conducted, because I liked Sead a lot. In the radio studio, he did not see himself as a genius or a suffering artist. Even if he did meet some requirements for being a neo-romantic player, the work of romanticising was done by the street fans — we needed him for the stories, we projected and completed his legendary profile. That was, now I understand, a crucial moment in my comprehension of football. It was around then that I shed the last residues of my boyish neo-romantic aesthetics.

(8) Romantic street artists were far more possible and present before the game of football became globalised and commercialised, before the money poured in, before unthinkable amounts came to be at stake, before the great players were able to sign astronomical endorsement contracts — all of which professionalised the game to the point of very rationalist discipline. Today's players pursue and project strength and health, taken to be necessary for any act of on-pitch brilliance and available in all sizes and flavours from the corporations they endorse. Even Ibrahimović, who grew up playing in a rough area of Malmö

and is as close to a street romantic
as any contemporary footballer, is a
consummate, ambitious professional.
Messi could be perceived as a solo artist
only if you somehow disregard the
perfectly attuned Barça orchestra and
have no memory of the romantic soloists
of the past.

And yet — and *yet!* — the street
dimension is still indelibly present in all
of football. After all, Neymar has just
landed in Barcelona.

A Man for all Seasons

Tomislav Ivić pioneered pressing and won league titles in five different countries

By Aleksandar Holiga

In January 2005, Tomislav Ivić gave a lecture in Herceg Novi, Montenegro. "Habit," he said, "is the second nature of man. We need to create habits — not as much physical or technical as mental. And you do that by constant repetition. A change in mentality is needed. You have to prepare your men psychologically for a new logic, so that over time they become eager to embrace it."

This wasn't a psychology congress on classic conditioning or applied behaviour analysis, but a seminar in football coaching. Ivić spoke about the subject of pressing and the sub-heading of his lecture revealed its extraordinary straightforward fashion: it read, quite simply, "How to beat a stronger opponent."

All coaches, especially the good ones, are behaviourists to some extent — such is the nature of their profession. But few of them have ever been so candid about their approach as Tomislav Ivić was. A rare breed in the football culture of the former Yugoslavia, which traditionally harboured an almost predeterministic appreciation of 'natural' talent and lionised individual artistry above all, he was a firm believer in the system. While he never dismissed the importance of natural ability, to him it was merely crude material which meant nothing

if not thoroughly processed, refined and given optimal use within a whole. He spoke a lot about "mentality" — but whereas in the Balkans that word usually has a negative, defeatist undertone in anything from politics and economy to popular culture, his interpretation was completely different. To Ivić, mentality was something to be constantly learned, reshaped and altered.

That he succeeded with these ideas in Split, a city so particular that it appears to be in a perpetual uprising against itself, is a true testimony to his greatness. And he did, winning three championships and four cups there while making Hajduk a force to be reckoned with in Europe. After that, nothing was too hard for Ivić. He went on to lift league titles in four other countries (with Ajax, Anderlecht, Panathinaikos and Porto; he also won the Copa del Rey with Atlético Madrid and the Taça de Portugal, the European Super Cup and the Intercontinental Cup with Porto. Sometimes he's also credited with winning the 1992 Ligue 1 title with Olympique de Marseille, but actually he only led them for a few months that season, remaining as an 'advisor' to his good friend Raymond Goethals for the rest of it. The Belgian coach admitted that Ivić helped him prepare tactics for the 1993 Champions League final, which he won against Fabio Capello's Milan).

League titles in five different countries is a feat yet to be matched by any other manager. All this silverware prompted *La Gazzetta dello Sport* in 2007 to proclaim Ivić the most successful manager in history. The trophy harvest also inspired José Mourinho, one of the three greats who have come closest to matching his feat, winning four — albeit stronger — national competitions (the other two are Ernst Happel and Giovanni Trapattoni). He first met Ivić back in 1988.

"José was a student of sports science and he'd often come to watch my training sessions in Porto," Ivić revealed in an interview with the Croatian daily newspaper *Jutarnji list*. Six years later, Ivić's second term at the club came to an end as he was replaced by Bobby Robson and Mourinho, his interpreter. Another decade later, the two men met at the Stamford Bridge after Chelsea's 2-1 win over Barcelona in the Champions League. Ivić was there as a pundit for Croatian television and, after the Special One had given him a signed copy of his biography, he showed it to the journalists. The inscription read, in Portuguese, "To the greatest coach of them all — I hope one day to win as much as you."

Many coaches are egomaniacs. Some are tyrants, some father figures and some try to act as players' mates. Tomislav Ivić was none of these things. You could say that he was a bit like Mr Miyagi from *The Karate Kid*, though: he always insisted on a set of very simple exercises, which were to be painstakingly repeated until the movements become automatic and instinctive. Ivić described some of those in that 2005 lecture and they appeared disappointingly banal — something you might expect to see when watching kids train, but not among fully grown professionals. For example, a small (35mx16m) pitch, with a wall at each end, was used for technique training: a player would run with the ball for a few metres, smash it into the wall, control the rebound, turn around, run with the ball, smash it into the other wall, control... And repeat. And repeat.

It's strange, given what a rationalist he was, how Ivić ascribed an almost mystical quality to those methods. In Herceg Novi, he told the coaches that most of the exercises he used had been devised by "the old Hajduk coach" — he meant Luka Kaliterna, easily the most iconic figure in Yugoslav football. The goalkeeper in the first Hajduk squad, in 1911, and a teacher to generations, Kaliterna is generally considered to be the father of football in Split. He was the first coach to win Hajduk a title, in 1927, and their first local coach after learning his trade from the dozen Czechs who preceded him. Yes, this goes all the way to the early 20th-century Central European football tradition — though, in this case, not to the coffee houses, but to the beer houses of Prague. In one of those, Hajduk was founded by four students from Split, including Kaliterna's brother Fabijan.

Although his idea of playing football was all about modernity, Ivić drew great pride from the fact that he was a part of this historical line. Himself a Kaliterna disciple — like pretty much every football coach that emerged from Split up until the 1970s — he often quoted his master's grains of ancient wisdom, like 'See everything, look at nothing' or 'The play, not the player, scores goals.' Whenever asked about his biggest influences, he'd always put Kaliterna first, then usually Rinus Michels and Hennes Weisweiler.

The players must have been less than enthusiastic about Ivić's methods — just as the Karate Kid Daniel LaRusso initially was when Mr Miyagi made him sweep floors and wax cars. It took them time to realise the value of endlessly repeating simple movements and tasks — but once they did, they became eager to embrace them. Dražen Mužinić, a long-serving Hajduk player in the 1970s, admitted he became so infected by the habits he had learned that he began "catching people in offside traps" when talking to them in the street. "I couldn't help it," he explained. "It was a reflex action for me." When Mužinić was transferred to Norwich City in 1980, he was so useless that Justin Fashanu remarked, "I don't think we got Mužinić. I reckon they sent his milkman instead." Besides not speaking a word of English, the player was immersed in Ivić's logic and found it too hard to function outside it. When Norwich cancelled his contract, he retired aged 29.

At Ajax, where Ivić coached from 1976 to 1978, between his two trophy-laden stints at Hajduk, he was initially met with a player rebellion led by Ruud Krol, who was supposed to be his sweeper and the commander of his defence. Had Ivić not been hand-picked by Rinus Michels himself to succeed him, this might have escalated, but the chairman Jaap van Praag intervened and the squad listened. In his debut season with the club, Ivić won Ajax their first Dutch title in four years — for the first time after the Ştefan Kovács era; for the first time without the likes of Cruyff, Neeskens or Rep. "The

older players like Krol had some trouble in the beginning, but they would later praise in particular his training methods," said Pim van Dord, a defender in that team. "What was special about those was how often he'd repeat certain things. In time we started to believe in his approach."

Ivić said that Michels had chosen him as his successor because the way his Hajduk played suited the ideals of Total Football. That may not be entirely so — while he did use the 4-3-3 formation, interchanging positions and intensive pressing, his football was never quite so easy on the eye or as attacking. In part that was down to a lack of extraordinary individuals but Ivić favoured automatism and a great deal of running, so his teams weren't as playful as the Ajax that conquered Europe. His was a more physical game.

"Split of the 1970s was not unlike some place in the north of England," said the *Jutarnji list* columnist Jurica Pavičić. "It was a city of blue collars and factory chimneys, where a company bus would pick up workers in front of their housing estate built by that same company. Split was experiencing a period of industrial growth and increased urbanisation. Football was its binding tissue, something everyone talked about. I cannot help but think it's no coincidence that Hajduk of that era made their name by playing what people usually call 'industrial' football."

As a young man, Tomislav Ivić worked at the docks and played for RNK Split, the city's second club which — coached by Luka Kaliterna — swept through the lower divisions to reach the Yugoslav top tier in the late 1950s. "They'd let him leave work a bit earlier because he was important for the club, but every day he had to walk for more than 10km — first from home to work, then home, then from home to the ground," Milorad Bibić Mosor, the late journalist and author who was probably RNK's biggest fan, told *FourFourTwo Croatia* in 2010. So if Ivić used to lead such a physical and industrial life, is it any wonder that it transferred into his coaching philosophy?

He was also often accused of playing defensive football. This probably had something to do with his methodology. "It's much easier to learn how to defend than how to attack," he used to say. "It also takes less time." Once he'd managed to fortify the defence, his teams would grow steadily and become more and more efficient in attack as well. In 1977-78, his Ajax team scored 23 goals more than in the previous season. But for various reasons, including his adventurous nature and in some cases money, he hardly ever stuck around in one place long enough to gain true recognition.

The time spent in Amsterdam influenced Ivić. Looking back, it seems that he learned how to manipulate space more efficiently there and that took his ideas to a new level. "In the second year with Ivić we started to put his counter-pressing approach into practice at a more fluid rate," Pim van Dord remembers. "We started to grow in terms of how he wanted us to play, but he had already indicated to us that he would leave at the end of the season — because of money. He was sad when he left us because he had us playing near to where he felt was the optimum under him."

It could be argued that Ivić returned to Hajduk in 1978 as something of a

pressing fundamentalist. He started talking about football in different terms, much to the bewilderment of local journalists. He became fascinated by the (bio)mechanics of team movement: "Pressing is the beating heart of our football," he'd say, describing the team's on-field shape as though it were a live organism, a muscle, explaining its contractions and expansions. His team was made to practise defending with a very shallow formation ("If you looked at it from a plane, the distance between the first and the last player should be about 30m"), from which they would 'organically' expand in transition to attack, following established and oft-repeated patterns.

In the late 1970s, Ivić was a man on a mission: he wanted to bring a European trophy to Split, which was probably the main reason he returned there in the first place. Although Hajduk had been a fearsome team in that decade, real continental success had eluded them — they had beaten Saint-Étienne 4-1, then lost 5-1 in the return leg; won 2-0 against PSV in Split, then lost 3-0 in Eindhoven. The coach wanted to change their mentality and shake off the 'home team' tag. In 1978, he was furious after being eliminated by Arsenal in the second round of the Uefa Cup. The Gunners parked the bus in the first leg and managed to pull off a promising 2-1 defeat, their away goal a long-range effort by Liam Brady. Two weeks later, Willie Young scored the only goal seven minutes from time at Highbury and Arsenal went through on away goals. In December that year, Hajduk's star striker, the 'King of Goals' Slaviša Žungul defected to America. It was a shock for everyone, but urban legend has it that

Ivić intentionally sent him on his way because they never saw eye to eye. He replaced him in the team with Zlatko Vujović, an incredibly fast young forward with prodigious stamina.

The following season, Hajduk stormed to the European Cup quarter-finals, in which they faced the great Hamburg side of Keegan, Hrubesch and Magath. Coached by Branko Zebec, who had been Ivić's predecessor in the Hajduk hot seat, it also featured Ivan Buljan, a former Hajduk player and a world-class defender. Ivić had four full months to prepare for the tie (the European break lasted from early November to early March) and became obsessed by it. In later interviews, he confessed exactly how far he took his thinking about this 'project'. For example, an article he read about Rod Laver's psychological preparation for five-set Wimbledon matches gave him an idea of how to prepare his men for the equally exhausting task he was about to give them. He also looked for ideas in other sports, like handball and even horse-racing. People would often see him in the street with one or two of his players, waving his hands frantically like some kind of mad scientist: he wanted to make sure they understood what he was asking of them, so he kept explaining. Over and over again.

This kind of obsessive behaviour remained a part of Ivić's character until his death in 2011. Journalists revealed stories on how he would rearrange chairs in their office to explain the Makélélé role. An acquaintance of mine told me how he was once on the same flight as Ivić: within minutes of introducing himself to the coach, he was presented with diagrams drawn on a piece of paper to explain how England should play if they wanted to have a chance of winning Euro 2004. To him, football tactics increasingly became something like a set of problems and equations which could be solved by proper analysis — something that can and needs to be mended. When, due to his deteriorating health, doctors instructed him to retire from coaching, he was still filling up his notebooks with tactical diagrams and new ideas on a daily basis. Even when he was admitted to hospital and banned from watching football on TV, he still drew his diagrams, straight from his head.

With his immense knowledge, understanding of the game and eye for detail, Ivić was one of the best TV analysts anybody is ever likely to see. But it was never too long before any football-related conversation with him returned to that 1980 Hajduk match against HSV.

In the first leg, Ivic's approach was very cautious, as was the norm for away games those days. Hamburg won 1-0 in an evenly matched game, which was seen as a decent result for Hajduk. Almost everyone in Split believed that the team could turn it around. Two weeks later, 52,000 people at Poljud stadium saw something they would never forget. Hajduk flew all over the pitch: they played one-touch football and swapped positions so quickly that it was hard even for the fans to keep track, let alone Hajduk's opponents. They moved in unison, contracted and expanded, as though all were controlled by some invisible brain or joystick. And they pressed the ball for the full 90 minutes.

This was avant-garde football — but it wasn't to be for Hajduk. Hamburg scored from what were their only two chances, while the player who had been the most reliable for Ivić let him down the most: he gifted Horst Hrubesch a goal after only two minutes and later missed a handful of sitters, including a penalty. That he scored to make it 3-2 four minutes from time was little consolation, by then it was too late and Hajduk were eliminated on away goals as they had been many times before and would be after. That player was Boro Primorac, Ivić's sweeper — the same Primorac who has been Arsène Wenger's assistant for almost 20 years now.

In plain terms, Hajduk were eliminated due to bad luck and human failings that could hardly have been foreseen. There wasn't much more Ivić could have done and that was the hardest thing for him to accept, especially because he was positive that none of the other three semi-finalists — Real Madrid, Ajax and Nottingham Forest — had an answer for the style he had developed. He was so disappointed that he decided to leave the club once again — this time for Anderlecht, where in his first season he brought them their first league title after a seven-year hiatus. As for Hajduk, they never won another Yugoslav title after 1979. In 1984, they reached the Uefa Cup semi-finals and lost to Tottenham — on away goals, of course.

Tomislav Ivić changed jobs many times in the years that followed and racked up so many wins that he even inspired the likes of Mourinho. But the impression is nothing ever meant as much to him as that one night in Split — not even that one-off game when he got to manage the Croatia national team and beat Italy, who were fresh from reaching the final of the 1994 World Cup.

In retrospect, that was the match that made Croatia as footballing nation: only their third competitive game ever (the first two were against Estonia and Lithuania). Their regular manager Miroslav Blažević had been suspended by Uefa, so Ivić took over. In Palermo, he set up a brilliant defensive strategy: Croatia played something like 5-3-1-1, with both Zvonimir Boban and Aljosa Asanović acting as deep-lying playmakers, the hard-running Nikola Jurčević alongside them and Robert Prosinečki as *trequartista*. Instead of a designated holder, Slaven Bilić and Igor Štimac took turns stepping out of the defence to help close down Roberto Baggio; Davor Šuker pulled wide all the time. The team of Arrigo Sacchi, a coach who had his own ideas about pressing, was given the ball but denied any space in attack. Frustrated, they lost balance and were less able to cope with Croatia's quick counters, so the visitors scored twice before Italy could manage a consolation goal in the dying minutes of the game.

The media at home were bowing to the genius of Ivić, but he didn't seem particularly proud. He set up those tactics against his own doctrine of how football should be played. He merely did what he felt was needed and 'mended' the team for Blažević. Given the time he had at disposal, that was all he could do, because "it's much easier to learn how to defend than how to attack."

He was a captivating speaker and a visionary. Football of the future, he predicted in 2010, a year before his death, "... will use formations consisting of only two lines, each of them including the best technician as specialist — the deeper one as a modified, new-age libero who can provide the best passes and act almost like a quarterback in American football, and the one up front to spearhead the attack not by power, pace or physique, but by creativity and positional intelligence."

But the glory and trophies will belong to those teams who'll be able to play at high tempo throughout the game, achieve automatism and act on instinct in transition, while constantly pressing on the ball very high up field — Ivić said that year when *FourFourTwo Croatia* spoke to him on the phone, trying to get him to write a column for the magazine (sadly, his health never permitted it, although he was very keen). "But is it possible to maintain that kind of intensity for 90 minutes?" — his rhetorical question was identical to the one in the very climax of that 2005 lecture, and so was his answer: "Yes, it is!

"You know, when Hajduk played Hamburg back in 1980..."

109
Writers

"Men such as Busby, Shankly and Stein were not only the beneficiaries of post-war working class social mobility, but also the instigators of that mobility."

The Thinker

Ivan Ergić on the competing draws of football and philosophy

By Vladimir Novak

"In transitional, post-war and post-socialistic society, sport becomes an institution which accumulates frustrations and reproduces nationalism, chauvinism and hostilities, and as such it is an ideal instrument for upholding a precarium and keeping unhappy youth far from government buildings, factory yards and students' dorms. Sport stands there together with all other forms of collectivity and mass events, in which the increasingly alienated citizen gains strength in collective delight. In that way stadiums and sports halls are transformed into incubators of nationalism and chauvinism and the descendants of the impoverished working-class and middle-class are transformed into a classic lumpenproletariat. The club consciousness, just like the regional and nationalistic consciousness, is a false consciousness, which prevents the development of authentic class consciousness. The national or the club flag replaces the flags and discourse about social justice, and the torch replaces the Molotov cocktail."

Who would you think wrote this? You probably wouldn't guess it was written by a professional footballer. But it was. This and many other remarkable articles — the paragraph above is of course only an excerpt — were written by the Serbian footballer (now retired) Ivan Ergić (born in 1981), who not so long ago was a star of Basel, put on shining performances in the Champions League and played at a World Cup.

❖ *Why did you decide to end your career so early, at the age of 30? You surely could have played on for at least for three or four more years?*

To tell you the truth, I finished my career mostly because of a certain saturation. I had had enough and therefore I decided to terminate my career. From the age of 14 I had been separated from my family; most of the time I lived alone, no matter where I was. After so many years I felt saturated with that way of life. As a matter of fact, in the last four, five years of my career I felt that in a way I didn't belong to this. But I still had the desire to play, because I loved to play football. I never had a strict plan of when I would play until. So when I turned 30, I thought it was time to quit. At the same time my health was important to me. Finally, I'd fulfilled my childhood dream. I'd played in big games, against great teams, great players, Champions League, World Cup... I no longer had any specific ambitions to achieve. So, all in all, I am happy with my career.

⟳ I read that in the last years of your career you became so occupied with reading and writing, often into the early morning, that you turned up at training without enough sleep. Is that true?

When I was 23, 24, when I started playing again, after that two-year-break I had because of depression, already then I started to go in a different direction. Literally, I started slowly to separate from all this. I was physically present, but my mind was more and more absent. To put it in a poetic way, just like the philosopher's owl turns up at night, also the muse comes in the night; so yes it did happen that sometimes I didn't sleep at all, because it was my passion to read, to think and to write. Normally, in the morning I was exhausted and sleepy. My coaches at Bursaspor and also earlier at Basel noticed that and as I was a key player, sometimes, of course not always, they scheduled training sessions for the afternoon, rather than the morning. That was an interesting episode. Maybe it was a bit unfair towards others, but I really got into that rhythm that often I didn't sleep during nights. But it was not a problem. It did not affect my performances. Matches were played mainly in evening hours, so in that period, I was always ready. For example, while I was at Bursa, I stayed in the club hotel, I rarely went out and there was a curfew and when we had morning training, our coach was confused why I was tired. But that thing with reading and writing in the night was stronger than me. It fulfilled me. The only exception was when we had pre-season preparations, when the programme was really hard, I always had a good rest.

⟳ What are you doing nowadays?

I'm *trying* to do some things, but unfortunately here in Serbia it's quite difficult. I'm involved in several things. I'm trying to do humanitarian work, but even that is not easy if you don't have wind in your sails from politicians or some influential people... Without it it's difficult, but I don't want it. I absolutely don't want any contact with anybody from politics, doing me favours. On the other hand, with just your own resources it's very difficult to achieve anything. For some time, even when I was in Basel, I've been involved in the project "Women — victims of violence". That story always touched me and I was always unhappy about the fact that in such social projects there were no men involved. I was also thinking I had to become active in the problems of refugees, because I, too, am a refugee. [Ergić's parents had to move from Croatia to Serbia when the civil war broke out in former Yugoslavia in the early 1990s.] But for the time being I'm trying to help the "Women — victims of violence" project, both in a financial and an organisational way. Apart from that, most likely I will get into theatre production. That's also a passion of mine. Together with a friend from a theatre we will try to stage independent plays, which will be politically engaged, which will deal with social problems. I think that I do have a talent for theatre. I also have long-term plans, like setting up a small culture centre to give young people more chances to engage and create. I meet so many talented and honest young people here in Serbia, but they are politically frustrated. They are disappointed and they do not have any frame in which they can find themselves.

⇔ *Those are noble goals. What other future plans do you have?*

Those goals are not short-term wishes. My long-term wish is really to put things into motion, to do something that will make sense. For example, I often say that in football I have achieved a lot, but in fact, in a human sense I didn't achieve anything. I represented my country when I played for the national team. But now — in the real sense — I want to help and represent my country. I aim to make a difference, to help those young people, to develop their huge potential, to get them out of apathy. I really have no dreams other than that.

⇔ *What about business and income? You speak only about non-profit work. Does that mean that you won't work for money any more, that you have enough?*

It depends what you mean by enough. It depends how much someone needs. I'm not used to a luxury lifestyle. All I really need is one room, full of books... I don't know, that's my micro-world. Of course, I'm aware that you have to be careful with the money you have earned. I know that there are many retired football players who unfortunately let it happen that one day all their money is gone. If you're used to having a lot of money and having a certain life style, it's difficult all of a sudden to switch to another lifestyle. I never got used to a grand lifestyle, so I have no problem in that regard. I wish to do with my money something that makes sense, something that will fulfil me. Whether I will succeed in having enough energy, spirit and financial resources to achieve that, we shall see.

⇔ *In the last two years, since you finished your career, have you ever considered a comeback? There were offers, weren't there?*

I must admit that I'm missing the game; the game as a game. It's true that I had offers from the Middle East and China. Actually, I considered perhaps going to China and signing for a club there. I had contacts with some Chinese clubs, but eventually I got fed up after I saw how many middle-men were supposed to be involved in the deal. Also with the Arabs it was a disaster. You cannot imagine how arrogant those guys are. They got rich overnight, they don't know anything, but they look down at you from a height. And when you turn them down, all of a sudden they sort of show more respect for you. They tell you things like, "My boss is offended, but he is ready to speak to you again," and so on and so on. I was in negotiations with a club from Qatar, but eventually I pulled out. So, all in all, there were no serious attempts for a comeback. I didn't speculate, I didn't wait for offers. Besides, there was never a serious offer like with Bursa, when the coach said that he wanted me, that he stood behind me, when we had decent and serious meetings.

⇔ *You wrote and still write articles for the Swiss paper* Tageswoche *and the Belgrade* Politika. *When and how did you get the idea for those columns? What was the main motive and inspiration?*

It was back in 2005 or 2006 when I started first writing for [the Swiss daily] *Tagesanzeiger*, but that didn't work out well. There were issues with making the pieces shorter, changing them, moving them from the sports pages to another section and things like that. Then I began writing for *Tageswoche* from Basel. The inspiration for those columns I got from everything I'd experienced in my football career; dealing with people from clubs, with agents, with criminals. I found myself in the middle of that story at the age of 19, with stories about millions and so on. Also the period before that marked me. Moving from place to place, being a refugee... All that was accumulated in me and it culminated at one point. So it was maybe natural that it resulted with some pathology [his depression]. After everything, it was for me a way of discharging, a way of dealing with everything. My basic psychological and emotional structure was in me, I couldn't reshape it; I kept everything, but I didn't hold it back any more — I decided to throw it out of myself. At the same it was a conscious decision, because I thought that people deserved to learn the truth. Sport, in general, is still keen to keep around it that aura of cleanliness. So it is still sort of a taboo. So I wanted, for example, youngsters and their parents to learn what is going on in this business. That was my main motive. I have to say that I was lucky with my writing, because I was at a club like Basel, which functioned a bit differently than other clubs.

⇨ *I was just about to ask you this. How did your bosses and teammates react to your writing? On the one hand you were making a living from professional football and on the other criticising the business severely in print. One could say that it's like spitting into the plate from which you were eating.*

The head coach [Christian Gross] was not happy about it. He was a strict guy. I had issues with him. Not so much because of my columns, but because I commented on our style of play. At one point we had

a team that could have played attractive, attacking football, but we played destructive football. So, sometimes I said that our main rival, FC Zurich, played better football, although they had poorer players than we did. That frustrated him. After each interview I ended up in his office. As for my columns, I noticed that people at the club were not happy with them, the president was not happy about it. But I knew the limits. I never wrote anything that could have had a negative effect on the atmosphere in the team and in the club. I wrote mainly about some general pathology in sport. So, in that sense I think that I managed to find some balance. But I cannot deny that I felt some sort of negative reactions, that I was regarded as a *Nestbeschmutzer* [someone who fouls their own nest], but I accepted it. After all, we lived in a democracy. Earning good money from football doesn't mean that you're not allowed to say something against it. When I was criticised in the club and from people around the club, as well as from fans and media, I replied that I thought that Switzerland was a democratic country, but that it seemed that it was not. But it was not polemical. It was my general attitude if there were complaints. Actually, it's ideal for the establishment to give a lot of space in the media to rich athletes and other celebrities, who have nothing to say, or who are not allowed to say it. As for my teammates, they didn't bother; they weren't interested in those columns.

⇨ *Did you maybe think about one day working as a professional journalist?*

No, not really. Especially not being staff writer in some company. But you never know. What attracts me is investigative journalism. I have the highest respect for that. But I think for that one has to have some sort of detective skills. I don't think that I have that talent.

Reading your columns, you get the impression that they were written by a sociologist or a psychologist, that the author is at the level of a university professor. Please tell me about your education.

Even when I was a little boy, I was keen to learn and to read. I come from a working-class family and my parents were quite severe. School was always very important. I was lucky that I received a scholarship from the Australian Institute for Sports and I finished high school in Canberra. Reading was always my passion. I wanted to study philosophy while I was in Switzerland and also later in Serbia, after I finished my career, but I didn't. I realised that formal education was not for me and that most people do it in order to get an academic title, rather than gaining essential knowledge. In a nutshell, I would say that I am an autodidact. As Chomsky said, formal education can make you blind rather than enabling you to develop critical thinking.

What kind of literature were you reading the most?

At one point I read a lot of stuff on psychology. It had also a healing effect for the emotional state I was in. I read also a lot of stuff on philosophy, sociology and politics, of course also a lot of literature per se. I can't tell you all the authors or titles, but I read so many books about philosophy, that it's no exaggeration to say that I could immediately get a doctorate in philosophy.

Last year you published a book of love poetry. Do you plan to publish more?

I have more poems. Some of them are a bit heavier, with more social and patriotic topics. I don't know if I will ever publish them.

Do you follow football? Do you go to games or watch football on TV?

Not so much. Usually I watch the Champions League highlights and some Spanish league games, especially Barcelona.

Please correct me if I'm wrong, but I had the impression that you never seemed integrated with the national team. Is that fair?

When I played my best football, when for example I was voted in the Champions League Team of the Week, I wasn't called up to the national team. Other players played instead of me and that hurt. At the same time the Australian Football Federation constantly pushed me to play for them. They gave me a lot, they invested in my football development, so I thought that it would be fair to play for them, but my heart decided to play for my homeland. I mean, I never regret that decision, but at the same time, you are right, I never identified myself with the milieu in and around the Serbian FA, with the people who were around the national team.

Everybody was puzzled when before the 2006 World Cup game between Serbia & Montenegro and Côte d'Ivoire you were the only player who loudly and proudly sung the old Yugoslav national anthem, an anthem of a country that hadn't existed for 15 years. What were you emotions then and how did your teammates react?

There were no particular reactions, although I think that they thought that I was strange. As for singing the anthem, I did it spontaneously and it meant a lot to me, because I was born and brought up in Yugoslavia and I loved that country. You know, I am a Yugoslav in a cultural sense. I cannot accept that [the Serbian writer Jovan] Dučić is mine and [the Croatian writer Miroslav] Krleža is not mine any more. That's as if someone cut off my arm. I cannot grasp why I cannot be at the same time a Serb and a Yugoslav. I even think that I am a bigger patriot than those guys who hold up three fingers all the time or wear some Chetnik [Second World War Serb nationalist paramilitaries] symbols...

✦ *Juventus spotted you in Australia and signed you. Still, in the end you didn't make a career with Juventus. Why?*

I was a 19-year-old kid and of course I was impressed when Juventus wanted me. I also had offers from some other big clubs, but I picked Juventus. They sent me on loan to Basel, where I played very well and at one point I was supposed to return to Juventus, but then I suffered a groin injury, I had an operation, the recovery took longer than expected [Ergić suffered at that period also from mononucleosis] and eventually I fell into depression. I was two years out of the game and in the meantime Juventus pulled out. They acted as if we never had a contract. Basel supported me; they were still counting on me, so that after my comeback Juventus was not an issue any more. I really felt a moral obligation to pay back Basel for the trust they put in me, during that difficult period I went through. Also Juventus were

in turmoil, they were in the middle of the corruption scandal, club officials were arrested... and when I saw all that, I said to myself, "I'm not interested whatsoever in Juventus," besides the fact that I was happy at FC Basel and that I owed them. Afterwards I was given the captain's armband, I was called up to the national team for the World Cup, I involved myself a lot in various club activities, in contact with our fans, especially in that tricky period when the club had to play six games behind closed doors [after a pitch invasion in May 2006]. I had credibility both at the club and with the fans. So I was practically an intermediary. I was also interested in how the fan culture functioned.

✦ *On the cover of your poetry book you wrote, "Football is my wife, poetry is my lover." You could say that maybe that was precisely the reason why you didn't have a bigger career, although you had the potential for it. What do you think?*

Well, probably I could have had a bigger career. I still keep that contract with Juventus as a souvenir and I believe that I could have played successfully for a bigger club, but I really have no regrets at all. Who knows, perhaps at a bigger club I would have struggled to cope with that massive machinery that surrounds the modern game. If I hadn't been with a club like Basel, which is not among the biggest clubs, but which is a respectable club in Europe, probably I wouldn't have had the space for my other interests. They were tolerant towards it.

✦ *Is it true that you never had an agent? Why?*

In the beginning, when I moved from Australia to Juventus, I did have an agent, but actually he was more a Juventus agent than mine. But later on I abandoned contacts with agents, although at some point it was suggested to me that I should have an agent, that I wouldn't find a club and that I wouldn't succeed in football without an agent. But I rejected the idea. I said that I didn't need an agent. I didn't want to change my mind.

⊕ *You were treated for depression and you didn't play for two years. At that point you even considered giving up your football career. How do you look back today at that difficult period?*

Yes, it's true that I wasn't sure if I could go on. I had a break of two years and you won't often find a club that will stick with their player in such a situation. But Basel held on, they were very correct and they extended my contract. It's not easy, when you're in a psychiatric clinic, to explain to people what kind of state of mind you're in. In such circumstances you don't think about life, let alone about your football career. So, at one point I told my psychiatrist that I didn't want to continue with football, but he tried to persuade me to go on. He was a big Basel fan and afterwards we became friends. He repeated all the time, "You will play again," and after I recovered, also the hope returned that I would continue my career. He worked a lot with me, he lifted my self-confidence. So, talking about football was part of my therapy. If I succeeded in re-socialising through football, it meant that I was ready again for life. Eventually I came out from it far stronger than I ever was.

⊕ *You wrote that professional sport is anything but healthy. Do you plan*

maybe one day to publish a book about that topic?

Yes, I wrote an article about that subject. I don't know whether I'll write a book. Besides, Duci Simonović [Ljubodrag Simonović, the former Crvena Zvezda and Yugoslavia basketball player, who is also a philosopher and publicist] has written about it his whole life, so I wouldn't like to repeat the same things.

⊕ *Fair Play practically doesn't exist any longer. You said that a fair game is more important to you than a victory. Did you have issues with coaches and teammates because of such an attitude?*

There were some situations with Basel, when they were not happy about it. For example, once when I told the referee, who gave a penalty-kick to us, that it wasn't handball and he changed his decision. Our coach [Christian Gross] called me into his office the next morning and asked me to give him an explanation. You know, it's the logic "to achieve victory by all means". Also from some teammates there was mocking. They told me that I was a pussy and things like that. So one could see that there was the logic of machoism, that one had to be aggressive, but it didn't bother me. Also the fans were divided. A few praised me, but most said that "victory is most important." They are raised from childhood like that. Of course I knew that I could never change things, but still sometimes I tried to turn around things a little bit.

⊕ *You wrote that you would like to experience the humanisation of football and professional sports. Is that too utopian an idea ever to happen?*

It's impossible to achieve as long as the society functions as it does now. Sport will become human only when society becomes human. Football cannot be humanised in the present circumstances.

✥ *Do you have a soul mate from the world of football or from other sports, someone with whom you share your thoughts, with whom you discuss ideas and arguments?*

I am in touch with Duci Simonović. He is a legend. In another age, he would surely be in a high position in sports. With the exception of some of his political views, I agree 99% with his ideas and views. But, in general, I don't have friends from football. Well, at Basel I had good relations with [Zdravko] Kuzmanović and with [Ivan] Rakitić. I was like their older brother, but we didn't have a relationship in terms of discussing the darker side of modern sport. **B**

THE BLIZZARD BY GOALSOUL
A PARTNERSHIP BORN OF FOOTBALL

BLZZRD03
COMPARING APPLE WITH ORANJE
SIMON KUPER AND DAVID WINNER

BLZZRD08
THE BICYCLE THIEF
LARS SIVERTSEN

The Blizzard by goalsoul partnership is a commitment to style and substance in equal measure. Our stunning and original story-inspired, graphic tees look and feel great. Lovingly hand screen-printed on 100% combed-cotton and shrink-resistant fabric – you can be sure of the highest possible quality, durability and wearability.

Available in sizes **S / M / L / XL / XXL** for only **£25** each, plus shipping.

THE BLIZZARD
GOALS ARE OVERRATED
JONATHAN WILSON

BLZZRD03
THE HARMONY OF THE SPHERE
PHILIPPE AUCLAIR

Exclusively available now from **www.theblizzard.co.uk** and **www.goalsoul.net**

More Important than That

David Peace discusses Red or Dead, *his novel about the life of Bill Shankly*

By Anthony Clavane

⇔ *In explaining why you wanted to write* Red or Dead, *you said: "I've written about corruption, I've written about crime, I've written about bad men and I've written about the demons. But now I've had enough of the bad men and the demons. Now I want to write about a good man." Some of us can't get enough of the bad men and the demons. The devil, they say, has the best tunes. Writers often find more depth and complexity in evil characters. In* Red or Dead *Bill Shankly comes over as a saintly man and a good socialist. So, how was it for you?*

Initially — instinctively, perhaps — I was drawn to Shankly by the mystery of his sudden resignation and retirement. And again, initially and instinctively, the temptation was there to focus solely on the resignation and the retirement; Shankly as Lear in the wilderness, as a Willy Loman or an Archie Rice figure. But that's not the story or, at least, not the whole story. Because I quickly realised that the story is in the work, in the acts of Bill Shankly; the determination and the struggle to take Liverpool Football Club into the First Division, to win the League and the Cup, and on into Europe. And the more I read about how he did that and the effect he had on the people and the supporters of Liverpool Football Club, the more that became the story.

And yes, it is the story of a good man. A socialist and a saint.

But I'd never written about such a man before. And, as you say, we are drawn to the bad men and the demons. But I don't agree the devil has the best tunes; he just has the more comforting and familiar ones; the ones which help us to accept and justify our own failings, perhaps. And, of course, it is always "easier to find inhabitants for an inferno or even a purgatorio" (to quote Ezra Pound). But, just personally, first reading and then writing about Bill Shankly was a very, very welcome change. And it was inspiring. And I hope people who read the book will also find it inspiring. And a welcome change from all the narratives of defeat.

⇔ *It's always been a mystery to me why Shankly suddenly retired, at the top of his game, in 1974 when he was 60, handing over to Bob Paisley who was only a few years younger. Part of his "goodness" was, as you make clear, his desire to spend more time with his wife and family. Do you think he could have 'done a Fergie' and gone on for another decade? And, if so, would Liverpool have been just as successful as they were under his successors?*

Well, it is a fascinating question but, obviously, an impossible one to answer.

I don't think we will ever know now exactly why Bill Shankly resigned when he did. But I do think — from all I have read and from what people who knew Shankly have said — that his retirement was often painful and he often regretted his decision. And undoubtedly he could have gone on and, with the team he had in 1974, I am sure they would have been successful. But, as I say, whether or not they would have been as successful under Shankly as they became under Paisley is an impossible question to answer. And I'd also be very, very wary of underestimating Bob Paisley.

✥ *As a Huddersfield Town fan, what do you think would have happened if Shanks had stayed at Leeds Road: would there have been a Herbert Chapman effect?*

Absolutely, yes! A return to the glories of the Twenties! Shankly himself said — and, of course, I wasted no time shoe-horning this into the novel — that had the Town board agreed to sign [Ron] Yeats and [Ian] St John, then Town would have gone on to win "all there was to win". And as with everything else Saint Bill said, I'll take that as gospel.

✥ *You listened to a lot of Shankly interviews and tapes. His voice was very stirring — it must have been a contrast to the cartoonish Scottish accent contemporary impersonators like Mike Yarwood went in for. I bet there weren't lots of "aaays". I remember Monty Python sending him up quite a lot. What is so unusual about this book is that Shankly is a hero rather than an anti-hero. After all your anti-heroes and their demons, what was it like getting inside Shankly's head?*

One thing I very consciously tried to avoid in the novel was reducing Bill Shankly to a cliché. Of course, he had many pithy one-liners and was extremely witty and so lends himself to being remembered as a funny man. But there was much, much more to him than that and I hope the complexity and depth of the man comes across in the novel. And again, as you say, he was a hero.

✥ *Given this, can you understand why Liverpool appeared to treat him so badly after he retired? It seems reasonable that Paisley wanted him out of the way — but it is astonishing to read that the board were so ruthless and insensitive towards a man who transformed the Reds into a British footballing institution.*

To be honest, I don't think Liverpool Football Club treated Shankly that badly. Or, at least, not intentionally. I think there were a lot of misunderstandings on both sides, particularly by Shankly. And I also think it's important to remember that both the board and Shankly were haunted by what had happened to Manchester United after the resignation of Sir Matt Busby; both Shankly and the board wanted to avoid any repetition at Liverpool Football Club. And, understandably, the club had to move on but, at the same time, understandably again, Shankly found it difficult to let go. And he must have had incredibly mixed feelings about the success of the club after he left which, again, I think is only human and very understandable. But by 1981, at the time Shankly died, I don't believe there was any bitterness or resentment on either side. And I hope that is what comes across in the novel.

✥ *Up until now, your work has focused on Yorkshire and Tokyo. You were brought up in God's Own County and have been living in Japan for some time. Was writing about Liverpool in the 1960s and 70s a big leap for you?*

Not really, no. I mean, writing about Japan and Tokyo during the American Occupation was (and is again now, now I am back writing the last book in the Tokyo Trilogy) much more difficult. I've got good friends from Liverpool and have spent a fair bit of time there down the years. But writing *Red or Dead*, I was very conscious of, for want of a better phrase, the "generation gap" between me and Bill Shankly. His background, for example, was obviously very different from my own and from most people of my age or younger. And also having not retired yet. But I was able, I suppose, to draw on things I knew about my own grandfathers and father.

↪ *Once again, I found the staccato, rhythmic prose style — familiar from the* Red Riding *series and* GB84 *— to be hypnotic, elevating the narration beyond mere storytelling. But it won't be every football fan's cup of tea. To play devil's advocate, what would you say to those who, for example, might baulk at the relentless repetition?*

As I say, "the work" is for me the most important part of the story. Shankly himself described football as a relentless river that goes on and on. And I wanted to show that in the text. And how consuming and draining that work is. I don't think it's enough to simply say, for example, "Bill Shankly trained every day with the players of Liverpool Football Club". I think you have to show exactly what that entailed, what it meant. And so I very much wanted the novel to be a

book the reader would experience and live, just as Shankly experienced and lived it. And in the same way, I think every game, and every detail of every game, is important. And I actually think most football supporters will appreciate that. Because even as supporters we all know how consuming and draining football is, let alone what it must be like for a manager. And, at the same time, we all know that all those very consuming and draining repetitions that make up football are also its appeal; the very things that give us comfort and sustain us.

↪ *You admire Shankly for his single-minded determination to transform Liverpool from also-rans to a European power — which he did —and his famous bond with the Kop. Don Revie, surely (as a Leeds fan, I know I'm biased...) did a similar thing and had a similar effect at Leeds, as did Sir Matt Busby at Manchester United. All three — Shankly, Revie and Busby —left league football at around the same time. Could a similar book have been written about these, and other, auteur-managers of the Shankly era? Or was he unique?*

Well, I do think Shankly was unique. To give only one example, I think the bond he created and fostered with the supporters of Liverpool Football Club, particularly the Kop, is different from the relationship that either Busby or Revie had with the supporters of Manchester and Leeds. Or, at least, so it seems to me. And for me, personally, Shankly's politics were also unique — particularly in his outspokenness, for example — and one of the reasons I was drawn to write about him. But equally, I think both Busby and Revie were unique, too. And so I am sure similar books could be written about both of them; in fact, Rob Endeacott has already written extensively about "the Don". And, of course, all that Busby went through and achieved, before and after Munich, would lend itself to a very compelling and dramatic narrative. That said, *A Strange Kind of Glory* by Eamon Dunphy would take some beating!

✏ *The Shankly-Revie-Busby-Clough-Stein era seemed, to me, to be about social mobility, working-class aspiration and advance. These were all working-class-lads-made-great. Heroic even. Do you see it as a golden age? How does it compare to the present football era?*

I agree with you, but I think it's also important to stress that men such as Busby, Shankly and Stein were not only the beneficiaries of post-war working class social mobility, but also the instigators of that mobility. Again, in what they believed, achieved and how they led their lives. For me, it was a golden age because of these men. We are constantly taught and told that those days are gone, that the world is too different now. And yes, of course it is different. But what these men — and the entire working class and Labour and trade union movement achieved — was born out of circumstances much, much more difficult than the ones most of us face now. And so I genuinely and honestly believe that if we are prepared to sacrifice, struggle and work as those men once did, then we — not as individuals, but as a team — can achieve anything we want. On and off the pitch.

✏ *When Alex Ferguson retired recently there was a great deal more fuss made than in 1974, when Shankly resigned from Liverpool. Clearly Fergie was a more*

successful manager. But how do you compare and contrast their personalities, legacies and politics? After all, Fergie, like Shankly, calls himself a socialist.

A fascinating, and very relevant, question. But very difficult to answer briefly; I mean, it took Oliver Holt an entire book (*If You're Second You Are Nothing*) to try to answer it! And you are right to say more fuss was made when (in a more fussy age) Sir Alex Ferguson resigned than when Shankly did in 1974. But at the same time, we should never forget or underestimate the great sense of disbelief and shock people felt when Shankly did resign. Thanks to YouTube, you can see that disbelief and shock in the report Tony Wilson did for Granada TV at the time. But to try at least partially to answer your question: Sir Alex Ferguson was a great admirer of Shankly and greatly influenced by him to the extent he used to play cassettes of Shankly speaking on the team bus when he was manager at Aberdeen (much to the annoyance of Gordon Strachan). And what Ferguson achieved at Aberdeen is perhaps when and where their two careers are at their most similar. Because when Shankly took over at Liverpool, his circumstances were very different from Ferguson's when he went to United and so it is difficult to compare their respective legacies. And perhaps it is more useful to compare Ferguson with Paisley (and let's never forget who won more European Cups). Of course, personalities and politics, particularly from the outside looking in, are also always very difficult to compare. But Ferguson seems to have more interests outside of football — wine and horses — than Shankly ever had and it will be interesting to watch how such interests help Ferguson cope with retirement. But finally, we should never forget how men like Shankly — and, of course Busby and Stein — in the way in which they changed how football clubs were managed and run, helped pave the way for the success of someone like Sir Alex Ferguson.

This feels to me, in some ways, to be a political book. Can you talk about Shankly's socialism and, perhaps, how his ethos towards football was a socialist one? You obviously admire this ethos: can you explain why? Is this a lament for a better era, both in a footballing and political sense?

To paraphrase Stokely Carmichael, I believe every book is political, whether or not the author or reader consciously is aware of the fact. But for me *Red or Dead* is a socialist book. And I think it would be impossible to write about Shankly any other way. I think his socialism — and also his Christianity, which is connected to his view of socialism — was fundamental and integral to every aspect of his life and work. And to put it very, very simply: it was about equality, on and off the pitch, and working for the people and the supporters of Liverpool Football Club. And also the city of Liverpool. It was never about personal glory. It was about communal work for communal success. And I do admire this and lament its absence. But I also hope the book is more than simply a lament and, as I said before, that people can draw inspiration from the story and from Shankly's life and work. And his beliefs that fuelled and sustained his life and work. Because there is no reason on earth — despite all we are taught and told to the contrary — why that "better era" cannot return again.

But do you not accept that that the game, like society, has changed, with individual greed replacing collectivism? For example, despite winning titles and other major trophies, winning the FA Cup in 1965 remained, for Shankly, his greatest day in football. Today, winning the Cup is not so special: a lower priority than avoiding relegation. In short, money conquers all; surely there are far more Gordon Gekkos around today than Bill Shanklys?

Yes, but there were a lot of Gordon Gekkos about when Bill Shankly began. I mean, Shankly's life encompasses two World Wars, the Russian and Chinese Revolutions, the General Strike, the Great Depression and the creation of the Welfare State. So I would argue that Shankly and his generation had to contend with just as many Gordon Gekkos, if not more. And from a much more difficult starting point. And when Shankly took the job at Liverpool, his preconditions were that he had total control of all aspects of the training and the playing. And that, as manager, he picked the team. This was unprecedented. And revolutionary. And those are the two words that perhaps sum up Saint Bill: unprecedented and revolutionary! And an example which I passionately believe is as relevant today as it was in 1959.

I was fascinated by Shankly's radio interview with the Labour Prime Minister Harold Wilson, which you reproduce in the book. Was this a verbatim reproduction? And, if so, what was the thinking behind it? Do you see a connection between their careers — or at least their sudden and unexpected resignations in the mid-1970s?

John Roberts, who ghost-wrote Shankly's autobiography, very kindly lent me some of the tapes of his original interviews with Shankly from 1975-76. And these tapes were a god-send in trying to capture the man in fiction; just to have Shankly's voice fill the room as I was writing was very, very haunting and emotional for me. And in among these tapes, John also included the original broadcast of Shankly's interview with Wilson from 1975 for Radio City. And the very first time I heard it, I just knew it had to go verbatim into the book. I mean, this was the Prime Minister of the day being interviewed by a former football manager; would that ever happen again? But more than that, I just felt every sentence they both said was so revealing about their own lives and the times they were living in. I also think their conversation has a poignancy and resonance for today, too. But yes, for a long, long time, I've been fascinated by Wilson and, once again, the mystery of his sudden resignation. And I hope to write more about Wilson later (as I see *GB84*, *The Damned Utd*, *Red or Dead* and *UK DK* — my book about Wilson — as forming a very loose quartet).

I have to admit, though, the interview was also another great opportunity for me to get Huddersfield Town into the book.

126

Polemics

"That is what has been lost:
identity. Individuality, tradition,
difference: all of the things that
once made football such a
gloriously varied menagerie"

Literally on Fire

How the game's relationship with smoking has changed over the generations

By Jonathan Liew

Stanley Matthews, Blackpool's quicksilver outside-right, has been capped for England no less than 33 times. Stan takes his training very seriously and soon discovered the cigarette which suited him best. "It wasn't till I changed to Craven A," he says, "that I learnt what smooth smoking meant."

Craven's ad, 1952

The problem with nicotine is not that it kills you, but that it makes you stronger. It's the other stuff in cigarettes that you need to worry about. In no particular order and by no means limited to: tar, carbon monoxide, formaldehyde, benzopyrene, a dash of cyanide, a trace of lead, a soupçon of polonium-210 (the substance that was used to murder Russian dissident Alexander Litvinenko in London in 2006).

Nicotine, on the other hand, is relatively harmless, at least in the microscopic doses you find in most cigarettes. In fact, it could be considered something of a tonic. Once it has been inhaled, it reaches the brain in around 10 seconds. It quickens the pulse, shortens breath, raises the blood pressure: all the symptoms, in fact, that one would normally associate with the 90th minute of a tight match. It floods your circulation with glucose and blocks the release of the insulin that

would soak it up. It improves reaction times and concentration. Once inside the brain, it overwhelms your synapses, stimulating its pleasure pathways and scattering endorphins throughout the body. Nicotine, for a few seconds at least, feels great.

It is hardly surprising, then, that long before phrases like "lung cancer", "second-hand smoke" and "take those filthy death sticks outside" entered common vocabulary, footballers used to smoke all the time. Virtually everybody did. A survey carried out just after the Second World War estimated that 82% of British men and 40% of British women were regular smokers. A third of men smoked more than 100 cigarettes a week.

And why not? They were cheap (around 22p a packet), freely available (while the government introduced bread rationing in 1946, they refused to do the same for cigarettes) and good for you. In fact, when Gino Bartali, the winner of the Tour de France in 1938 and 1948, went to his doctor complaining of low blood pressure and a slow heart rate, he was prescribed three cigarettes a day. All doctors smoked too, by the way.

Cigarette companies, keen to make explicit the link between smoking and sporting success, used sportsmen as a central plank of their advertising strategy. In 1896, Marcus & Company produced the first set of football-themed cigarette cards, the first concerted attempt to link the rapidly-growing sport with smoking. Matthews's endorsement of Craven A was something of a subterfuge — he was in fact a committed non-smoker. But two decades earlier, Dixie Dean appeared in adverts for Carreras Clubs with the slogan "the cigarette with a kick in them!" Dean would be paid around £50 a pop for such endorsements — big, big money to someone earning a mere £8 a week.

Of course, there were dissenting voices, and earlier than is popularly believed. In 1904, for instance, the Tottenham Hotspur captain JL Jones wrote, "I cannot find words strong enough to express my disapproval. The habit of smoking, once started, may lead to grave disasters."

Some managers frowned upon the habit, too, most notably Herbert Chapman. Chapman would ask prospective signings whether they drank or smoked before signing them. Not even star players were immune from his wrath. David Jack, a notorious chain-smoker, was signed from Bolton in 1928 for a world record £10,890 fee and, soon after, failed to turn up for training. Chapman despatched the trainer Tom Whittaker to Jack's house, where he was found sitting in his armchair with his feet on the mantelpiece, smoking a cigarette. Jack was hauled into Chapman's office post haste.

Later, Bill Shankly and Brian Clough would famously disapprove of their own players smoking, even though the latter did himself smoke occasionally. But by

and large, the practice was tolerated and at times even tacitly encouraged. During the 1950s, Newcastle United would pay their players a packet of 20 cigarettes every week, along with their wages and win bonus. Most of the squad didn't smoke, so they would give theirs to a man who absolutely did: Jackie Milburn.

Here's the thing about nicotine: once the body decides it likes it, it wants more and more of it. First the body submits, then it demands, making every cigarette less potent than the last. Once you try to give it up, the brain is flooded with exactly the opposite feelings to those nicotine used to produce: anxiety, depression, irritability, lethargy. Ulcers are common. Once nicotine has you in its grip, every cigarette is a grim, compulsive and ultimately futile attempt to feel a little less miserable for a little longer.

The Watford manager Gianfranco Zola told me about a former team-mate of his at Parma: "I probably shouldn't say this, but there was a player who would smoke in between the first half and second half. No, actually he would vomit first — because of the stress, you see — and then he would smoke and then he would go out again. You see it's less common today, but some players still do."

According to one US study, 90% of smokers eventually return to tobacco in some form or another. Milburn was one of them. He was one of the game's legendary smokers. Just before the 1951 FA Cup final, he slipped off for a fag and was, as he later wrote, "shocked to discover four of my teammates puffing away in the toilet. They told me they'd cadged them off fans beforehand." After the 1955 final, he claimed that cigarettes had helped him to ignore the pain of an injured stomach muscle.

Milburn won 13 England caps and three FA Cups, all before the age of 33. In 1957, his fitness in decline, he moved to Linfield and never played top-class football again. How much more might he have achieved without his smoking habit? In the event, he only decided to give up cigarettes after he had retired from the game.

As Milburn's son Jack wrote in the book *Jackie Milburn: A Man Of Two Halves*, "At just 33, he was beginning to feel like a much older man... He felt the need to change his way of life. He was suffering some fairly nasty withdrawal symptoms, both physical and mental, as he attempted to chuck the fags. He tried desperately to stick to his guns and resist temptation, but in reality dad felt quite lost without them, and when fag-less certainly became more of an introvert. He would last a few days and then buckle."

These days, around a fifth of Britons smoke daily. Around a seventh of Swedes do and about a third of Greeks. But across the board, the picture is more or less uniform: though a significant number of young men in every part of the world still smoke, the number is declining. Smoking is becoming niche.

Search online for "footballers smoking" and you will find dozens of web pages and stories dedicated to compiling lists of transgressors. Just as drugs have inflected the history of popular music with a thrilling jeopardy, so too smoking and sport. Puffing on a cigarette when your livelihood depends on remaining at your physical peak requires a nonchalance, an indifference to consequence, perhaps a tinge of sexy self-destruction, that lends the concept of the smoking footballer a vaguely macabre fascination. The shrill initial reaction — how dare he? — quickly gives way to a grudging admiration: how does he? Where the smoking footballer was once a commonplace and then a pariah, now he possesses something of the giddy aura of the anti-hero.

Consider the list of genius footballers of current or recent vintage who have been known to smoke. Ronaldo. Zinédine Zidane. Roberto Carlos. Wayne Rooney. Alessandro Nesta. Gianluigi Buffon. Mesut Özil. Mario Balotelli. Fabio Coentrão. Dimitar Berbatov. Aaron Lennon. William Gallas. Fernando Torres. Dozens more that we know about. Probably hundreds that we don't. Rui Costa only admitted to his habit in a newspaper interview after he retired: "Today, I can tell you: I always smoked. Never said I did, especially to not give a bad example to the young lads and future players. I know that it is not good for an athlete. It is a bad habit and I have decided, very soon, to stop." That was in 2009. He's still smoking.

Managers, coming from a different generation and with different responsibilities, have fewer scruples. Only in June, Marcello Lippi was pictured puffing on a cigar as he watched his Guangzhou side from the stands. Roberto di Matteo is another, saying in 2010 while at West Brom, "I'm trying to do it less and less. But it gives me five minutes to collect my thoughts after a match and my press officer can debrief me." Slaven

Bilić, Walter Mazzarri, Gianluca Vialli and Martin Jol are others. Roy Hodgson too, until his wife stopped him.

Part of the perverse glamour of smoking footballers is bound up in taboo. Watch the tabloid castigation that follows whenever a nameless flea with a long lens camera catches a player having a cheeky fag on holiday. Coentrão was hauled over hot coals for his moment of smoky ignominy outside a nightclub in March 2012. He claimed that the cigarette was "one isolated act" on his birthday.

Özil, meanwhile, was snapped in the summer of 2011 having a smoke on a yacht. "It was because I lost a bet," he said, perhaps the least convincing excuse any sportsman has ever produced in any situation. "I assure you: I do not smoke."

This is the thing about smoking, you see: everybody does it, yet nobody can admit it. In this age in which footballers are hyper-sensitive to criticism, a vice like smoking can be used as a conduit for criticism, held up as an example of indolence or fecklessness. It makes them less attractive in the transfer market and may violate the terms of their club's medical insurance. So they smoke in secret, and then later pretend it was the only time they had ever touched one of these 'cigarettes' — is that how you pronounce it, guv? Any other explanation simply isn't worth the hassle.

And yet while smoking still lends a man a certain sophistication in certain contexts, in others it takes on a dirty shame as distasteful and unwelcome as the chesty cough that follows. "I tried to smoke an ordinary cigarette once, but never liked it," reads the autobiography of one prominent Premier League footballer. "I've never taken drugs of any sort, although like everyone else I knew who the dealers and druggies were on our estate." Any ideas? Why, it's Wayne Rooney, written before he was pictured urinating in an alleyway with a cigarette in his hand and before he tipped a hotel worked £200 for getting him a packet of Marlboro Lights during his well-publicised session with a Manchester prostitute in 2010.

Rooney's smoking habit raises interesting questions about smoking and public image. Paying a prostitute for sex, clearly, is not cool. But what was even less cool, it seemed, was Rooney's choice of cigarette. One commenter on the *Guardian* website wrote — with deathly seriousness — "As it was a packet of Marlboro Lights then that tells me that he is an image-smoker only and uses his nancy-boy fags as a percieved [sic] cool prop. If he's blown 200 for a packet of Golden Virginia or 20 Lucky Strike I could have empathised, but blowing a half-decent wedge on 20 Marlboro Lights just to look the part, then that's just ridiculous." "Unsophisticated council flat rubbish," weighed in another correspondent.

And here we come to a fundamental north-south divide in the way smoking is perceived. In the *Journal of the National Cancer Institute* in 2009, a group of epidemiologists led by the French scientist Gwenn Menvielle looked at the relationship between smoking and social class in a number of European countries. Until the 1970s, smoking was a largely classless activity. The rich were as likely to smoke as the poor. But as more information about the health risks of tobacco became known, the better-off slowly began to give up smoking. Now, in Britain, the disparity in smoking rates between the rich and the poor is startling. Around 15% of men in the highest social classes smoke, rising to around 45% in the lowest social classes, 70% amongst adults living on or below the poverty line, and about 90% for the homeless. Despite rising prices, cigarettes are now an emblem of deprivation.

This was a pattern repeated in Scandinavia and the Netherlands. But Menvielle's team found something quite different in southern Europe. While working-class men are still more likely to smoke than the better-off, the disparity was much less pronounced. Amongst women, in fact, the trend was reversed. In Spain, Italy or Greece, women with a degree are more likely to smoke than those who never went to secondary school.

Which may go some way to explaining why we can look a picture of Gianluigi Buffon puffing away on a cigarette next to his bikini-clad wife and think, "That is cool." And then look at a picture of Rooney doing the exactly the same thing and think, "That is not cool." As Owen Jones demonstrates in his book *Chavs*, smoking is a trope that is often used to demonise the working class in Britain.

And yet cigarettes eat away at your respiratory system at exactly the same rate whether you live in Naples or Newcastle. After giving up cigarettes, Jackie Milburn would allow himself the occasional miniature cigar. Soon, though, they became more regular until he was smoking almost as many cigars each day as he once had cigarettes. In early 1988, he went to the doctor complaining of breathlessness and heavy coughing. He was struggling to climb the stairs and

was so weak he would often spend the whole day in bed. In May, he filed his last ever match report for the *News of the World*, headlined "Newcastle's Gascoigne Magic Has 'Em Reeling". In July, he was diagnosed with terminal lung cancer. On October 9, 40 years to the day after he made his debut for England, he died. He was 64. As well as many other things, this was not cool either.

Jimmy Greaves looks a little sad. He is sitting in one of the function rooms at Wembley Stadium at the launch of Royal Mail's "Football Heroes" stamp collection. There are hundreds of journalists in the room, but none of them appear all that interested in talking to him. Instead, a scrum amasses around Denis Law, Bobby Charlton and Bryan Robson. A few hours earlier, you see, Sir Alex Ferguson announced his retirement and now the entire sprawling corpus of the English football press is scrabbling around for reaction.

Greaves has little to say about Sir Alex. But there is something I want to talk to him about. As well as being one of English football's legendary goalscorers, Greaves is one of its legendary smokers. "About half of us used to smoke in that Tottenham dressing room," he says. "Ronnie Henry did. Bill Brown smoked a pack a day. Maurice Norman. There was nothing wrong with it in those days."

There is a reason I am so keen to canvass Greaves on this. Recently he gave up smoking following a series of health scares and he has now been off the fags for around four years. With the odd lapse here and there, obviously. As of 8 May

2013, it had been around seven weeks since his last cigarette.

Meanwhile, it had been over five months since mine. After around nine years of puffing away on a succession of increasingly unsatisfying Camel Lights, I finally gave them up at the end of December 2012. My last cigarette — and you always remember it — was outside Alexandra Palace after midnight after watching the semi-finals of the World Darts Championship with my friend Jack.

For me, the final straw was that NHS advert where a guy is standing out in his back yard smoking, and the cigarette gradually mutates into a malignant tumour before our very eyes. Partly it was grotesqueness of the image, but partly too the humiliation implicit in it. Someone at the Department of Health clearly decided it was necessary to pay a graphic design company to create an animation of a throbbing CGI tumour in order to get me to quit. Wow, I thought. They must really, really want me to quit. So I quit.

And it was fine, for the most part. I put on a little weight, as every time I felt like a fag I would have a snack instead. But eventually I got used to not smoking and began to tick off some of the benefits. I noticed my bank account swelling a little. I got more work done. I was even able to perfect the self-satisfied leer of superiority you give someone when they nip outside to indulge their habit in sub-zero temperatures. But all the while, there was a little nagging doubt in the back of my skull. And it was while researching this article that things came to a head.

Part of giving up smoking, you see, is making a little pact with yourself and convincing yourself at all times that you got the better side of the deal.

As a result of not smoking:
1) I will look less cool and get tetchy sometimes.
2) But that's OK, because I'm now fitter and have more money.

And that works just fine, until you log on to Getty Images and see a picture of Berbatov or Özil or Socrates puffing away on a cigarette and looking like the coolest bastard in the world. In that instant, Berbatov is not only cooler than me, but is also fitter and has more money. So what was the point of giving up? I may never have the talent of the physique or the money of Berbatov, but at least I can emulate him in one crucial respect.

It is for this reason that seeing a prominent footballer smoking a cigarette, wilfully singeing their genius, is a more potent image than a thousand pictures of tumorous lungs. So I want to know if Greaves feels like all those years of smoking were worth it. More simply, I want to know whether I did the right thing.

"I enjoyed smoking," he says. "The doctors were always telling me to cut it out and I finally did a few years ago. But I still have a sneaky one now and then. How old are you?"

The answer is twenty-seven. Greaves snorts.

"Oh, you're still young," he says with a note of disgust in his voice, as if I have been wasting his time all along. "You've got plenty of time yet. Go and get yourself some fags. I might come and join you." Ⓑ

The Death of Mystery

Is the modern thirst for knowledge taking the fun out of football?

By Rory Smith

In the space of three weeks in the summer of 1989, two things came to pass. On the face of it, they are entirely unconnected, two events from different worlds, but it is worth considering them in conjunction nevertheless. A thread runs through them. An echo sounds from one reality and into another.

24 May 1989: AC Milan lift the European Cup for the first time under Arrigo Sacchi and etch their place in history. Steaua Bucharest are their pliant victims, two goals from Ruud Gullit and two from Marco van Basten putting Anghel Iordanescu's side to the sword. Milan will go on to retain the trophy the following year — the last team to do so — and they will reach the forgotten final of 1993, too, before finally regaining the cup in 1994.

15 June 1989: Europe goes to the polls for elections to the parliament at Strasbourg. In the United Kingdom, some 2,292,695 people choose to cast their ballot not for Labour or Margaret Thatcher's Conservatives or even the newly-founded Liberal Democrats. Instead, some 15 per cent of the voting electorate give their support to the Green Party.

It was the greatest result in the organisation's brief, somewhat muddled history. To some, it heralded the birth of a fourth political power in Britain. True, the vagaries of the first-past-the-post system meant that, despite a sixth of the country voting for them, the Greens won no seats at all in the European parliament. But the message was clear. The Green Party had arrived and Britain would change forever.

But what unites these two disparate events, a European Cup final and a European election, is not triumph. There is no similarity between what the summer of 1989 meant for the Greens and what it indicated for Sacchi's Milan. This was not the dawn of a political dynasty; just a footballing one.

Within a year, the Green Party had separated into individual units in Scotland, Northern Ireland and England and Wales. They would never again come so close to establishing themselves as a major party (though they do, at least, currently have one Member of Parliament at Westminster). Where Sacchi's and Milan's time was just starting, the Greens' was already coming to an end.

The link, instead, is in the eventual defeat. There was no shame in the Greens failing to break the three-party system in British politics; that they came so close should be a source of pride. There was no shame in Steaua losing to that Milan side, either, to a team of Maldinis and Baresis and Donadonis and those three sublime Dutchmen. Iordanescu and his team have the right to be proud, too.

It is what happened to both, afterwards, though, that is of most interest. Their fates run parallel, an object lesson about how the world deals with nascent forces, how the big and the strong and the rich and the powerful adopt and assimilate them to maintain the status quo.

What happened to the Greens is best summarised by Richard North, writing in the *Independent* in 1992, when Sara Parkin, the public face of the party, left for pastures new: "[The problem faced by Green parties across Europe] is they are now surrounded by voters and politicians who want to be some shade of green, are increasingly going to some pains to work out what that means, and are even acting on it. The greens are being challenged where they live: they are no longer unique, only uniquely committed."

Their success in 1989 was their curse: the main parties realised, belatedly, that green policies were vote-winners. (It would be nice to assume they also realised they were morally the right thing to do, that the Greens' message about the planet being in danger had got through, but let's not be naive.) By the time the 1992 General Election rolled around, everyone was a little bit green. Suddenly, there was no need to vote for a specifically environmental party; your green policy came rolled up in a package of other beliefs and values, like free texts when you get a new mobile phone.

Steaua were undone by a similar process. On December 22 of that year, Nicolae Ceauşescu and his wife Elena fled Bucharest by helicopter. By Christmas Day, they were dead, shot by firing squad after being captured by police and handed over to the army. As in much of the rest of the former Soviet Bloc, the collapse of Communism granted football players the chance to travel abroad for the first time in their careers. Within two years, nine of the side who started that defeat to Milan in 1989 had moved west. They were adopted and they were assimilated and the team that had given them their chance was left with nothing.

Much the same process occurred to Crvena Zvezda, winners of the European Cup in 1991, and not only the last eastern European side to win the competition, but the last Eastern European side to reach the final and, Dynamo Kiev in 1999 aside, the last eastern European side to get anywhere near it. Within a year of victory in Bari, the exodus accelerated by the threat of the Balkan civil war, all of that Zvezda side had departed the crumbling Yugoslavia.

In both cases, the impulse was the same: if you can't beat them, take them. As Labour and the Conservatives took the Greens' policies, so too teams in Italy and Spain and Belgium and Sweden — and in Ştefan Iovan's case, Brighton and Hove Albion — cherry-picked everything they wanted from the East as soon as the political climate allowed them to do so. Just when Zvezda's moment and Steaua's moment, seemed to have arrived, it was over.

That process had ramifications way beyond Steaua and Zvezda, beyond

Bucharest and Belgrade, and beyond the former Soviet bloc. Infinitely more significant things happened in 1989, of course, across a continent in ferment and infinitely more tragic things happened that year in football: the loss of 96 lives in the Hillsborough disaster, which set the path for everything English football would become. But, just as 1989 was one of those years in which the world changed irrevocably, dramatically, beyond all recognition, it was also a year in which something just as seismic started to happen to football.

The seats in Nelspruit's Mbombela Stadium are black and white, like a zebra's hide, its 18 russet roof supports are designed to look like giraffes. It is just a few miles from here to the Kruger National Park. The ground could easily be mistaken for a gigantic steel-and-concrete advert for the wildlife on offer.

Few of those seats are ever occupied. Since the 2010 World Cup, the stadium has served as the occasional home of the Premier Soccer League side Bidvest Wits and one of two home grounds for the Pumas rugby franchise. Of all the stadiums built for Africa's first World Cup, the Mbombela has emerged as possibly the greatest folly; given the competition, that is quite an accolade.

On 21 January 2013, though, the stadium buzzed with noise. Busloads of Ethiopian fans had been arriving at the ground for hours in anticipation of their opening African Cup of Nations tie with Zambia. The men came with flags hailing Haile Selassie and T-shirts of Bob Marley; the women with their hair

piled high and their heels vertiginous. They danced and sang and blew all of their breath into the devil's hornpipe, the vuvuzela.

I sat in the sunshine, in the quiet end of the ground. My ticket had cost just a few rand, proffered by an underemployed tout outside. Out came the two sides: Ethiopia, all in white, and the green of the Chipolopolo, the reigning champions. A few of the Zambians were familiar — Christopher Katongo, Collins Mbesuma, Chisamba Lungu. Their system certainly was: raiding full-backs, holding midfielders, Katongo dropping deep. They were as well-organised as you would expect continental champions to be.

Ethiopia, though, were something else. Not one familiar face, not one familiar name. The number seven emerged as the star of the side: a nimble, quick-witted forward. But the number eight, too, had something about him. His long stride, his barrel chest, looked for all the world a little like Sandro, of Brazil and Tottenham Hotspur.

I did not know their names. Saladin Said and Asrat Megersa, I know now. But then, they were new, alien. And the way they played, too: not chaotic, not at all, but a style of their own, home-grown, uniquely theirs. Megersa roamed around the pitch, occasionally dropping deep, occasionally emerging as a forward. That should be no surprise: Ethiopia is a market that remains almost entirely untapped by Europe. All of that side, bar Said and Fuad Ibrahim, a young forward, played and play in their homeland, untroubled by scouts or agents or being streamed in Europe. It is a world that exists on its own and it is a world that does not exist any more.

There will never be another Steaua Bucharest. There will never be another Crvena Zvezda.

That is in part simple economics: the collapse of the Iron Curtain exposed the former Soviet bloc to football's unabashed free market, a bazaar in which they lack the financial clout to compete.

As soon as Romania or Serbia or wherever produces a single decent prospect, he is enticed west, a migrant in search of riches in Paris or Milan or London. The chances of any club in the east holding on to a single generation of players for long enough to threaten to captivate Europe is all but zero.

But it is not just about players. It is about styles, too. Football has no borders in Europe, in much of the world, now. Not only can players transfer easily to wherever they can earn the most money or fulfil their ambitions, but so, too, can systems and tactics and approaches.

In such a climate, individual identity is all but lost. For all the hand-wringing the English indulge in over why their national side cannot compete with the best in the world and for all the self-adulation they afford themselves about the product on offer in the Premier League, if you look — as the authors of *The Numbers Game* did — at the end result of what football is — passes, shots, dribbles, goals — the numbers are remarkably similar across all of the major leagues, in England, France, Germany, Spain and Italy.

There are slight variations of tempo, of course — influenced by the climate and how much referees deem illegal — but, broadly, at the elite level, it is the same game wherever you go. The technical gap is miniscule; so, too, the tactical. Most teams in Western Europe play a formation that is somewhere close to a 4-2-3-1 or a 4-3-3 (which is probably more accurately characterised, on the pitch, as a 4-1-2-2-1). There are a few three-man defences in Italy, of course, and in England the 4-4-2 makes an occasional appearance, giving the game in question the air of an Ocean Colour Scene reunion gig. You see it and you're immediately transported back to the 90s.

The days of each nation having its own individual style, its own unique approach to the game, have gone. That is true away from the bright lights of the Champions League's latter stages, too: Europe's minor leagues are full of Spaniards and Brazilians on the pitch and French, Germans and Dutchmen in the dugout. Best practice disseminates rapidly, eroding identity.

That is what has been lost: identity. Individuality, tradition, difference: all of the things that once made football such a gloriously varied menagerie. Football is a homogenous game now. Everywhere you look, it looks the same. Gone are the days when Dinamo Tbilisi might be the best side Liverpool face on the way to a European Cup final. Gone are the days when Steaua or Zvezda might take the continent's breath away, developing a team almost in secret, playing football in their own unique way.

The big leagues have taken all of the players, strangling any nascent golden generation at birth. Look at Borussia Dortmund; when they cannot stave off the predators, what chance Legia Warsaw or Levski Sofia?

And in exchange they have sent their reservists and fringe men as missionaries, to teach the poor and the deprived and the savage how to play the game the right way.

But it is not "the" game. There is no such thing as "the" game. It is their game, and it is our game. Football has myriad different interpretations, different emphases. It is wonderful, of course, that best practice can spread around the globe. It is wonderful that advances made in fitness or nutrition in England can be picked up in Slovakia, and vice versa, too.

But there is a dark side to this globalisation: as each nation loses its individual style to the proselytisers, as well as its best players to the merchants, its teams are condemned to play an inferior version of the football on offer in the Champions League. Football functions in a similar way to the Roman Empire: it takes the elements that it wants from conquered peoples and inserts them into its own culture, so they feel part of the conquest, while at the same time superimposing a version its own hybrid culture on each nation it touches.

So Zvezda and all the others are taught that there is one way to play; if they have any good ideas or any good players, they are adopted by the status quo and added to the cant. This is condemning the host nations, these lesser leagues, to a life-time of second best. It is depriving them of the hope they once had, that

they might be able to compete by virtue not of being better but of being different. It is taking their game away and making a low-quality copy of our game.

We suffer, too. Gone is that capacity to surprise that the game once possessed. By virtue of social media and the internet and ESPN and Fifa and *Football Manager*, we as fans know, too, exactly who is coming through in which league, where all the brightest prospects are. But that means we are never surprised, our imaginations never captured by this strike force at Dynamo Kyiv, or this number 10 at Steaua, or this wondrous team emerging in Belgrade. Football can never take your breath away, not quite as it once did. The mystery has died.

There are still pockets that survive. In Ethiopia, of course, where St George and Dedebit dominate the national team and the scouts tend not to venture. In much of east Africa, in fact, football has seemingly been written off; strange, given how many players west Africa has always produced, that nobody should think there is likely to be just as much talent across the continent, amid the vast populations of Kenya and Tanzania. Perhaps here, isolation shelters individuality.

In South Africa, that is certainly the case. This was meant to be Africa's forge of greatness, once apartheid was ended and the Rainbow Nation emerged blinking into the world. It looked that way, in 1996, when the African Cup of Nations was lifted, but the conveyor belt has never quite clicked into gear; the factory was never built. In some part, that is down to the traditions football developed during apartheid: it is a game here of skills and tricks. That is what the crowd want; that is what, in many cases, the players know. It may be ineffective at international level. It may infuriate vast numbers of players and coaches in the PSL. But it is their game. It is not ours.

In Egypt, too, before the revolution and the bloody chaos that followed, before Port Said and the suffering of the Ahlawy, a unique football culture had developed. There were still foreign managers, of course, playing in foreign formations, but most of the players were Egyptian: when the country is working, when the league is running, the money is good enough here to remove the temptation of moving abroad.

It is the same in Mexico: true, some of that country's most famous names –

Javier Hernández, Giovani Dos Santos, Rafael Márquez – have made their careers in Europe, but there are many who remain in the Liga MX, aware that they can have the lifestyle they want in Mexico City and Guadalajara and Monterey, playing in a high-quality league and retaining their international ambitions without needing to leave home. The influence here comes from Argentina, from the south, but this is still a football culture that has developed its own mores, its own codes, its own character.

These are the places where the game is still theirs, where Europe's colonialism has not yet permeated. This is where the talent has not yet been adopted and the ideas not yet assimilated. These are the places where 1989 has not yet happened. These are the places where the mystery lives. Ⓑ

An Extra Edge

Is football really clean, or does the sport have its head in the sand?

By Colin O'Brien

It might have been at the opposite end of the stadium, but the second it happened, we knew. Thierry Henry had handled the ball before passing it to William Gallas, who duly scored the tap-in, thanks very much. In the 13th minute of extra time in a crucial World Cup qualification play-off against the Republic of Ireland, one of France's greatest ever players had cheated in front of 80,000 people in the stadium and millions more at home. It was a cognisant breach of the rules, in plain sight and on the record. And I bring it up because of a conversation had just before kick-off.

We were in town for the football. But it being Paris and me being a cycling fan, the talk drifted to the Tour de France. Giovanni Trapattoni's tactical nous is not exactly a fertile source of pub banter, after all. That summer Lance Armstrong had cheated his way through the last of his Tour de France abominations. There was no evidence revealed as of yet, no lifetime ban or farcical heart-to-heart with Oprah, but you didn't have to be among the Texan's closest friends to know that he'd been a drugs cheat all his career. Alberto Contador, meanwhile, went home in the yellow jersey. He looked cleaner than the American, but doubts remained.

The discussion centred around the fact that cycling was a sport for "junkies"

— my colleague's word, not mine — and that everything else wasn't. Not exactly a nuanced argument, but top marks for directness. I maintained that cycling appeared dirty simply because it was the only sport actually trying to clean up its act up, but he stuck to a "show me the evidence" approach. For anyone interested in the cancer that is performance-enhancing drug use in professional sport, it's a familiar one.

"I've never tested positive," was Armstrong's go-to defence. *Show me the evidence.*

Say what you like about him, but he's clever. It's not a denial of drug taking, simply a statement of the fact that he'd never been caught by a drugs test. A familiar note echoed through Henry's comments after that night in Paris. "Yes, there was a hand," he said: "But I'm not the referee." Sure, I broke the rule— but I wasn't caught.

Later that night, the continued junkie debate was a welcome distraction from the disappointment. And it's one that I've been having on and off with people ever since.

Henry wasn't the first or the last footballer to cheat on the pitch (and there is, perhaps, a moral distinction to be drawn between an opportunistic, instinctive breach such as Henry's and a systematic, premeditated programme of doping), but because it was a somewhat personal experience it stuck with me. If a footballer is willing to do that in front of millions just to offer his side the slightest chance of victory, what would he be willing to do behind closed doors?

Every week there's shirt pulling, fighting, violent tackles, diving, offside goals celebrated... all out in the open. Clear breaches of rules and flaunting of sporting principles. But doping? Hardly ever a whisper. Something's not right with that.

I don't mean to say that every single footballer on the planet is up to his gills in performance-enhancers every week, but it seems ridiculous that we're supposed to believe that in such a bunch of chancers no one's willing to use illegal substances that will give them an edge in what is the world's most competitive and lucrative sporting environment.

To illustrate, Norway's independent anti-doping database dopinglist.com currently has 24 provisional suspensions and nine disqualifications on record from last summer's Olympics. There were 14 cases in track and field alone, out of 2,231 athletes.

In contrast, Fifa says that it tested 28,587 blood or urine samples in 2011. Of these, just 19 tested positive — five of which were from the North Korean women's team. There are clear similarities to cycling's approach to the problem in the 1990s when only the workaday, insignificant among the peloton were ever found to be guilty of infringements.

The Professional Footballers' Association has 4,000 members in England and Wales and the last high-profile doping case there was when the Portuguese full-back Abel Xavier was banned for 18 months in 2005 while playing for Middlesbrough — for taking anabolic steroids. That's eight years without a high-profile bust.

The more dope-fluent among you might have scoffed at Xavier's choice of poison. Steroids, after all, are so passé.

Sure, they can be handy occasionally, if you've got a solid alibi. Armstrong kept a chummy doctor nearby who was always good for a back-dated prescription. But it's easy to trace and there is a plethora of performance-enhancing drugs out there which are more difficult to test for.

Take GW501516 for example, a drug so trendy it doesn't even have a proper name yet. It's a receptor agonist that stimulates enzyme production similar to those produced when exercising and was developed with the aim of treating obesity. When combined with proteins like Acadesine, used to treat leukaemia, it also greatly increases aerobic endurance — and causes cancer. An article in the *New Scientist* earlier this year warned that the product originally developed by GlaxoSmithKline "rapidly causes cancers in a multitude of organs, including the liver, bladder, stomach, skin, thyroid, tongue, testes, ovaries and womb." Nothing's perfect, right?

Despite the dangers, GW501516 made its way onto the black market and is now making headlines. The Russian track cyclist Valery Kaykov has been banned already and there are unconfirmed reports that more bans in other disciplines are to follow. Impressively, for fans of acts of unbridled stupidity at least, Kaykov's positive test came just weeks after the World Anti-Doping Agency (Wada) actually warned potential cheats that the drug was one of the more dangerous illegal options available to them.

In a bid to protect these athletes from their own ignorance, Wada took the unusual step of releasing an official warning, as they put it: "to ensure that there is complete awareness of the possible health risks to athletes who succumb to the temptation of using GW501516 for performance enhancement."

Not everything is so risky, of course. A footballer could partake in a simple bronchodilator like Clenbuterol to improve his lung capacity and then, having spoken to Spain's Contador, found out the most convincing way to blame the drug's appearance in a urine sample on contaminated food.

Or they could blood dope with transfusions, whereby several units of blood are withdrawn when the body is in optimum condition — preferably while training at altitude, say for instance, at one of those popular summer training camps held away from prying eyes—and re-injected when the athlete needs a boost.

Then there's Erythropoietin. EPO is a naturally-occurring hormone produced by the kidney that controls red blood cell production. The doper's dope, the synthetic version increases red blood cell levels in the body, thereby increasing the body's aerobic threshold. Basically,

the hormone travels around in your system until it comes into contact with special receptors in the bone marrow where it starts a chain reaction that creates many more red cells. The EPO-receptors in these new cells are replaced by new receptors which are attracted to iron-transporting proteins. Elsewhere, globin proteins combine with haem molecules — they contain iron — to make haemoglobin, which collects oxygen in the lungs and is then carried by the iron-loving red blood cells to the body's muscle tissue — fuelling the fire, so to speak.

In athletes, the synthetic EPO allows them to perform at peak level for much longer because the improved supply of oxygen to the muscles delays lactic acid build-up. This is especially useful in a sport in which repeated changes in tempo and bursts of pace without the hassle of recovery time might be useful. Like cycling... or football.

The downside of it is that super-rich blood becomes a dark red gel and when the body's not running at full tilt there's a significant danger of a horrible death. Anecdotes abound of cyclists spending the night in their hotel rooms on training machines to keep the blood flowing — after riding for hundreds of kilometres during the day. The upside is that it's almost completely untraceable.

In recent years, some sports have spent a great deal of money trying to eradicate EPO usage. The biological passport, an electronic record of indicative biological markers in an athlete's system that can be observed to detect spikes and irregularities with much greater precision than standard urine testing, is proving useful.

Obviously, it's not yet been adopted by football. In fact, almost no modern doping tactics have been embraced, even if Fifa is in the process of playing catch-up. According to Wada's president, John Fahey, "team sports players can go their entire career without being tested once." Not exactly confidence-inspiring.

In a recent statement, the sport's governing body said, "Fifa is developing plans to introduce this new tool, including a steroid profile through urine and a blood profile, for the ... 2014 World Cup in Brazil, where in and out-of-competition tests would be conducted on all participating players."

This sounds promising from a football perspective, but as fans of other sports will tell you, it still leaves a lot of questions. Questions like when, where, how and who?

If most athletes can avoid testing or at least be warned well in advance, then what's the point? There's a crucial 'glow-time', the period when a performance-enhancing drug (PED) will show up on tests and once you can predict the tester's movements it's easy to hide. Then there's the 'hematocrit holiday', whereby an athlete in the know is left out of a squad if his doctors are afraid of his red blood cell levels arousing suspicion. Which makes you wonder if some managers might be 'resting' players for other reasons than recuperation.

Any efforts to stem the use of PEDs should be applauded, but the problem with Fifa's first serious steps towards facing up to the problem is that while they're inexperienced in the field, the people they're up against are seasoned pros.

As the Operación Puerto probe in Spain proved, doping cross-pollinates. The man at the centre of the scandal, Eufemiano Fuentes, has repeatedly insisted that while he was stung by cycling investigators, he was never exclusively used by cyclists. It was hoped that the investigation would name and shame several high-profile athletes, tennis stars and footballers, but though investigators currently have 216 blood bags in their possession, Judge Julia Patricia Santamaría ruled that revealing the owners would be a breach of doctor-patient confidentiality. The Italian National Olympic Committee, Wada and the International Cycling Union are just three of the groups who disagree. They've appealed against the decision and Fuentes has already said he'll name all the owners. It promises to be an interesting list and one that almost certainly includes several high-profile footballers.

Another interesting list would be the number of "therapeutic usage exemption" issued across all professional sports every year. A TUE justifies the use of banned substances for medical reasons, but they're commonly used as nothing more than a bureaucratic way to excuse doping. A skin cream for a rash, for example, can contain steroids and produce similar signals to illegal PEDs in tests. So a simple note from the club doctor would make a serious problem go away.

The Premier League's testing is handled by the FA, which says that it not only adheres to Wada guidelines, but actually exceeds them. Wada disagrees. You decide who to believe, but the records show that the only players to do be caught doing anything wrong in the last two years have been Barnet's Mark Marshall and Sunderland's Lewis Gibbons, who tested positive for cocaine use rather than a PED.

On the continent, it's much the same. The former president of Real Sociedad, Iñaki Badiola, has admitted that the club ran a systematic doping campaign between 2001-07 and has hinted at a connection to Dr Fuentes. Sociedad's president at the time was José Luis Astiazarán, the current president of the Liga de Fútbol Profesional.

The doctor himself maintains that Real Madrid have an unpaid bill to settle with him, unrelated to doping but surely indicative of a close relationship, and a trusting one too because the Spanish club called the doctor as a witness against the French newspaper, *Le Monde*. But despite this, the last case dopinglist.com has on file for Spain dates from 2002, when the Athletic midfielder Carlos Gurpegi was suspended for steroid use.

In Italy, the investigating magistrate Raffaele Guariniello pursued Juventus for much of the 2000s over evidence he'd collected that suggested there was a PED system in place in Turin, but little came of it. The trial lasted five years and it proved that Juve and other Serie A sides had used illegal substances in the 1990s. It also found that a Turin-based doctor had almost certainly supplied EPO to a host of *bianconeri* players but the club escaped punishment because the court couldn't prove that it had ordered the usage. Video evidence was discovered of Fabio Cannavaro injecting himself while playing for Parma, although he claimed it was vitamins.

The first judge found the club not guilty, the state appealed and in 2007 a revised verdict found Juventus guilty of sporting fraud — after the statute of limitations had expired.

Everyone got away with it. The only person to be caught since is Sassuolo's Leonardo Pavoletti, who failed a drugs test before a Serie B game last year. *Calciopoli*, the match-fixing scandal that hit Italian football in 2006, seemed to suggest that Serie A's problems lay elsewhere and little has been done since to tackle the problem of doping.

The system Fifa plans to implement will be a welcome addition to anti-doping measures, but it will mean little to the sport overall if more is not done domestically. Part of the reason that the biological passport system has been so successful in athletics, cycling and other sports is that athletes are now tested all the time, wherever they are in the world.

There are fewer and fewer opportunities to cover up the glow-time and as the punishments become more severe and the odds of being caught shorten, few young athletes are willing to start off on that slippery doping slope.

If any dopers heading to the World Cup only have to worry about being caught in Brazil, they'll simply tailor their PED regime to ensure that their tracks are covered and the work that Fifa does hand-in-hand with Wada will be for naught.

In 2014, Fifa plans to conduct in and out-of-competition tests on all participating players. It's a commendable goal, but as Lance Armstrong never tired of saying, he spent his whole career without testing positive. He was protected by his teammates, managers, national coaches, doctors and a network of political allies within professional cycling. Fifa must make sure that no such Machiavellian systems exist within football if they're going to succeed.

At least one high-profile figure within the game doesn't seem convinced that Fifa's anti-doping dealings will be completely transparent. Speaking recently about the measures, the Arsenal manager Arsène Wenger openly doubted the system's effectiveness. "It is very difficult for me to believe that at a World Cup," he said, "where you have 740 players, you come out with zero problems. Yet mathematically that is what happens every time."

Wada's president John Fahey is more optimistic but added an important caveat to his praise of Fifa after meeting with Sepp Blatter to discuss the matter. "We are very interested in continuing the work on biological profiles," said Fahey in the Fifa statement. "Wada is very satisfied with the commitment of Fifa on the biological profiles. There is always more which can be done in the fight against doping, but we know Fifa has always been serious in this domain, [but] we think the domestic leagues can complement what Fifa is already doing."

That's an understatement. Perhaps part of the reason that little has been done openly to confront the possibility of doping in football is that the stakes are a lot higher than they are in other sports. At the Olympics, the athletes compete as individuals. Fans will celebrate success happily enough, but there's no commitment to sharing the burden of

a heavy loss or the blame for a scandal. Pro cycling's teams exist at most for a few years and are then replaced by new sponsors and new riders. There's never the generational, socio-geographic connection that exists between football teams and their fans and the world's biggest cycling events continue regardless of who rolls up to the start line.

Football, in contrast, is fuelled by emotional and historical bonds between the clubs and the fans and political and financial bonds between the clubs and the leagues. La Liga would mean little without Barcelona or Real Madrid, after all, and the Premier League's importance would dwindle should a club like Manchester United or Liverpool cease to exist.

The betting scandals that have rocked Italian football over the last decade provide a glimpse of the dangers. Serie A's decline in recent years has been unquestionably exacerbated and complicated by Juventus' legal problems and subsequent relegation, as the league became less competitive at home and less influential abroad without the Old Lady's muscle.

There's a lot on the table. A few key figures could bring the whole house of cards down — and the powers that be are aware of this and understandably hesitant to test fate. Taking Fahey's advice to "complement" Fifa's commitment could bring disastrous consequences, but ignoring the problem threatens a future far more ruinous.

The clubs could start by explaining their dealings with people like Fuentes. Or they could be more open to the idea of allowing greater testing freedom to impartial organisations like Wada. They certainly need to at least join the conversation and admit that, as Wenger suggested, it does seem a little odd that there are no problems in football.

There's doping in athletics. There's doping in golf. Cycling was riddled with it. There are six doping cases registered on dopinglist. com from billiard sports and eight related to roller skating. It's a universal problem, one that grows exponentially with money and fame. And there are none more rich or famous than footballers. Ⓑ

Importing "¡Puto!"

What a chant reveals about attitudes to homosexuality in US stadiums

By Nicolas Poppe

Although the stadium is so frequently described as a kind of secular sporting temple that its comparison to a house of worship seems worn out — especially given that what is frequently mythologised as play has now been commodified as spectacle to be consumed by an increasingly global television and internet audience — it is inevitable that those who love the game will create deep bonds with some of its most important rituals, not least of which is chanting. Like most supporters' passion for some aspect of football, the love of chanting often emerges from a germinal state upon experiencing a match in person. It can be absolutely electric. It becomes meaningful.

Semantically more important than mere song and syntactically not limited to the repetition of a single sound or word, chanting endows supporters with voice, allowing them to express themselves and participate in the match in different ways. Extensions of those who sing them, these chants also implicitly or explicitly reveal a wide-range of cultural practices and understandings. Even in the most insipid chants like Club Brugge KV singing the White Stripes' "Seven Nation Army" as Andrés Mendoza banged in an away goal against AC Milan in a Champions League match in October 2003 — there is an excellent *Deadspin*

article on its history by Alan Siegel — or the Chicago Fire supporters group Section 8 belting out the popularised-by-Tetris "Korobeiniki", chants say something not only about what is happening on the field but also about those who sing them in the stands.

One of most resounding chants in US football in the early twenty-first century originates in Mexico. It can be quite difficult to pinpoint the genesis of a chant but it is often said that this one began in Guadalajara in 2003. Oswaldo Sánchez — who, after a spell at Club América, returned to *la perla del occidente* not with his previous club Club Atlas but with the local giants, and bitter rivals, CD Guadalajara, more commonly known as Chivas — lined up to take a goal kick. Reverberating in the stadium, fans' voices collectively united to roar: "¡Puto!"

Puto is a fascinating word. Employed as an adjective, it frequently functions as an equivalent to the English word "fuck" (for example, "*¿Dónde está el puto control remoto?*" or "Where's the fucking remote?"). Used as a noun, according to the *Diccionario de la Real Academia Española*, the term means "*Hombre que tiene concúbito con persona de su sexo*" or a "man who has coitus with a person of his sex."

Although dictionary definitions help us understand how words are used, their descriptive or prescriptive natures never quite fully encapsulate how speakers actually use language. It is useful, therefore, to question how words are used in particular contexts. In Mexico, *puto* is not a synonym for other terms like homosexual or gay, two frequently employed words in Spanish, but rather it frequently acts as a derogatory obscenity more similar to words like *joto*, *maricón* and *puñal*. It is, in that sense, similar to words in English that range in texture from the ostensibly less offensive "bender", "fairy", "fruit" and "homo" to the more clearly offensive "faggot".

Even the harshest opponent of the chant would not argue that most fans who yell "*¡Puto!*" at an opposing keeper do so thinking its level of offence is equal to the English word "faggot". It is, as apologists would argue, much more likely that it were used to indicate a coward, a kind of easily frightened shadow of a man. Putting aside that *puto* takes a deeper, more-hateful meaning on other occasions, as well as in many other places in the Spanish-speaking world, the word never really escapes its odious origins. That is, it never really loses its meaning as being other, as lying outside of what is heteronormative. The *puto* — in this case, the opposing keeper — is simply not a real man. (Parenthetically, Mexican crowds seem to be equal opportunity abusers: as reported by the daily newspaper *Milenio*, in a women's national team match against Chile in the Pan American Games in Guadalajara in 2011 fans yelled out "*¡Puta!*" or "Whore!").

In the context of the United States, those who participate in the chant most probably do so for cultural reasons: its crescendoing build-up and appealing roar replicates something that has become hugely popular within the past 10 years in Mexico. Heard sometimes — not always, however, as Univisión and other channels sometimes censor it in the US — when watching the Liga MX or the national team, it has been imported into the stadium in the United States. Although that has been the case for several years when *El Tri* visit the United States for one of their many friendlies, it recently has come to be chanted in several Major League Soccer stadiums. Perhaps most curiously, this year it has been yelled in the first, as well as what might be called the most "American", of all soccer-specific venues in the United States: Columbus Crew Stadium.

When support for the US national team is at a premium, Columbus Crew Stadium has come to be used as a *de facto* national stadium. Although several nations draw huge crowds in specific metropolitan areas — Haitians in Miami and Salvadoreans in Washington, DC are two obvious examples — there are few places in which fans of *El Tri* would not outnumber, if not dwarf, fans of their northern rivals in a game played in the US. In order to maintain a home field advantage, US Soccer has placed our *clásico*, our Concacaf derby, in Columbus.

Crew Stadium, like other grounds, is not merely an edifice but is also a nexus of individuals. Its fans are drawn from a wide range of backgrounds but in the stadium everyday practices and understandings are suspended and new ones are employed. Among these is another chant hurled at an opposing keeper taking a goal kick, a full-throated

"You suck asshole!" which primarily but not exclusively emanates from the Nordecke, the supporters section. Used throughout MLS — despite frequently attempts of the league and clubs to eradicate it by both carrot and stick: Red Bull New York, remarkably, offered supporters' clubs $2000 dollars each if they could go four games in a row without deploying the chant — it has come to be followed by the imported insult of "¡Puto!"

Of those who watch their local side, it is the member of the supporters group — the club officially recognizes Crew Union, Hudson Street Hooligans, La Turbina Amarilla, and the Buckeye Brigade — who is most redolent of Eduardo Galeano's description in *Soccer in Sun and Shadow*: "Although the fan can contemplate the miracle more comfortably on TV, he prefers to make the pilgrimage to this spot where he can see his angels in the flesh doing battle with the demons of the day." To use Galeano's mythologising language, the fan is many. The individual becomes the collective. As is the case throughout MLS, a league that strongly courts Latino fans, America — or perhaps rather, its twenty-first century incarnation as 'Merica' or 'Murica' — and América — the Spanish word used to refer to both Americas, North and South together, as well as a corresponding broader continental identity — are unified. America and América as one, even in the stadium that hosted USA v Mexico in World Cup qualifying in September 2013.

Expressions against discrimination and for equal rights for homosexuals have pervaded MLS stadiums in 2013, ranging from rainbow LGBT pride flags in Columbus, as well as most if not all other stadiums in the league, to an enormous, impressive *tifo* created by the Timbers Army in Portland in a game versus Chivas USA whose two banners read "Pride, not prejudice" and "Football fans against homophobia". Coupled with a much-publicised agreement to work with the You Can Play Project, a group "dedicated to ensuring equality, respect and safety for all athletes, without regard to sexual orientation" according to its mission statement, the league has taken proactive steps in fighting homophobic discrimination. Despite this, however, very little has been expressed publicly about the import of "¡Puto!"

Much has been made about the return of Robbie Rogers to MLS and professional football. If the ex-Crew player, who played with Andrés Mendoza at Columbus in 2010 and 2011, is to not be subjected to homophobic abuse, this matter must be addressed by individuals, clubs, and organising bodies like MLS. In addition to broader anti-discrimination awareness campaigns like MLS's Don't Cross the Line or the UK charity Kick It Out, direct and practical interventions demand to be made. An excellent — and undeservedly mocked, at least in the nether regions of Twitter — first step was recently made by Liverpool: the compilation of a list of words deemed offensive and unacceptable by the club. In addition to clear communication from club to staff and, later, to supporter, teams like the Columbus Crew must also take decisive steps toward standing up for tolerance. Measures, which should range from expulsion from the ground to longer, perhaps lifetime, bans for both individuals and supporters groups and their members, need to be taken. If not, might we someday live in a world in which the Red Bulls attempt to pay their fans not to hurl homophobic slurs at players?

If homophobia is to be unrooted from the game, powerful organizations like US Soccer, Federación Mexicana de Fútbol Asociación, Concacaf and Fifa must step in. If that is to happen, individuals need to not only admit that the problem of homophobia in the football stadium exists but rather also be willing to act to eradicate it. If the fan is many, the fan cannot stand idly by and permit discriminatory behaviour, much less participate in it as ritualised spectacle like ¡*Puto!* Given football's track record with race, it seems like a long, perhaps interminable, road toward meaningful progress awaits. It is, however, the right road to go down, even if this is just the beginning. Ⓑ

The Voice of a Nation

The commentator Victor Hugo Morales is controversial, but makes football matter

By Dan Edwards

In the same way that a great footballer can be immortalised with a single flash of brilliance, so those who comment on the sport through the mediums of radio or television can be elevated by a few moments. The right words to mark an inspirational goal or a great victory become the soundtrack to history, linking player and commentator in posterity. Is it even possible now to think of Geoff Hurst's goal in the 1966 World Cup final without Kenneth Wolstenholme's voice in the background?

In Argentinian football, one man more than any other has earned the right to be described as the voice of the national game. Victor Hugo Morales has commentated on matches for almost five decades since beginning his career as a radio announcer in 1966. But it was one game in 1986 that cemented his place as a giant of the microphone.

Morales was covering Argentina's bid for a second World Cup triumph in Mexico that year, the first time the nation had entered the competition since the end of military dictatorship and the return of democracy in 1983. Working for national station *Radio Mitre*, he was in the press cabin when Diego Maradona seized hold of the tournament. One goal would define the No. 10 — and Morales:

"It's coming to Diego, now Maradona has it, two mark him, Maradona steps on the ball, the genius of world football is moving for the right, he leaves them standing and he'll pass on to Burruchaga... Still Maradona! Genius, genius, genius! Ta-ta-ta-ta-ta-ta-ta... Goooooool... Goooooooool... I want to cry! Dear God, long live football! What a goal! Diegoooooo! Maradona! I'm so sorry, it brings tears to your eyes. Maradona, in an unforgettable run, in a move for all time... You barrel-chested cosmic phenomenon... What planet did you come from to leave so many Englishmen in your wake, to turn the country into a clenched fist screaming for Argentina? Argentina 2 England 0, Diego Armando Maradona, thank you God, for football, Maradona, for these tears and this Argentina 2 England 0."

Argentina, of course, won that quarter-final 2-1 and went on to lift the trophy as Maradona dominated the latter stages of the tournament as no other individual ever has. Morales's inspired, honest, emotionally raw but impeccably articulate monologue, meanwhile, has, in Argentina, become almost as famous as the goal itself.

Less well-documented, naturally, but equally powerful was the commentator's reaction to Maradona's first goal, the infamous 'Hand of God' incident. "For me there was a hand, the referee messed up, the linesman messed up... He put it in with the hand, but he celebrates with the soul," ran Morales's almost sheepish recognition of the other, dark side of his idol's genius. The second goal was the crowning point of the then 35-year-old journalist's career.

Yet the man who would become so closely associated with Argentina's favourite sport is not even Argentinian. Morales was born in the tiny town of Cardona, across the Río de la Plata in Uruguay. At 19 he began work as a radio presenter in the nearby city of Colonia, before becoming sports director of Montevideo's *Radio Oriental* in 1970, while still in his early 20s. It was a post he would fill until 1981, when he made the move to Argentina — a decision, he later revealed, that was motivated by the persecution he felt from the Uruguayan military dictatorship. He even spent 27 days in jail following what he described as "a fight which football produces in its hundreds in heated moments" during a charity match.

Shortly after crossing the Río de la Plata he made the switch to Radio Mitre, forming part of a sporting team that included some of Argentinian journalism's most venerable names — the current head of the government-run *Fútbol Para Todos*, Marcelo Araujo, and the *FoxSports* lead commentator Fernando Niembro, to name two — before moving on to *Continental* in 1987 as sports director and commentator. His beautifully flowing, cerebral, at times esoteric, at times acerbic, approach to journalism both over the airwaves and in print mark him out as a standard-bearer

for quality reporting in an age in which new media and the quest for brevity and dramatic quotes cheapen the profession.

Take, for example, this extract of an article from 2007 criticising the decision to name the local tournament after the communications giants Cablevision rather than a recently deceased colleague: "They have called the championship Cablevision. It could have been [Roberto] Fontanarrosa. But in the end, in a flash of honesty, they have given that name to this miserable creation spawned from the copulation of the devil with a drunken witch. Parents of a crippled, helpless creature, football television and the rest of the decision-makers rise like an army of hulks, who appear from behind the mountain and become ever stronger and more invincible."

With such forthright views, as well as his ability to branch out from football and comment with equal clarity on current affairs in a way almost unimaginable in the UK, Morales has made more than a few enemies over his career. His current support for President Cristina Kirchner, at a time when commercial media have turned away from the head of state in their droves, actively encouraging opposition, has particularly marked him out as a target.

One of his most vehement critics is Jorge Lanata, the journalist responsible for founding the left-leaning newspaper *Pagina/12* in the 1980s, a publication which more than any other promotes human rights and calls for transparency regarding events that happened under the last military dictatorship. The journalist is seen by many on the right as the figurehead of opposition to the

Kirchner government, using his Sunday night television show to uncover the supposed failings and misdealings of those in charge. Included among the Cristina supporters, Morales has also found himself in the firing line.

In 2012, Lanata launched an astonishing attack. Brandishing a copy of a book written by the Uruguayan journalists Leonardo Haberkorn and Luciano Álvarez, he described how the book denounces Morales as a collaborator of the military dictatorship in Montevideo, an accusation that carries grave political weight both in Argentina and his home country. Lanata made clear the links between the regime in one nation and the other. "Here the names are not too familiar," he said. "If you say 'Florida Battalion' [the regiment with which Morales is alleged to have been close], it does not ring a bell, but can you imagine Victor Hugo Morales having a kickaround in the Esma [the military academy in Buenos Aires that was used as a torture centre]? ... We are sick and tired of people who invent for themselves a past worthy of Che Guevara which they never had."

The response of Morales and those who chose to support him was swift and vitriolic. The Uruguayan admitted that he had played football at the Florida Battalion camp and that he had formed a relationship with high-ranking officials such as Juan Carlos Grosso, but flatly denied ever being a supporter of the dictators. Such friendships —forged through countless media football matches — did not stop him from spending almost a month in jail and Morales received the support of human rights organisations such as the Madres de la Plaza de Mayo. Another

body that spoke out in his favour was the Frente Amplio government headed by the Uruguayan president José 'Pepe' Mujica, a former guerrilla who spent 13 years in prison because of his battles with the military. Meanwhile, Morales pointed out the hypocrisy of his new adversary in speaking out against him while working for Hector Magnetto, head of the massive *Clarín* media group and a man widely suspected of having worked alongside the dictators in exchange for help making his corporation the strongest newspaper, radio and television force in the whole of Argentina.

"It is a mystery," Morales said in a recent television interview when asked why he was the subject of Lanata's attack, his voice steeped in irony. "It is still hard for me to confront him because we were pretty pally on the air. Never friends, but acquaintances. I find it hard to think why he has been so tough on me, I think he is projecting. Jorge cannot be earning less than US$300,000 a month and I think it's too little because what he's done for Magnetto is worth a million per day."

Morales emerged bruised but not beaten, having lost a few followers thanks to his stance in favour of the government but with his reputation still firmly intact. In a sense, the fact that a journalist primarily known for his work in sport can inspire such strong feeling speaks volumes for the conscientiousness and integrity of what he does, two qualities that are less than universal in the often shabby world of football writing. The Uruguayan represents a dying breed in the profession: those who are journalists first and foremost and football fans second. How many of the current generation of football writers could comment with as much authority on the election of Jorge Bergoglio as Pope Francis, say, as they could on Messi's position inside the current Argentina national team?

Alongside Morales, there is another figure in Latin America who personifies this fusion between the literary, journalistic and sporting worlds, another Uruguayan. Eduardo Galeano, a contemporary of Morales and another who was exiled because of his differences with the military government, leaving in 1973. The crusading author is best known for his book *The Open Veins of Latin America*, in which he lays bare the effect that centuries of colonialism, foreign intervention and exploitation have had on the South American continent. Galeano is also a rabid football fan and his homage to the game, *Football in Sun and Shadow*, combines a deference to and respect for the sport with a ready willingness to criticise it, expressed in a style that is both accessible and challenging to the reader: "The history of football is a sad voyage from pleasure to duty. At the same time that the sport became an industry, it began to banish the simple joy that is born from just playing for the sake of it," Galeano laments in the opening line of the book, which goes on to chart the story of the game from its beginnings in Buenos Aires and Montevideo, through the first World Cups and on to the present day. It is an intellectual critique of how football has lost its way and lost its soul over the decades, imparted with the belief that a new innocence and golden age can still be discovered.

Without a synthesis of these skills —a journalistic background and an ease with language that is not confined to

dressing room cliché and jargon — we are left with a coverage that is a shadow of the reflective analysis the likes of Galeano and Morales give us. The paucity of quality writing, the tribalism, transfer rumours and idle chatter are easy fodder for the kind of intellectual that pours scorn on the game, but these figures also leave themselves most open to ridicule. Galeano makes no effort to hide his contempt for whom he dubs "the conservative intellectuals", who believe that in football "animal instinct imposes itself on human reason, ignorance crushes culture and the vulgar masses get exactly what they want." It is intellectuals such as Morales and Galeano, who write about the game they love with a passion that transcends the stands and with the awareness to look at the current system and see a rotten core, who hold the key to understanding football's place in our hearts, more capable of doing so than the legion of weary transfer commenters and cynical detractors combined.

So what does the future hold for Morales who, at 65, shows no sign of reducing his hectic workload? As well as his exhausting duties for *Radio Continental*, the Uruguayan hosts an investigative television show in which he explores the world of politics and current affairs, most notably hitting the headlines with a recent episode that examined Hugo Chávez's presidency. He continues to court the contempt of much of Argentina's commercial media thanks to his reserved support of Cristina Kirchner, from whom in December he received an award saluting his work in human rights. Of the president, Morales has rarely hidden his admiration. "She is on the way to being recognised in history as an important stateswoman," he commented recently following Kirchner's meeting with Pope Francis, a figure who, as archbishop of Buenos Aires, fiercely criticised initiatives such as gay marriage and proposed changes in the abortion laws. "What she has done with the Pope speaks of a person who rises above the masses. She has reached her highest level ever in this relation constructed so that he is now Francisco and not [Jorge] Bergoglio, who was a player in local politics and now plays on a much higher stage."

Many may loathe him, but there are few from whom he does not command respect for years of exemplary work in sports journalism. The truth is that, in a profession changing almost day to day thanks to the influence of the internet, the prevalence of social media and the slow death of traditional print publications, every day there is less space for a man who will dispense with the ease of a 140-character tweet and liken the naming of a championship to the bastard child of the devil and a drunken witch. But all is not doom and gloom; all indications suggest that the veteran will continue to bring us the beautiful game for many years to come. And let us not speak too harshly of the internet — thanks to its inexhaustible memory, moments such as Morales's wonderfully-charged eulogy on Diego are not only preserved for the ages, but can be accessed at the click of a button from Buenos Aires to Bangalore.

155

Fiction

"It was clear that Juan Carlos
was destined for things much
greater than ploughing fields and
slaughtering cattle."

Los Cincos y los Diezes

A letter changes the life of a young footballer forever

By Rupert Fryer

1. The Letter

We had been waiting six months for that letter, for the day my brother, Juan Carlos, would become the first Caballero to leave. I always thought he'd eventually sign for Instituto, but a scout from FC Huracán had spotted him during a school match and said right there and then that Juan Carlos would be the greatest 5 in Argentina: that's the defensive midfielder who wears the number 5 shirt and gobbles up all the loose balls. He's a worker, the one who gives everything for those around him. His jobs are to win the ball from the opposition and to take it from his defenders and move it forward to those more imaginative, and also to block the opposition's number 10.

The 10 is the magician. The creator. The guy with who is a better player than everyone else. I often wonder about 5s and 10s — that the two most famous positions in the sport that we adore so much should be exact opposites; the only thing we seem to love as much as an artist is the man who can kill his art.

I always thought Juan Carlos should play as a 10, as an *enganche* who connects the forwards to the midfield. Juan Carlos could have been the ultimate 10: he was blessed with an intelligence and balance that few kids of his age possess. I used to tell him that he would be the best 10 in the Córdoba Province, but he was always content to be a 5.

Like every other family in Argentina, mine was mad about football. My father didn't really talk, not to anyone, about anything, except during or after a game. He would speak to Juan Carlos after his school matches, asking how it went, how the team was looking and whether the rest of them were working as hard as his son.

My brother was never much of a talker either, though, so I started going to his games in order to tell my father about them when we got back. By then I'd begun listening to the games on the radio and had been through every one of my uncle's old boxes of *El Gráfico*. I fell in love with football and inside a year I'd read every football book in the local library. My father was always too busy to talk to me about the games, though, and so as I got older and more knowledgeable, we began to talk about less and less. He took my brother to see Instituto once a month but I was never allowed to go, apparently because it was too dangerous for a girl to be in the popular. It was there, on the concrete terracing, that the *barra brava* banged their drums and led the chants. I must have listened to over a hundred matches on the radio before I saw my first game at a real stadium. Juan Carlos would take me with him once a fortnight when he started getting free tickets. My mother would just say we were visiting our cousins.

I had by then developed an understanding of the sport that was far superior to all of Juan Carlos's coaches. At half-times, my brother would come to me and ask for advice. His friends found it hilarious that a little girl was telling her big brother what he should be doing on a football pitch, where the space is and what mistakes he had made. But they wouldn't dare make their feelings known. Juan Carlos's performances earned him too much respect for that. He would jog over, pouring with sweat, and I would consult my notes and remind him always to show their 10 onto his weaker foot or to give the particularly skilful ones an extra yard so they didn't ghost past him, but never to allow two yards to those with the vision to execute a pinpoint through-ball. Twice a week we did this, and twice a week Juan Carlos would do exactly as I said when he went out for the second half. I was always amazed at how much he had taken in and by how perfectly he'd adapt his game to my instructions; not least because he would usually be flirting with any number of female admirers that stood along the touchline during our tactical discussions.

My brother was a handsome man, blessed with my father's strong jaw line and jet-black hair; but whereas my father's face was stern and dark, eternally cast in shadow by the perennial mopping of the sweat from his brow, Juan Carlos's was bright and gregarious, welcoming and content. He would let the sweat pour off him, forming tiny droplets that hung from his chin like triumphant symbols of all the heart he put into his work. And that's how he saw his football: as work.

People called him an idol. The local media had been writing about him since he was 12 years old and scored 12 goals in one match for the school. "One for every year this little genius had been on earth," one particularly chirpy local journalist gushed. They even interviewed him for the local news. Everybody was so proud. "A Humble Hero" ran the headline in *El Diario Córdoba*. "The most important thing was that the team won the cup. We are all champions," Juan Carlos told them. "I was only able to score the goals because of my teammates." In fact, anyone who knew anything about the game could clearly see he scored those goals despite his *compañeros*. The final score was 12-8.

From then on, he had his pick of the girls in town, but rarely did he have a girlfriend. The longest relationship he ever had lasted about three months. Alicia was the prettiest girl in school. She was smart, too. She spoke English and Italian and read poetry, and her father was the mayor. My mother had heard the gossip and asked Juan Carlos about her one evening at dinner.

"So what's this I hear about you and Alicia Canteros?" she asked, with a wry smile.

"The mayor's daughter?" snapped my father. "You think you're good enough for the suits at the mayor's office?"

"It's all hearsay. She is not my girlfriend," sighed Juan Carlos, never once looking up from his plate.

The next day I found Alicia crying by the football pitch at school. She said Juan Carlos had broken up with her.

The Caballeros were farmers; farmers and housewives. We always had been, ever since arriving from old Italy nearly a century ago. The men worked on farms and the women worked in the home. But I wasn't going to be anyone's housewife and it was clear that Juan Carlos was destined for things much greater than ploughing fields and slaughtering cattle. He would be a national idol. He was already halfway there. And me, I would be the one who wrote about people like him. I would not only be the first Caballero to go university, but also the first woman in Argentina to commentate on a live match on the radio. I could already speak faster and more intelligently than any of the men who called the games in Córdoba.

I would sneak off on Sunday evenings and run to a phone box near town to call the radio shows. I said I was a boy, and that's what they called me: *"El Pibe"*. I became something of a favourite on *Radio Impacto*. Every Sunday night the presenters would give *El Pibe* at least three full minutes to deliver his take on the evening's major talking points. They even started calling me back after I was once cut off because I had ran out of money. I had to start using different phone boxes in case they sent someone to bring me into the station one evening for a live show. It was something the presenters had joked about before making the invitation official after my prediction that the Talleres forward Humberto Rafael Bravo would score as many goals as Diego Maradona.

I practiced my commentary into a mini tape recorder my mother had given me

for my 13th birthday. I had tapes and tapes of Juan Carlos's games. They would be priceless in 10 years. I always told myself that when my brother won the Mundial I would present them for archiving. Imagine that: *La Nación*'s most famous journalists writing about the life of the country's greatest player whilst listening to tapes of a 13-year-old girl calling school matches somewhere in the provinces.

It was the just beginning. We were ready. And it would all start with a letter.

My father and Juan Carlos were out in the fields when it finally arrived. I raced through the front door and swept through the kitchen when a sudden realisation brought me to an abrupt halt: I didn't know to which of them I should hand the letter. I asked my mother, who was drinking maté and watching the bread bake.

"Give it to your father," she said, her arm outstretched, offering me some tea. "He will decide."

"But it's not his."

"Isabella, why must you complicate things?"

"Having to decide whether or not to hand a letter to the person to whom it is addressed is something that has to be debated in this house, and I'm the one complicating things?"

My mother laughed. Every time I thought she'd snap, she instead let out a devious chuckle. The corners of her mouth turned up ever so slightly, less than a millimetre perhaps, in perfect sync with the narrowing of her gracious, green eyes. Her head tilted ever so faintly to her left, just enough to allow her glistening dark fringe to lean away from her forehead. I used to misinterpret that look as one of intrigue, but it was actually one of humour; one that acknowledged of the lunacy of the world around us and told me that she appreciated the ironies of our plight on this farm.

"Come on, my love!" she screeched, grabbing my hand and skipping out of the kitchen towards the fields.

I was slightly disappointed by the envelope itself. For something that had been anointed with the responsibility for protecting a young man's dreams, it was rather dull — just a piece of folded paper, a strip of adhesive the only thing between us and words that signalled a new beginning. There wasn't even a club crest stamped on the corner.

What I mostly remember about that moment is seeing my father smile. It wasn't a big one, his mouth hardly moved, but I read it as enough to convey the sense of pride I imagine he must have felt at that moment. Perhaps I saw a tear in his eye, but it was hard to tell as he wiped clear the remnants another hard day's work. My father had been spending more and more time in the fields over the last few years and less and less time at the markets — the only other place I'd ever seen him communicate with anyone. I often asked to help out, but he always said that he and Juan Carlos could manage the work. They would often be out there until the early hours of the morning, even when Juan Carlos had a game the next day. But all that would be over now.

My father took a knife from his pocket and skilfully slipped it under the seal, slicing

it open with one, efficient stroke of his blade. Juan Carlos stood motionless, staring at that envelope as if it was the only thing in his world. My father pulled the letter free and began to read, but the look I had previously interpreted as one of joy became increasingly distorted. The sun's smile was so strong that it hurt my eyes to look at the bright, white paper he held in his worn, discoloured hands. I could clearly make out from the back of the page that there couldn't have been much more than 200 words on that piece of paper. I wanted to ask him what on earth was taking him so long. He stood so still; as static as I had ever seen a living thing. Then his eyes travelled back up to the top of the page. Was he really going to read that damn thing twice? He scanned back down and the look on his face began to change again, almost by the line. He dropped his arms to his side, engulfing the letter in his shadow. He handed it to my mother. I would normally have dived over her shoulder, but I couldn't take my eyes off him. She dropped the letter. As it fell, it float down to the dry, grey soil at her feet before catching a breeze, darting between my parents and back up into the air. Juan Carlos and I followed its flight, but didn't move a muscle. My father stepped forward, rested both hands on my brother's shoulders and looked right into his eyes. He looked into mine once. I think it was on a birthday, or maybe it was that Christmas he handed me my first notebook for Sunday school.

"You will do the name proud won't you, Son?"

"Of course, Father," Juan Carlos nodded

"Isabella, your brother is going to be a soldier."

2. Sólo un Chico de las Malvinas

16th May, 1982

Alright, love,

I hope things are well at home? How's Jenny's dancing going? Tell her I was asking about her and about Mary's diary, too. I hope she's writing in it every day like she promised? Let her know I've kept my end of the bargain and that I'll read it to her when I get back. Let everyone else know I'm missing them like mad, but that I'm fine and I'm enjoying my holiday.

We're pretty much wrapped up here now, I reckon, so I expect to be home soon. Hey, you ain't traded me in for a younger model since I've been gone, have you? So sorry I didn't get the chance to see you again before all this kicked off. We were ██████████ ███ and were rushed back and then straight out here. We took off so quick ██████████████████ one of its propellers wasn't working. Can you believe that? ██ █████████████████. The banter on the way over here was brilliant, as always. We were all telling jokes about their top man and some of the lads even had T-shirts made up. I've kept hold of a shirt for you that says, "Start crying for us, Argentina!" It's always good to have a laugh. Anything to pass the time, really, and believe me, there was a lot of time to pass. It took so long to get here that I think most of us forgot we were actually going somewhere.

It's an odd place, really. They say we're on the other side of the world, but you wouldn't know to look at it. "You'll travel the world," they told us. First Northern Ireland and now this. Not exactly what I had in mind. It's all cold, wet and green. It looks sort of like the Scottish Highlands or the Isle of Man. It reminds me of our week in the caravan with the girls last year actually. It was right weird when we first met the locals. This young girl came rushing over to me waving a notepad. I almost wet myself when she asked for my autograph in the broadest Cornish accent you've ever heard in your life. In a funny way, it kind of makes you feel like you ain't that far from home after all, though, which is quite good.

We ██████████, ███████. We took ████████████ pretty quick, and

██████████████████. When we rendezvoused ████████ we knew we were golden. There was a lot to do, of course, but ██████████ ██████████████████. They seem a little chaotic, to be honest. Like they've ran headlong into something they weren't ready for. The only moment of doubt was after ████████████████. I was gutted, we all were. You remember ██████? You had a chat with his ████, ██████████, last May at the barracks I think. He was on it. I didn't know him that well really but it sort of brought it all home to me, you know what I mean? It sounds selfish to say it, especially when I think ████████████████████████ must be going through, but in a way I was sort of glad. Glad is the wrong word actually, but when something really bad happens we all try really hard to find the good in it. You always find the good in things. We could do with more people like you, both over here and back there. One of the fellas here with me (a lad called ████████, clever little bastard, he is) said it's just the way we cope with it all. I don't know, but it made me hate them more and hate can't be a bad thing to have in war. I danced a bloody jig when we ████████████████... Gotcha!

Anyway, what I meant by glad was that it made me think about you and the girls. I think about you all the time of course, but this was different. I don't think I really have the words, love, but it really made me think of you all. It made me think of you loads. For hours, I reckon, and that made me smile. These islands don't feel like the sort of place that sees many smiles. I'd bloody kill to see one of yours when I get up every morning.

Anyway, I have to get my beauty sleep. ████████████████████ ████████... I'm still trying to get used to sleeping through the whistle of the wind. This has to be the windiest place on earth. Give the girls a massive kiss from their dad. I miss you, love. I'll be back before you know it.

All the love in the world from the other side of it,

Tom xxx

_____

1st June, 1982

Alright, love,

How are you? You probably still haven't got my last letter, so don't worry about writing back to me. Just knowing you're all there is enough. Some of the lads here ain't got a lot to go home to. They're the ones who really get into all this stuff, talking about brothers in arms and all that. Shame really. The best part about going away is coming back. Along those lines, and yeah, yeah, I know I said this last time, but I reckon I'll be back soon. Some of the lads been saying they reckon she'll ███████████████ ████, ███ ███████████████████████████████████████. I don't know much, but I don't reckon she wants us to, if I'm honest. I remember your dad saying she █████████████████████████████████████ folk like us. Guess she ████████ now. I been chatting to a couple of the new guys, especially the interpreter. We have one with us just in case. He's an interesting fella. He's been teaching me some Spanish words. Did you know that they speak Spanish in Argentina? Spain used to own them, see. They used to own the land I'm lying on right now. According to one of the journalists I met on the way here, so did the Dutch and the French. It had to be given back to the Spanish, though, so God knows how we ended up with it. Probably because nobody else wanted it. Anyway, You believe that? Me speaking Spanish, ha ha. Ola me amor x!! I'll take you out for a slap-up meal when I get back with candles the lot. I'll speak Spanish to you, as well. I'm going to be one romantic old bugger with that lingo in my arsenal. Bloody irresistible.

Right, got a really early start as ██████████████████████ ██████████████████████ so must dash. That ████████████ will be along to collect the letters soon and if you don't have them ready to go as soon as he gets here then he ██████████████████████. ██████████████ ████████, ███ ███████████████████████████████. Tell everyone I love them and that I'm enjoying myself.

I miss you more than I can ever say on a piece of paper like this. I'll be with you soon, love.

Tom xx

12th June, 1982

Alright, love,

How are you? I could really do with one of your hugs today. I'd

give my left arm for your sausage and mash and one of those pretty
smiles to go with it. Anyway, obviously I'm fine because I'm writing
this letter now, so don't worry as you read on but you'll see it's
been a pretty strange day.

I found this fella, see. Well, this kid. He couldn't have been no
more ███████. I found him crouched ████████████████████ inland
of ████████████. He clearly couldn't walk. The left knee of his
uniform was soaked red with blood. God knows how he managed to
get half way across ████████████, we were the ones doing all the
bloody yomping. So, yeah, I'd wandered off for a pee when I heard
this shuffling coming from a little ditch. I crept over to it, rifle
drawn, and there he was. ████████████████████████████████████,
████████████████████████████████████. ████████ and shouted at him
to stop. I don't quite know why I did that, not like he was going
anywhere. Then he hauled himself up, dead straight, and held out
his Argie blade. You get used to your blade, to all the stuff
they give you. They sort of become a part of you, like an arm or a
leg. They're what makes us different, see. Not to each other, but
from them. Enough of them had already felt the sharp ends of our
bayonets, so it was sort of funny that he should hold his blade out
to my rifle. His leg was shaking like mad.

It's weird the things that fly through your head at times like that.
I was 100% focused on him, on my duty, but in those few seconds I
still remember thinking all sorts of stuff. I stood there, aiming
a gun at a kid, and I wondered ████████████████████████ all this,
love. How can ████████████████████████████ an enemy? Yeah, we can
all ██
████████████████████████████████, ████████ what's in the pull of a
finger? When you actually get up close, though, so close that you can
see them looking back at you, ████████████████████████████████ I
know nothing about Argentina. I know nothing about their government.
Christ, I don't know much about my own. You see they don't clog our
brains with that ████████. ████████████ here to do a job, I suppose. And
so was he, I guess. And you know what? I bet he didn't want to be
crouched there freezing his bloody knackers off any more than I did.
He was a brave bugger, though. I'll give him that.

'Como say yama?' I shouted, which is how you ask someone what
they're called in Spanish, but the boy just stood there looking
straight at me. I asked again and then he replied, but with a load
of words in Spanish that I didn't understand.

'Rendursee,' I shouted, which means to surrender. He just kept looking at me, though. It felt like we were there for about half an hour. Eventually, he threw his knife down. I called the lads and we took him away. I'd never had a prisoner before. I don't want another one.

I count my blessings he didn't have his gun and that I still get to come home to you all. I'll count my blessings every day for that. Thing is, though, at the same time I couldn't stop looking at him. One of the lads ██ ██████. I guess lads are like that in war. Maybe I was. At least I used to say things that would make people think I was. But, love, how can I shoot a kid? I don't want to ███████████. I don't really ██████████████████████████.

I ██████████████████ and all the lads were cheering and patting me on the back as we passed them.

There was something about this kid, though. I don't know what it was, but he was different and sort of the same. That don't make sense, I know. I think I respected him. Once he'd dropped the blade, I think I even sort of liked him. I don't know if that makes any sense. It's at times like this when I wish I'd studied more in school and maybe gone to a proper college or something. I don't think I can really explain to you what I was feeling.

He had a piece of paper on him. You know I ain't one for reading and that, but it was sort of beautiful, I think. Once we realised that it wasn't important or nothing, ███████ let me keep it. I've copied it out for you because what's beautiful about it is how it looks. Here it is…

> Soy un diez.
> Soy un cinco también.
> Después, hoy soy un soldado
> Y lucho por mi país y por mi pueblo y por mis colores.
> Quiero a mi hermana, a mis compañeros, y mi casa en Córdoba.
> Quiero a mi madre, a mi padre, y a Argentina.
> Pero soy solo un chico de las Malvinas
> Mis pies una vez fueron mi gloria
> Ahora están frios y húmedos

Funny, isn't it? The shape I mean. Like it works up to something and then falls away. ███████ translated it for me. Apparently it says he's a soldier and stuff and then the long line says all he really wants is to be back at home with his family. I recognised

the third from last line. It's what he said when I asked his name.
He says he's just a boy.

It made me think about us and how ████████████████████████
████. The more I learn about ███████████████████████   them
equally. ████████████████.   ██████████████████████████████
██████████████████████████   in power longer. ████████████████
█████.██
███
█████.██
███.   ██████
███
█████.

But you're not, we all know she is and he probably knows they are,
too.

I'll never forget that kid.

Tom xx

3. Las Malvinas: From Caudillo to Pibe

Juan Carlos Caballero: A Life Lost in Las Malvinas

At 12 years-old, Juan Carlos Caballero was tipped to be an idol of Argentinian football. Thirty years later, the veteran of Las Malvinas remembers a dream that died one afternoon in the South Atlantic.

By Martín Gutiérrez

3rd April 2012

We stand in silence — a long and tranquil silence that I dare not break. It's the first time we've met in over 30 years, and for over half an hour we've hardly said a word.

In June 1976, as a trainee journalist on the news desk of *El Diario Córdoba*, I was sent to a local school to conduct my first ever newspaper interview. I was there to speak to a 12 year-old boy who had just become the first player in the history of Córdoba boys' football to score 12 goals in a single match. Young Juan Carlos Caballero was the talk of the town, having single-handedly delivered the Junior Cup to his school for the first time in its history.

I met him at his parents' farm on the outskirts of the city, where he was already working in the fields with his father. A stern and misanthropic man, Sr Caballero remained by his son's side at the dinner table in total silence as the young boy ran me through each of his goals. I would see Juan Carlos play a handful of times over the next four years before I moved to Buenos Aires

to take up a position here at *La Nación*. Whenever our paths crossed, we'd stop and chat, his sister, Isabella, never failing to ask me when I'd come to interview her big brother again. While I'd never been able to kick a ball more than a few feet, I saw something familiar in Juan Carlos. I, too, was an ambitious young boy from the provinces hoping to make my way in the world and so I tried to stay in contact with him — a journalist lives and dies by his contacts and I quickly realised he could one day be one worth having. After my piece was published, the chief scout from Club Atlético Huracán had phoned me at the newspaper to find out just how good the kid was; the local sides Belgrano and Instituto had also expressed their interest to the Caballeros. I expected to see much more of Juan Carlos in years to come.

But this week, we meet for the first time in more than 30 years. And not at a club training ground or a posh awards ceremony, or even the family farm back in our hometown, but at Plaza San Martín in the heart of the Buenos Aires. We stand side-by-side, motionless, entombed in what feels like a sacred silence, facing Monumento a los Caídos en Malvinas. As a boy, Juan Carlos looked like the archetypal *pibe* — a devious smile perpetually on his handsome young face. It was one that I read as conveying an excitement for the life that lay ahead. For the dreams he would go on to live. And for the fame and reverence an illustrious career in Argentina's national sport brings those talented enough to make it. Today, however, the reverence the man commands is an entirely different one.

He wears a three-piece suit beneath a jet-black trench coat, and polished black loafers. Juan Carlos is unrecognisable from the boy I met three decades ago. "A lot has changed," he says. "I recognise some of the names [here]," he continues. "That boy was a 5, like me. He was from Rosario... [That one was] from Mendoza, a 10 who used to sneak wine from the vineyards at night. I was going to... go and visit him... [but] he never returned."

There's a crack in Juan Carlos's voice as he speaks about his *compañeros*. The adolescent grin has been replaced with something perhaps best described as a sort of empty gaze. Having removed his hat when we arrived, the rain water now ran down the length of his face before falling to the puddles at our feet. They perhaps mask his tears; I can't be sure. The silence has returned, and it lingers until the rain stops.

"Did you remember me?" Juan Carlos asks later that afternoon as we sit watching Las Madres walk the Plaza de Mayo. With his question arrives that boyish smile that first greeted me at a Córdoba family dinner table all those years ago. "I played as a 10 [that day]," he tells me. "Seba, who usually played

as the 10, was sick and so I was pushed forward. Until that season everybody said they saw me as a 10, but Seba and I were quite far ahead of the rest of the boys in our school and he could play only as a 10... I could play anywhere. At our first training session, I told the coach that to get the best out of us both, I should play as the 5."

Between his sips of maté, I notice his feet twitching as he talks, as if actively reliving the kick of every ball that day. "We won the cup, so I guess it was a good idea... From the back I could organise those around me. And by working hard for the team, by being what they now call a Pacman, I earned the respect of my *compañeros*, so they listened [to me]. Football is about movement. You don't always have to be going forward, but you always have to be moving." Juan Carlos seems to move only when discussing the sport.

I want to ask him about Las Malvinas; we've been together for over two hours now and I'm becoming increasingly aware that I'm not getting enough copy for an interview commemorating the 30th anniversary of the conflict. I attempt to steer the conversation that way, asking what he thought of the islands when he first arrived. "It was cold and wet," he replies. "In fact, one of the British soldiers told me he thought it was like Britain... It was hardly La Plata in November," he adds, chuckling quietly. His feet have settled. He pulls a notebook from his breast pocket and scribbles something down. I notice what looks like a football formation sketched out on the adjacent page and ask him what he uses the notepad for? "For my thoughts," he replies. I press him on what thought it was that he's just added. "Just an image... I'll unpack it later [...] I went to a couple of writing classes last year and everyone had one. It seemed like a good idea... I write essays, short stories and lots of poetry. I began [writing poetry] on those islands. The heart of a 5; the mind of a 10," he adds with what I think was a wink.

And just like that we're back to football again. "My career ended in Las Malvinas," he says. "It was like playing without a crowd. In every corner of those islands, there was nothing but silence. One that the wind carried with a palpable menace." I never thought of war as being silent, I tell him. "It was deathly silent," he shoots back. "Until one day... when it was broken by the sound of bombs falling. All around me, my *compañeros* fell. I joined them on the turf when something flew into my knee." Juan Carlos had been hit by a piece of shrapnel. "That was the moment that changed my life forever... they say 649 Argentinians lost their lives in Las Malvinas. But it was many more than that. I am still here, but for me a life ended that day. I feel lucky that I was able to start a new one... Many were not so fortunate."

Juan Carlos hid in a ditch for two days after a series of explosions had separated him from his troop. He was eventually found by a British soldier and captured as a prisoner of war. A few days later, the war was over and he was released. "I thought that was it for me," he says when I ask him how it felt coming face-to-face with the enemy. "I was tired, wet, and in a lot of pain... But I wasn't going to go down without a fight. [The British solider] pointed his rifle at me; I pointed my knife at him. I say I wanted a fight. But maybe I wanted something more." It's at

such gripping memories that one would expect to see a man speaking with his body as much as his words, but whenever he speaks about the war, Juan Carlos remains still. "I froze, waiting for him to shoot. I remember thinking about how it would sound. How it would feel. But the guy just stood there looking at me... [then] he tried talking to me in Spanish."

That British soldier, Tom Jenkins, died in 2002, aged just 45. "I always wondered... what he made of me. Thankfully I found out [a few years after his death] when I received a letter from his widow. He had written about me in his letters home... He found one of my poems, which had later inspired him to start writing his own. Mrs Jenkins and I email each other about once or twice a month now and she continues to send me scans of his work."

Juan Carlos places his hat back on his head and closes his eyes. I ask what he sees in the darkness. "I know what you are getting at," he says. I'm aware by now that Juan Carlos is an intelligent and thoughtful man: little gets past him — either on or off the football field. "I do not have to close my eyes to remember," he replies. "I see them when I am awake."

He stands and asks me to walk with him. We stroll to the centre of the Plaza, where he stops and looks out at the Madres pacing their circles. "The mothers of my *compañeros* should be walking with them," he says, squatting. "Marcelo Bielsa squats on the touchline. He says you can see more at ground level, that it's easier to decipher the patterns of play. Bielsa is an idol for me; more so than [César Luis] Menotti. But I have already seen the play from the ground." He rises back to his feet, and for the first time I notice what an imposing figure he has become. He stands around 1.85m, but at a slight angle. "My dodgy knee won't allow me to squat for that long anyway," he adds with a grin. Another chuckle escapes the boyish smile that returned to his face as soon he mentioned El Loco Bielsa. "He understands that creativity and individualism must be allowed to flourish, but in a way that benefits the collective."

The silence returns and I take the opportunity to ask him what he's been up to for the last 30 years. "When I returned [from the war], I couldn't play anymore... so I went back to Córdoba and helped my father sell the farm. We moved to a smaller house and I got a job in the factory. It was fine, I worked with the union and there was lots of time to read on the shop floor." I ask him if he ever pursued another sort of career in football, a question I think I ask mainly to try and coax that smile back out of the earnest man that has returned to my side. "I did some coaching courses and became the DT of my old school team in 1988... We won the Junior Cup, the second in our history. I was offered a job with a very small club in Buenos Aires... but by then my mother was very ill and my father couldn't manage. My sister had left for the capital by then. She was doing very well and I couldn't make her come back."

His sister, Isabella, is now a prominent football writer at *Clarín* and occasionally commentates on televised games. It wasn't until we met at a football writers' dinner in February that I realised she was the same Isabella I had met three decades ago. A week later, we sat in her San Telmo apartment listening to an old audio tape of her commentating on the Junior Cup final. When she told

me what had become of her brother, I asked her whether she would help me secure an interview. "Good luck getting him to talk about anything other than football," she said, with a devious smile which I now recognise as something of a Caballero trait.

Juan Carlos left the factory last July, after nearly a quarter of a century on the shop floor. When his father passed away, he sold the house and took early retirement on medical grounds, and has since taken up writing full-time. "I've had a few short stories here and there and *El Gráfico* published one of my poems," he says. "A villanelle about Boca's 10, Juan Román Riquelme, and River Plate's 5, Matías Almeyda — two great binaries of Argentina... Both are integral to their teams, but both represent completely opposite ends of the spectrum; as footballers [and] as Argentinians... For me, what is so great about them is that they know what they are. We need them both... The thing about the 10 is that while he is an individual, given the freedom to express himself, he cannot truly flourish without his antithesis — the 5."

I once again attempt to steer the conversation back to Las Malvinas, asking Juan Carlos for his thoughts on who should hold sovereignty over the islands today. "People get in the way of politics. People should come first." I ask him about the Junta and the approach taken to the conflict. He removes his hat and turns to the Madres, who have finished their march and are now chatting and embracing one another. "I always come here whenever I am in Buenos Aires on a Thursday. Their march is deeply moving, but for me what is even more emotive is the way in which they greet one another when the walking stops. I imagine many of them meet just once a week, brought together by the most unthinkable of things."

Juan Carlos seems to see the contrasts in everything. I press him on the tactical deployment of our troops during the conflict. "OK," he says, turning on the bench to face me for the first time all afternoon. "The England team charges full-steam ahead... like that lad [Bryan] Robson. I have never seen a 10 play for England, except for Paul Gascoigne — boy, what a player. He's a *pibe*, you know, like El Diego." It's at this moment when I realise Juan Carlos is using the word '*pibe*' as anthropological term as much as a colloquialism. "Their problem is that all they have are bad 5s, and when they get a good one like that lad [Ray] Wilkins, who always retained possession and kept his team moving, they don't realise it. Our problem is we have these people who are 5s but... they make it to the top and then they behave like the most incompetent of 10s: from Caudillo to Pibe. We were

too English in our approach to Las Malvinas. War is not a game."

For hours I had been trying to coax Juan Carlos into talking to me about war and politics, to direct our discussions away from football and address something more important, but perhaps that is exactly what he had been talking about all along.

Now I feel as if I have so much more to ask him, but my time is up. "I am writing a book," he tells me as we say our goodbyes and agree to meet up in a few months' time. "It is a collection of short stories and poems, entitled *Los Cincos y Los Diezes: Los Pueblos de Argentinidad*."

Juan Carlos Caballero is still here, but he is one of many who lost his life in Las Malvinas. Speaking to him today, however, 30 years after the conflict, I get the impression that amid all that loss, he seems to have found something.

Translated by Richard Hartley

171

"It was one of those exceedingly
rare individual fixtures that
distinctly divided eras in the
competition's history."

AC Milan 2 Benfica 1

European Cup final, Wembley Stadium, London,
22 May 1963

By Miguel Delaney

After a few seconds of silence, the issue that has simmered for years is finally brought up. It's the 24th anniversary of the 1963 European Cup final and, in order to commemorate the occasion, the Italian state broadcaster RAI have gathered Cesare Maldini, Mario Coluna and the renowned journalist Gianni Mina into a studio to watch and discuss AC Milan's 2-1 win over Benfica at Wembley. The panel have just seen the pivotal moment in the 59th minute, when Gino Pivatelli fouled Coluna and

(to?) put him out of the game. The incident didn't just reduce Benfica to 10 men in the absence of substitutions, it removed their most influential player. In a period of perceived attacking innocence, Coluna was the architect who gave the defending European champions clear direction and design. Now, the question is how much direction and design lay behind the foul.

So, Mina eventually broaches it. "Awful challenge, eh? Lads, after 24 years, can we say whether that foul was ordered or not?"

Maldini, who was captaining Milan from centre-half that day, is insistent: "Absolutely not. Clearly it was a foul, but..."

An agitated Coluna cuts him off, pointing at the screen as a translator relays his words.

"Look how far away the ball is. Pivatelli got nowhere near it!"

"Coluna said it decided the game," Mina interjects.

Undeniably.

The game itself, meanwhile, did more than decide that season's European Cup. It was one of those exceedingly rare individual fixtures that distinctly divided eras in the competition's history; a meeting of two ultimately dominant teams at opposite points of their cycle.

Because of the improbability of so many elements aligning — right down to the luck of the draw — there have only really been three such clutch contests in 58 years of the competition.

In the 1972-73 quarter-final, a fully formed Ajax brutally illustrated to Bayern Munich just who the continent's best team were. Many of the German players cited that resounding 4-0 defeat as the most traumatic match of their careers, but also the final lesson that transformed them from domestic champions into European champions. After that elimination, Bayern immediately embarked on their own three-in-a-row. Four years before that, Milan had much

the same effect on a more callow Ajax by beating them 4-1 in the 1969 showpiece.

In 1963, though, it was a nascent Milan that showed much greater savvy than the reigning champions Benfica. That wasn't the only aspect that marked this match apart. It was also unique in the manner that one moment so distilled all of the defining traits of those eras and those sides, effectively bringing two decades down to a single kick.

In that, Pivatelli's foul was as layered as it was lasting. Because, even if an injury was not intended, it was the ultimate consequence of Milan's distinctive approach.

Their manager Nereo Rocco had specifically detailed Pivatelli — a notional wing-forward — to shackle the playmaker. Moreover, he had dropped the prolific Paolo Barison in order to do so. Never before at such a vaunted level had a team so conspicuously compromised their existing attacking approach. It perfectly illustrated Rocco's new pragmatism.

After eight years of free-scoring European Cups in which creators like Coluna had space in which to innovate, a more calculating breed of team and coach were now seeking to shut them down. Innocent attacking had started to give way to a singeing cynicism. The Pivatelli foul did not just symbolise a new era; it set the template for it.

Wembley was witnessing the rise of *catenaccio*. First, Rocco had to figure how to bring about the fall of Benfica.

As the 1963 European Cup final kicked off, it was difficult to see where a sea change to more constrained football was coming from. Milan began in assertively direct fashion, immediately taking the game to Benfica. Within seconds, José Altafini had latched onto a loose ball and charged straight at goal. Within minutes, the refined Gianni Rivera had attempted a perceptive through-ball that fell just short. The Italian fans in the Wembley crowd even booed when Benfica had no option but to pass the ball back to their goalkeeper Costa Pereira. This was not *catenaccio* as it came to be recognised.

For their part, the Milan squad always bristled at their association with the philosophy. Cesare Maldini especially despised it and frequently pointed to the team's fine goalscoring record. The statistics certainly make a statement. In winning Serie A in 1961-62, they hit 83 goals in 34 games, 22 more than the next most prolific attack. In reaching that 1963 European Cup final, then, they hit 31 in eight — the highest ratio in the competition's history. Even if 14 of those goals were against Union Luxembourg in the preliminary round, eight went past Galatasaray in the quarter-finals and five past Bob Shankly's Dundee in the semis.

The great misconception about *catenaccio*, however, is that it was a fundamentally negative approach. It was not; it was an inherently pragmatic one. Realism was always Rocco's great skill and, for all the players may have despised their association with the philosophy, there could be no denying their manager's career was intertwined with it.

Rocco was the coach who made *catenaccio* mainstream in Italian football and he would do the same on the continent. Adapting the system from Gipo Viani at Salernitana in the 1940s, he added a more clinical form of counter-attacking and then applied it to unprecedented effect at both Triestina and Padova. As those provincial sides powered up the table, the noted football journalist Gianni Brera, following Lev Filatov, notoriously described *catenaccio* as "the right of the weak": finding some cleverer strategy to trump superior opposition.

This was the crux of that 1963 final.

For all the apparent bravery that Milan showed in the opening minutes, an anecdote from the build-up betrays their true mood. "We were pulling into the Wembley car park when Rocco noticed the fear in our faces," Maldini has said. So often severe and authoritarian with his players, the coach knew this time to use humour. "He stood up and shouted, 'Anyone who is scared shouldn't bother getting off the bus.' Then he sat down and pretended to be frightened. We all burst into laughter and the tension evaporated."

That might have helped Milan as they prepared kick-off but Rocco knew it would not be enough over the course of the entire game. Ultimately, his squad were intimidated by Benfica because they were inferior.

The Portuguese side had proven their lasting quality not only by lifting the European Cup in successive years, but by proactively going toe to toe with the competition's benchmark sides. There was no luck of the draw. Benfica admirably went for the win. In the 1962 final, they beat Real Madrid 5-3. A year earlier they had defeated the only other side to eliminate Real in Europe, Barcelona.

Moreover, the team were at the forefront of football's dominant attacking philosophy at that point. Their previous manager, Béla Guttmann, had been at São Paulo in 1957, directly influencing the Brazil side that would win the 1958 World Cup in such vibrant fashion. With Guttmann taking that approach on further at Benfica, it could even be argued that they represented the culmination of that era of attacking football in continental club football. The 1962 final against Real Madrid certainly represented it, finishing 5-3 and bringing together all that had been great about the first seven years of the competition: its two best teams and only champions, glorious attacking football and great players fully applying their talent.

Although Guttmann departed in controversial fashion immediately after that victory, to be replaced by the Chilean Fernando Riera, Eusébio would later argue the team was so intensely integrated by that point that any manager was irrelevant.

Rocco would have to prove otherwise. Realising that it would only tempt defeat to take on Benfica in an open game, the Milan coach tipped the balance. He invoked "the right of the weak". Although Paolo Barison had scored six goals from the right flank en route to the final — three of them genuinely important strikes — he was dropped for the more functional Pivatelli. The squad was surprised, primarily because the 30-year-old's career as a forward had faded and he was by then only intermittently used as a defensive option. Now, he would

have the most important defensive job of all: to track back and stop Coluna at left-half.

The scale of the challenge was emphasised by how quickly the playmaker seized hold of the game. Although Benfica were initially hemmed in by Milan's abrasive attitude, it was an 11th-minute drive and long shot from Coluna that characteristically brought them back into the match. For the first time, Milan were pinned back and suddenly forced to re-assess how open they'd been.

Within seven minutes, those pre-game fears had been born out. Shortly after the effervescent António Simões had started to unravel the Milan defence with an intricate run, the rest of the Benfica attack prised them apart.

Collecting a loose ball in his own half, Coluna immediately flicked it forward to José Antonio Torres. The 6'3" forward controlled the pass at waist height and poked it on for Eusébio in one movement. From there, about 35 yards from goal, the forward displayed his devastating acceleration to tear away from two Milan defenders. Every stride only opened up more space, until Eusébio was left to angle the ball in off the inside of the post.

The entire move was the perfect combination of poise, power and precision, taking just nine seconds from Coluna's right boot to the back of the net. For the next 10 minutes or so, Benfica were buoyant, bouncing the ball around the pitch with joyful ease. One swift interchange reflected the attacking integration that Guttmann had worked so hard to develop. Milan were struggling to keep up and in danger of being swept away.

It was around that point the game saw its first key change, but not from Rocco. Although the 3pm Wednesday kick-off time had brought the Wembley crowd down to just 45,700, the noise made it impossible for the Milan players to hear any instructions from the bench. So, they took matters into their own hands. In truth, it wasn't entirely without authorisation. As domineering as Rocco often appeared, he placed great trust in his senior players. A group consisting of Rivera, Maldini and Giovanni Trapattoni formed the coach's 'internal commission' whom he would regularly consult before games. It was also telling how many of Rocco's players, in contrast to Helenio Herrera's, succeeded in management. At a fraught stage of the 1963 final, they would illustrate why. Maldini told Trapattoni to take over the job of marking Eusébio from the ailing Víctor Benítez.

In the previous season's final, the then 20-year-old forward had signalled his emergence as European football's dominant star by besting both Ferenc Puskás and Alfredo Di Stefáno to score the double that won the trophy. Puskás handing Eusébio his shirt after the game was seen as a symbolic passing of the torch. A year on, there seemed no one on the continent to match him in terms of box-office quality or sheer talent.

Trapattoni, at least, began to match his every movement. Conspicuously, after 29 minutes, Eusébio was left limping and requiring treatment. It marked another shift. Rivera also made his mark on Coluna, stealing the ball before

nutmegging a defender. Milan began what was probably their best period of the game, pummelling Pereira's goal and forcing him into all manner of flaps, but with no end product. At that stage, Altafini was enduring a miserable afternoon. On 35 minutes, the defender Mario David hooked a hugely inviting ball across the face of goal, which seemed only to require a touch. Instead, Altafini completely missed it, compounding the error with the awkward manner in which tried to lift his right leg to turn in the cross. It was not the movement of a confident forward. Altafini could immediately be seen holding his hands up to winger Bruno Mora.

Although the Brazilian would go onto become the fourth-highest scorer in Serie A history, his reputation was rarely beyond reproach. On first taking over at Milan in 1961, Rocco railed against Altafini in public more than any player apart from Jimmy Greaves. The coach felt the duo were disconnected from the rest of his developing system and unwilling to work for it. "These two need to understand," Rocco once bellowed, "that during a football game you get kicked and not just well paid."

To a degree, the dilemma further demonstrated the manager's fundamental approach to the game. Blessed with two of the game's greatest-ever goalscorers, he sought to force them into a system rather than facilitate their main ability. It failed to function, with Milan dropping to seventh in the table by the November of the 1961-62 season.

To his credit, Rocco eventually found a solution. Fed up with the unhappy

Greaves's indiscipline off the pitch as well as on it, the coach replaced the English forward with Brazilian passer Dino Sani. Altafini was spared. In theory, the move represented another regressive step, given that it involved the use of a midfielder at the expense of a forward. In practice, it immediately gave Milan balance and unlocked their attack. From Sani's debut against Juventus, Milan took 31 points from the next 34 available to win the title. There was suddenly a clear line from Sani through Rivera to Altafini. In that match against Juve, the forward scored four goals in a 5-1 win.

By the 50th minute of the 1963 final, though, Altafini had already squandered four glorious chances. On the stroke of half-time, he followed the miss from the David cross by heading straight at Pereira from just yards out. Two minutes after the break, he drove wildly across goal. Moments later, he somehow put the ball over from just under the bar. It was because of occasional wastefulness like that that Brera nicknamed Altafini *'Conileone'*: supposedly combined the weakness of a rabbit, *coniglio*, with the fierceness of a lion, *leone*.

This match at Wembley would sum up that contradiction, even if it would also finally banish the accusation that he never produced in big games. Because, out of nothing — or, at least, out of a bad Benfica miss — Altafini equalised.

On 57 minutes, Eusébio picked the ball up in his own half and started to power through Milan in much the same manner he had against Madrid in the 1962 final. Instead of cutting inside as in that game, though, he was forced to pass wide. The ball was floated across the box, only for

Torres to head it back the same way with the goal at his mercy.

Reprieved, Milan eventually worked the ball up the right through David. He lofted it inside for Rivera, who attempted to hammer it at goal. The shot was blocked but took a lucky bounce for Altafini opportunistically to fire it into the corner. Milan were deservedly level.

As intermittently poor as Benfica had been by their standards, the goal couldn't have been described as a true turning point. It wasn't something the Portuguese were unaccustomed to, given how they normally set out simply to outscore the opposition. The approach had worked in the previous two finals.

In 1962 in Amsterdam, they had suffered the supposedly devastating psychological blow of Puskás putting Real Madrid straight back into the lead after Benfica had pulled back a 2-0 deficit, only to fight back again to win 5-3. And in 1961 in Bern, they had recovered from an early Sándor Kocsis header to defeat a brilliant Barcelona 3-2.

Coluna had scored key long-range shots in both of those finals and was now similarly attempting to alter the course of this one. Although Eusébio personified that Benfica team through his goals, his Mozambican compatriot undeniably powered them. In fact, it was arguably the arrival of the young forward in 1961 that allowed Coluna truly to flourish. The transfer meant Guttmann could move the playmaker back to left-half, from where he had even more scope to dictate games with his precision and influence from deep. Rocco recognised this more than anyone, which explained his surprising decision to pick Pivatelli. "He had practical intelligence, common sense and was extremely intuitive," Rivera later said. "He always knew where the least expected danger would come from."

It was well inside his own half, about a minute after Altafini's equaliser, that Coluna intercepted a Pivatelli pass and strode forward. As the Benfica number six raced away to surge through one of the gaps that were so prevalent in European football of the late 1950s and early 1960s, Pivatelli immediately sought to close it — just as he'd been trying to do all afternoon.

At the moment the Milan player reached out, though, Coluna evasively and intelligently poked the ball away. In full flight, he was about to force a propitious three-on-two. Until Pivatelli reduced it all to one kick. The Italian lifted his leg and sent Coluna crashing to the ground. The action of the trip itself seemed minimal, almost innocuous. The consequences were both instant and immense.

Most conspicuously, it took Coluna a few moments to get up before he had to be helped off the pitch with a broken foot.

The injury didn't appear immediately to affect Benfica. They remained on top for the next few minutes, with Simões seeing a lot of the ball down the left. For all their charges, though, there were no actual chances; no one suddenly to open up the increasingly enclosed space around the Milan box.

The offset, of course, was vast tracts at the other end of the pitch. On 65 minutes, Milan gave Benfica something

of a warning as Altafini flicked Mora through to bring a save from Pereira. The warning was not heeded.

With the Portuguese side pushing forward moments later, Rivera stole the ball in the centre-circle, deftly set himself up and threaded a fine ball through for Altafini. One on one with Pereira, the Brazilian — perhaps inevitably — saw his first effort saved. There was nothing to stop him finishing the follow-up. Milan, for the first time, were ahead.

Coluna has remained indignant about the entire incident ever since, at least right up to an interview with Ben Lyttleton in 2004. "I ran past him but he chased me, fouled me from behind and broke my foot," he said. Perhaps more interestingly, the playmaker thought Trapattoni was responsible. "I never spoke to Trapattoni again, not even when he was managing Benfica in 2004-05. Nothing. I don't want to talk to him again. He meant to do that. After the game [a match between Benfica and AC Milan in 1987], an Italian TV station invited me to go to Milan to meet him live on a TV show. Trapattoni never showed up. This proved me that he really wanted to injure me."

While Trapattoni evidently got unfair blame for that foul, he deserves a lot of credit for the effectiveness of Milan's defending thereafter. At one crucial juncture, the left-half put in a cast-iron — but entirely clean — challenge on Joaquim Santana that ended a Benfica attack in the Italian box and allowed his side to keep the ball. It wasn't far off the perfect tackle.

Riera didn't see all of Milan's efforts that way. After the final, he was reportedly shocked at the "ungentlemanly" approach of Rocco's side. That was somewhat surprising given that the Benfica coach had been in charge of the Chile team involved in the notorious Battle of Santiago against Italy during the 1962 World Cup, with many of his players keenly trading blows. The Milan right-back, Mario David, had even been sent off in that game for kicking Leonel Sánchez in the head after taking a punch to the face from the Chile forward.

Either way, the last 20 minutes of the Wembley final fell into a pattern that was to become all too familiar over the next decade and beyond: an Italian team resolutely defending; an opposition side in charge of the ball but vainly chasing the game.

Coluna would hobble on again about 10 minutes from the end, but to predictably little effect.

In Benfica's two previous finals, the relentless willingness to attack created an element of doubt about the outcome right until the end. Here, there was no grand rally, no rousing late chance. Milan had closed out the most open era in European football.

With one kick, the entire climate had seemingly changed. Rocco's club were European champions for the first time, shifting the continent's centre of power from Iberia to the burgeoning city of Milan. The trophy would spend four of the seven seasons that followed in the Giuseppe Meazza stadium.

Across the famous arena, Angelo Moratti was already looking on enviously at all Rocco had achieved. The Internazionale president was so fed up with failure that in 1961 he went and paid a record £35,000 for the best manager in the business, Helenio Herrera. It was part of a period of Italian football driven by what the English press called "the lure of the lira". The excess off the pitch, however, was contrasted by the economy on it. Although Herrera's Barcelona had been one of the highest scoring sides amid even the abandon of the late 1950s, he gradually realised the tactical canniness of Serie A required a much greater degree of calculation. *Catenaccio* was now too widespread. In October of the 1962-63 season, after a defeat at Atalanta to yet another inferior side successfully practicing Rocco's style of pragmatism, the Argentinian made his Faustian decision. Inter would convert to *catenaccio*.

Characteristically, Herrera did not just adapt the philosophy. He took it to extremes.

Inter immediately produced what was statistically the meanest defence that Serie A had ever seen to win the title and then a series of the lowest-scoring ties the European Cup had yet experienced. The 1965 final was a nadir, as Herrera's side beat Benfica 1-0 with a performance of astounding austerity.

Away from the pitch, though, there was an even grimmer aspect to their glory. Evidence soon arose of Inter using their riches to fix European semi-finals, while Herrera was accused of doping players. Unlike Pivatelli's own evasion of the rules in that 1963 final, there could be no disputing the intentions there.

There could also be no denying that catenaccio had started to condition the sport as a whole, even if most teams were never going to go as far as Inter. The 1963 final marked the mid-point of a period in which the then frenzied sport cooled to a recognisable version of its current form. The World Cups either side provide a telling barometer. In 1958, the average goals per game had been a thrilling 3.6. By 1966, it was a more moderate and modern 2.6.

More than anything, Pivatelli's foul brought all this to the fore. While aggressively targeting opposition players was nothing new, it had never quite been as systemised as this. There was deeper method to any malice.

The 1963 final did not just lose Coluna. Football lost some of its innocence.

Miguel Delaney is currently writing a history of the European Cup and Champions League, to be published by BackPage Press in 2014.

181

Eight Bells

"Northern Ireland... ARE ON THE
SCORESHEET AGAIN."

Computer Games

A selection of key moments in the development of the football simulation

By George Osborn

 **International Soccer
1983**

If computer games can be considered an art form then the games developed in the late 1970s and early 1980s are the equivalent of prehistoric cave paintings. With processors on most home computers at the time barely strong enough to power a modern day microwave, game developers had to make significant sacrifices with graphics and gameplay to ensure their titles worked properly and didn't accidentally immolate the console (or, in some cases, the tape deck) playing it.

And for early football games, things were no different. The initial batch of football games were so simplistic that they barely represented the sport printed on the box. The first game commercially marketed as an interpretation of the sport was *Binatone Football*. A plug-in TV game made for a dedicated console in the late 70s, the game was simply *Pong* with the word "Football" appended; an unimpressive start to the genre.

But in the 1980s, games began to appear that really could be recognised by gamers as a genuine representation of football. One of the first to achieve that was the 1983 title *International Soccer* which debuted on the Commodore 64.

Developed by Andrew Spence in his bedroom (the natural habitat of a British game developer in the 1980s) players could choose from six different team colours and play a rudimentary game of seven-a-side football against the computer or a friend.

And I really do mean rudimentary. Despite sporting the alternative title *Cup Final*, what *International Soccer* really resembled was a low-grade kickabout down the park. With no offside rule, fouls or set pieces, you were left with what appeared to be two teams of obese men kicking a ball around in front of a white noise generator that was programmed to blare whenever a goal went in.

So *International Soccer* was far from the hyper-realistic footballing package we've come to expect today. Nevertheless, it is recognisably a football game. Even with the basic graphics and game-play simplicity, *International Soccer* offered gamers the chance to play football and it wasn't long before it began inspiring a legion of successors throughout the 1980s that sought to expand on the formula.

The *Match Day* series, fondly remembered despite being utterly rubbish, arrived on the Spectrum in 1984 and boasted ball deflections to add randomness to the gameplay. In 1988, the successor to *International Soccer*, *Emlyn Hughes International Soccer*, introduced lobs, backheels, tournaments and a basic management sim to the gaming mix (as well as branded endorsements). And in 1989, the *Kick Off* series brought order to the anarchy of football games by adding fouls, cards and set pieces to the virtual pitch for the first time.

So while *International Soccer* may not look like much now, it sits at the top of the football sim family tree as the game that kicked off the genre. And, despite its simplicity, there hasn't been a game since which allows you to seal-dribble the ball into the goal Kerlon-style. Not bad for a 30 year old.

Footballer of the Year
1986

While *International Soccer* was all about playing as a team, in 1986 Gremlin Graphics launched one of the first games that tried to capture the narcissistic thrill of being a professional player: *Footballer of the Year*.

Starting life as a board game, the makers decided to shift it onto the ZX Spectrum and brought the footballer's life to video gamers instead. On the first boot up, you started out as a lowly lad who has £5000 in his pocket and 10 "goal cards" that could be used to turn the tide of the match in your favour. After signing for a lower-league side, your aim is to get to the top of the footballing tree on the pitch and be a commercial hit off it with a number of business sidelines.

Unfortunately, in most senses *Footballer of the Year* was a terrible game. On a fundamental level, the attempt to shoehorn the mechanics of board game into a computer game doomed it to failure. With no effort being made to remove the bizarre card system in favour of a more natural fit for a games platform, reviewers laid mercilessly into it as ill-conceived and disconcertingly random.

Crash magazine gave the game a lowly 54%, lambasting it for being both too easy in the arcade simulation section and lacking depth on a strategic front. Meanwhile, *World of Spectrum* gave *Footballer of the Year* a pitiful one out of five after the reviewer's character earned a measly £75 a week despite banging in 30 goals for Juventus in a single season (though a profitable gambling addiction kept food on his family's table, thankfully).

Despite all that negativity, *Footballer of the Year* has remained an influential game simply because it was one of the first to thrust the player into the shoes of a budding pro. While the execution was flawed, the dream of rising from nobody to footballing hero remains an intoxicating idea that other developers have capitalised on more successfully. A prime example of this was the 2013 Bafta Award winning app *New Star Soccer*, another game which gets you progressing from hero to zero, whose developer Simon Read cited *Footballer of the Year* as a key influence on the development of his game.

So while it may have been a stinker in terms of execution, *Footballer of the Year* laid out the blueprint 27 years ago for a genre of football game that is still going strong today.

Championship Manager
1992

With developers getting gamers playing football as a team or working their way up as a pro, the last area left was the world of football management and the associated challenges that came with creating the football equivalent of the God sim.

As usual, it was 1980s hobbyists who came up with the first stab at a football management sim. The *Football Manager* series created by Kevin Tom for the ZX Spectrum provided the basis of all the sims to follow by giving players spread sheets to analyse, control over team sheets and the ability to make transfers as well as a match engine that meant the player could control little of what was happening on the pitch.

But it was the *Championship Manager* series, which launched in 1992, that transformed the genre from game to, for some players at least, full time occupation. Initially, things got off to a slow start. With established rivals *Premier Manager* and *The Manager* already on the market, *Championship Manager*'s text based match engine, Microsoft Excel gameplay, handful of leagues and fake player names made a limited impression in the broader management sim market.

The driving force behind the game wasn't a desire to make money but a passion for the game that put quality and fun top of the priority list and that proved its salvation. The developers Paul and Oliver Collyer, looking back at the series during an interview with *Eurogamer* in 2001, said that they simply wanted to make something they were proud to play: "We

didn't wake up one morning and think, 'I know, let's make some money out of computer games.' It was more like, 'We like footie, so let's make a game that we'd want to play.' We're just continuing the same philosophy really."

It was that approach which led to the defining feature of the series: tangible yearly updates from the developers that clearly improved the core game play. From purchasing licences to scouting more players and deepening the game-play options, Sports Interactive dedicated their time to slowly and steadily evolving the game. Early updates built on the game engine and tinkered with the idea of playing in foreign leagues (such as in the *calcio*-themed *Championship Manager Italia*) ensuring that the game evolved significantly over the coming years, slowly establishing a growing base of hardcore fans to tap into.

That meant that by 1995 and the launch of the next generation of the game, *Championship Manager 2*, the series had reached a point at which its level of detail, player control and flexibility had the gaming press enraptured by the completeness of its offering. With that success and a strong sales base to mobilise from, Sports Interactive established their series as the best management sim on the market and, like a development version of Sir Alex Ferguson, dedicated themselves to a philosophy of constant evolution to improve the game and drive on to new levels of success.

 Sensible Soccer
1992

Most of the games on this list were dreamt up by developers who had football on the brain and a football game as the clear ending to their thought processes. So it comes as something of a surprise to learn that legendary arcade classic *Sensible Soccer* owes its creation to something outside of the world of football: a strategy game called *Mega Lo Mania*.

Inspired by the game *Civilization*, *Mega Lo Mania* had players battling across various technological epochs. However, after building the game, the team realised that the 2D engine would be perfectly suited to creating a top-down football sim in the style of *Kick Off* and set about making one with the tools they had assembled.

The result was *Sensible Soccer* (or *Sensi* to its adoring fans), an utterly frantic and accessible game. With a single button for shooting, passing and tackling and a control stick to guide your players and the flight of the ball, anybody could get a good game going and, more importantly, add a stupid amount of curve to their shots to bamboozle goalkeepers from 30 yards out.

Under the surface, though, was a game that was well ahead of the time. On a gameplay front, *Sensi* was one of the first football sims to reward passing. With the game played at a lightning pace, circulating the ball accurately from front to back was crucial to actually getting yourself in a decent shooting position. The result of that possession-based approach to the genre, along with an enormous roster of teams and players spanning the world, was the base for one of the most solidly built football sims of the 90s: offering depth and fun in equal measure despite technical limitations.

From 1992 until 1998, Sensible Software released new versions of the game to ensnare newer fans including giving the series a new name to reflect the significant upgrades made to the gameplay. *Sensible World of Soccer* boasted a management sim and career mode, creating a simple hook to drag you further into the arcadey brilliance. Whether you were transforming Cambridge United into Premiership champions or leading Rosenborg to European glory, the management aspect allowed players to turn their skill into unrealistic (but entertainingly won) prizes.

It wasn't to last. As consoles developed rapidly in the 90s, with graphics improving considerably and gameplay options growing for hardcore players, the simplicity of *Sensi* couldn't survive. From 1999 no new top-down Sensible games were released; with the series living on only in arcade form on the Xbox 360 (an unsuccessful 2006 reboot aside).

But, even now, whenever I see a player bury a 40-yard piledriver past a despairing keeper, I like to imagine that somewhere a nine-year-old kid is slamming the control stick to guide the ball into the back of the net.

 International Superstar Soccer 64, 1997

Until now, the games we've looked at have been British interpretations of football. But football is, of course, an international game and that means international variants. So, while British developers ensconced themselves in bedrooms, developers abroad were doing things a little differently.

This included Konami, the Japanese developer behind the *International Superstar Soccer* (*ISS*) series. Originally appearing for the NES in 1991 under the Winning Eleven series name, ISS moved west, first in 1994 for the Super Nintendo, before really entering the western consciousness with the 1997 N64 game, ISS 64.

It made a huge impression because it took serious steps forwards in both graphics and gameplay within football titles. In terms of appearance, ISS's motion-captured character models produced what was, at the time, a startling level of realism. As the internet reviewer Mr N64 said, "There's an astonishing attention to detail in ISS 64. From the ref writing in his notebook as he issues a red card, to the coin toss, to slipping on wet turf during the rain, to the victory dances... It's all extremely detailed."

As for the gameplay, *ISS* was able to leverage the increased graphics powers of the new 64-bit console to offer an experience with greater depth and realism. With the game boasting lob-passes, through-balls and a selection of tricks you could perform to beat your man, *ISS* allowed the player to exploit space more intelligently while moving the ball around the ground and through the air more convincingly.

However, despite all the positives, there were areas where the game betrayed the slight cultural differences between Japanese developers and other parts of the world. The instruction manual and in game options were often baffling, particularly the bit where you could select the number of players per team and eleven was defined as "many".

And the commentary was downright terrible with the announcer yelling and whispering phrases like "Northern Ireland... ARE ON THE SCORESHEET AGAIN" with all the coherence of a badly programmed rail-announcement system.

But the most jarring part of *ISS* was the alternative player names. While many games decided to circumvent licensing issues by going for completely made-up names, *ISS* took the route of slightly misnaming famous players instead. The results were memorably bad with players like Revemalli, Kleimann, Belbiero, Griggs, Laurup and Zaundes (Dean Saunders, in case you missed it) all lining up for your pleasure. While certainly not a deal-breaker, in the age when football really began to grow into a commercially recognisable global offering, the fake names stood out like a sore thumb.

Nonetheless, even with these slight problems, *ISS 64* was the making of the series in the west, with the emphasis on high-quality controls and generally decent presentation making the series a hit. While *ISS 2000* flopped slightly due to its release coming late in the N64 era (as well as featuring a curate's egg of an RPG mode), its initial successor *ISS 98* sold well and paved the way for the excellent *Pro Evolution Soccer* series to arrive on the original Xbox and PS2; a move that turned Konami from international rivals to a dominant development power.

6 Football Manager 2005, 2004–2005

If the Collyer brothers' dedication to quality made them Ferguson-like paragons of renewed excellence, then their split from Eidos in the build-up to the 2004-05 season had all the hallmarks of a classic Fergie falling out.

It all happened two years after their biggest success. *Championship Manager 4*, which was released for the 2002-03 season, became the fastest selling PC game in history as the text engine was finally replaced by a 2D top-down, offering both the most accessible and most detailed version of the game. With the game's scouting network identifying players like Kaká, Wayne Rooney, Wesley Sneijder, Arjen Robben, Rafael Van der Vaart and, err, Lenny Pidgeley as wonderkids, *CM 4* was backed up by a level of research that dripped with authenticity.

But internal tensions between Sports Interactive and Eidos led to conflict between the two former partners within three years. While details of the exact reason behind the falling out remain hazy and shrouded in legal secrecy. SI walked away in February 2004, taking the source code for the game with them. But, with Eidos retaining the name, it meant the SI team were forced to find a new publisher and a new name for the series, leading to the emergence of the *Football Manager* series (unrelated to Kevin Tom's 1980s games) which were published by the newly software-only Sega.

Football Manager won the battle against Eidos's new *Championship Manager* series (created by Beautiful Games Studio) fairly easily when they went toe to toe in 2004-05. While Eidos were forced to start from scratch, the team behind *Football Manager* released another excellently refined management sim featuring a plethora of new features such as managerial mind games, pre-

and post-match summaries and coach reports to help analyse a team's strengths to heighten the brand. So, when the average reviews came in for the new *Championship Manager* title, *Football Manager* 2005 waltzed away with enough sales to become the fifth fastest selling PC game in history, blowing Championship Manager to pieces.

Since then, *Football Manager* has established itself as the leading management sim worldwide. By adding greater depth to managerial communication, adding player roles and duties to give tactics infinite levels of customisation, a 3D-match engine, the development of a scouting network so good it has apparently been used by Everton and mobile versions of the game, *Football Manager* has become so detailed and adaptable that it eats away the hours of millions of players across the world every day.

Fifa 2012
2011-2012

The Fifa franchise may be successful and sport a worldwide fan base, but it certainly hasn't been universally loved due to its commercial partnership with Electronic Arts and, historically, an attachment to production values over balanced gameplay that meant individualism was privileged over teamwork. But from 2006 onwards, the Fifa style changed dramatically. While production values remained at the forefront of EA's mind as, from 2003, they set about creating a "televisual" footballing experience, the arrival of Xbox 360 and PS3 and the increased power on show allowed the development team to switch focus from eking power out of the graphics card towards evolving the gameplay. And the result of these evolutions to the series would eventually make it the most convincing simulation of football ever made.

Even before 2012 a number of changes had been made to give the game more tactical depth. The greater development emphasis on team chemistry from 2006, improved passing accuracy in the 2008 game and better off the ball pressing in 2009 edition slowly transformed the game. From rewarding players who put a big guy at top with tricky wingers to slalom through the defence, Fifa evolved in a way that suited players who wanted to keep possession or build up play.

But this approach reached its peak in *Fifa 2012*, which radically altered the foundations of the football sim in general and the expectations of players by introducing a proper defensive system. Until 2012, football games had tended to lack depth on the defensive side. With the dual 'hard' slide tackling and a 'soft' lighter tackling forming the basis of the game play, you were essentially forced to defend in an 'English' style; pick a defender, employ a thunderous tackle to grab the ball and boot it clear.

What *Fifa 2012* did was to introduce the idea of pressing to computer game defending. With the help of the shoulder buttons and your own intellect, *Fifa 2012* encouraged you to keep your defensive shape and look to nick the ball before attempting either to break or build your own counter. As the possession-based

aspect of gameplay improved with the introduction of 12-way passing (which took advantage of improved control stick technology), any player ignoring those options and sliding in recklessly was likely to be punished as a result of the more incisive passing options available.

The result of this shift was profound. Until that move, Fifa games (as was true of the majority of the genre) tended to be little more than end-to-end affairs with multiple goal scorelines the norm but, after 2012, they produced matches with realistic final scores, which possessed a natural ebb and flow all over the pitch as established styles (from a Barcelona-like pressing and possession style to disciplined counter-attacking approaches) flourished over individualism.

So after Fifa had spent the best part of 20 years trying to create the most realistic football experience they could through the addition of context-driven commentary, flashy graphics and player-controlled celebrations (introduced in *Fifa 2007*), they made more progress in a single edition simply by making defending as a unit an art worth mastering.

 ## Score! Classic Goals 2012

Since the first football games came out, developers have worked to make their games more involving and more complicated. With games like *Fifa*, *Football Manager* and *Pro Evolution Soccer* improving their gameplay, databases and production values, football games have become both higher quality and, at the same time, more difficult for non-gamers because of the myriad buttons needed to play the average sim properly.

But with the arrival of gaming on smartphones and tablets, developers have been forced to design games with simplicity at their core. With apps accessible to billions of players across the world, game studios have had to create experiences that fit with newly dominant and simplistic gesture-driven touch screen interface to ensnare users. And that has meant new types of football games to fit with that reality.

Score! Classic Goals was one of the first to adapt properly to the platform. Rather than being a traditional sim, *Score!* challenges you to recreate classic goals in history by accurately drawing with your finger the path of the ball into the back of the net. Crucially, each goal only takes about 30 seconds to complete. So whether you're recreating Gascoigne in 1996 or Van Basten in 1988, on completion you're awarded up to three stars and rapidly moved on to the next goal.

The result was a brisk window into football's back catalogue. By reversing the trend for complexity and difficulty in most modern games, *Score!* tapped into the new mobile market by reinventing the football game as a puzzle accessible to the casual gaming audience. While retaining a hardcore commitment to football more broadly by offering an experience rooted in the history of the game, *Score!* opened the genre up to a mass market that would not necessarily have come to a hardcore game like *Fifa*.

And that is forcing developers to confront a new reality: that they have to make their games appeal to a newly broadened audience. Already, *Football Manager 2013* has embedded a Classic Mode into the game to accommodate players who can't make the game a full-time job. So in the coming years more developers, particularly those working in mobile formats, will have to come up with innovative new types of games that are accessible not just to hardened football gamers but to football fans in general.

Contributors

The Blizzard, Issue Ten

Tom Adams is deputy managing editor of the Yahoo!-Eurosport site. He has previously written on football for ESPN,Sky Sports and Setanta's online presences. His father, who contributed vital research to the piece, is retired. **Twitter: @tomEurosport**

Philippe Auclair is the author of *The Enchanted Kingdom of Tony Blair* (in French) and *Cantona: the Rebel Who Would Be King*, which was named NSC Football Book of the Year. His biography of Thierry Henry has just been published. He writes for *France Football* and *Offside* and provides analysis and commentary for RMC Sport. **Twitter: @PhilippeAuclair**

Andy Brassell writes and broadcasts for the BBC, the Independent, ESPN, Four Four Two and Talksport among others. He is the author of *All Or Nothing; A Season In The Life Of The Champions League* and was the European correspondent on BBC FiveLive's *World Football Phone-In* for seven years.

Mike Calvin, chief sportswriter of the *Independent on Sunday*, has twice been named Sports Reporter of the Year and has also won the Sportswriter of the Year award. He contributes to BT Sport and Talksport. His book, *Family: Life Death and Football*, a season spent behind the scenes at Millwall was shortlisted at the British Sports Book Awards in 2011. His latest book is *The Nowhere Men*. **Twitter: @CalvinBook**

Anthony Clavane is the author of *Promised Land: A Northern Love Story*, which won Football Book of the Year and Sports Book of the Year at the 2011 British Sports Book Awards. His second book, *Does Your Rabbi Know You're Here?* was shortlisted for Football Book of the Year at this year's awards. He writes about sport for the *Sunday Mirror*. **Twitter: @lufcpromised**

Miguel Delaney is an Irish-Spanish football journalist based in London, who writes for ESPN, the *Irish Examiner* and the *Independent*. He is the author of a history of the Irish national team called 'Stuttgart to Saipan', which was released in 2010, and in 2011 was nominated for Irish sports journalist of the year.

Dan Edwards has been based in Argentina since 2009 and is the South American Editor for *Goal.com*. he is a contributor of *Hand of Pod*, a podcast on Argentinian football. **Twitter: @DanEdwardsGoal**

Richard Fitzpatrick is the author of *El Clásico: Barcelona v Real Madrid, Football's Greatest Rivalry*, which is published by Bloomsbury.

Rupert Fryer is a freelance journalist and co-founder of SouthAmericanFootball.co.uk. He has written on South American football for the likes of *Fox Sports*, the *Guardian*, the *Observer* and *Sport360*. **Twitter: @Rupert_Fryer**

Aleksandar Hemon is a Bosnian-American writer and novelist. His novel, *The Lazarus Project* was a finalist for the National Book Award and the National Book Critics Circle Awards. His most recent book is a work of non-fiction, *The Book of My Lives*. **Twitter: @SashaHemon**

Aleksandar Holiga is an independent football writer. He maintains a

column for Tportal in Croatia and has contributed to the *Guardian*, the *Herald*, *FourFourTwo*, *11 Freunde* and *When Saturday Comes* among others.
Twitter: @AlexHoliga

Simon Kuper is author of *Football Against the Enemy*, a winner of the William Hill Sports Book of the Year, and *Ajax, The Dutch, The War*. His latest book, *The Football Men*, was published by Simon & Schuster in May 2011. He is a columnist with the *Financial Times*. A new expanded edition of *Soccernomics* was published last summer.

Jonathan Liew writes about sport for the Daily Telegraph and is a former Young Sportswriter of the Year.
Twitter: @jonathanliew

Felix Lill is a German freelance journalist who last September moved from London to Tokyo, where he now works as an author for *Die Zeit*, *Die Presse*, *Der Spiegel*, *NeueZürcherZeitung*, *Tagesspiegel*, *Zeit Online* and others. He was awarded the Austrian Sports Journalism Award in 2010, 2011 and 2012. He was awarded the Austrian OEZIV Media Prize 2012.

Vladimir Novak is a freelance journalist based in Belgrade. He writes for *World Soccer*, *Titan Sports* (China) and *World Soccer Digest* (Japan).

Colin O'Brien is a freelance journalist based in Rome, Italy. He covers Italian football and cycling for several publications worldwide.
Twitter: @ ColliOBrien

George Osborn is a freelance tech journalist and app marketer who presents

The App Show podcast. He is interested in the increasing cross over between football and technology and tweets.
Twitter: @GeorgeOsborn

Michal Petrák is a chief reporter of iSport TV who has previously written for Sport, a Czech sports daily, and *Hattrick*, a football monthly.
Twitter: @michalpetrak

Nicolas Poppe is Assistant Professor of Spanish at Ball State University. His work on Latin American cultural studies has appeared in several books and peer-reviewed journals such as the *Arizona Journal of Hispanic Cultural Studies*, the *Journal of Cultural Geography* and the *Journal of Latin American Cultural Studies*. **Twitter: @nicpoppe**

Javier Sauras is a Spanish journalist and photographer based in London.

Rory Smith writes about football for *The Times*, as long as someone with a foreign-sounding name is in the news. He ghosted Rafael Benitez's first memoir, *Champions League Dreams*, and moved some commas around on *The Numbers Game*.

Henryk Szadziewski is a researcher and writer based in Washington, DC, who has published extensively on human rights in China. His work about football takes a look at cultural identity and he is currently researching supporters groups in the United States. **Twitter: @putbolchi**

Jonathan Wilson is the author of *Inverting the Pyramid*. He writes for the *Guardian*,the *National*, *World Soccer*, *Foxasia* and *Sports Illustrated*.
Twitter: @jonawils

Blizzard Subscriptions

Subscribe to the print version of The Blizzard, *be the first to receive new issues, get exclusive Blizzard offers and access digital versions of all back-issues FREE*

Subscription Options

Set Price for Four Issues

Get a four-issue subscription to *The Blizzard* — for you or as a gift — for a flat fee including postage and packing (P&P):

UK:	£35
Europe:	£45
Non-Euorpe:	£55

Recurring Pay-What-You-Like

Set up a quartely recurring payment for each edition of *The Blizzard*. The recommended retail price (RRP) is £12, but pay what you like, subject to a minimum fee of £6 plus P&P

See www.theblizzard.co.uk for more

Digital Subscriptions

If the cost of postage is prohibitive, or you just want an excuse to use your new iPad or Kindle, you can set up a subscription to digital versions of *The Blizzard* for just £3 per issue.

See www.theblizzard.co.uk for more

Information for Existing Subscribers

Free Digital Downloads for *Blizzard* Subscribers

Whether you have taken advantage of our set price or pay-what-you-like offer, for the duration of your subscription to *The Blizzard* you are entitled to download every issue FREE.

See www.theblizzard.co.uk for more

We very much value the commitment of our print subscribers and have a policy to make available new issues, special offers and other limited access events and benefits to print subscribers first.

About *The Blizzard*

Distribution & Back Issues
Contact Information
About Issue Ten

Buy *The Blizzard*

We want as many readers as possible for *The Blizzard*. We therefore operate as far as we are able on a pay-what-you-like basis for digital and print versions.

Digital Version (Current & Back Issues)

All issues of *The Blizzard* are available to download for Kindle, Android, iOS and PC/Mac at: *www.theblizzard.co.uk*.

- *RRP: £3*
- *Pay-what-you-like minimum: £0.01*

Printed Version (Current & Back Issues)

Purchase a physical copy of *The Blizzard* in all its luxurious, tactile, sensual glory at: *www.theblizzard.co.uk*. If you haven't felt our rough textured cover-varnish and smelled the inner genius, you haven't properly experienced its awesome true form. Read it, or leave it on your coffee table to wow visitors.

- *RRP: £12 (+P&P)*
- *Pay-what-you-like min: £6 (+P&P)*

Contact *The Blizzard*

All advertising, sales, press and business communication should be addressed to the Central Publishing Office:

The Blizzard
Ashmore Villa,
1, Ashmore Terrace,
Stockton Road,
Sunderland,
SR27DE

Email: info@theblizzard.co.uk
Telephone: +44 (0) 191 543 8785
Website: www.theblizzard.co.uk
Facebook: www.facebook.com/blzzrd
Twitter: @blzzrd

About Issue Ten

Editor Jonathan Wilson
Publisher The Blizzard Media Ltd
www.theblizzard.co.uk
Design Azure
www.azure-design.com

Copyright

All content is ©Copyright The Blizzard Media Ltd and may not be reproduced without explicit consent. Thanks to Jeanette G Sturis at the Kingsley Motel, Manjimup, for kind use of Warren Walker's original sketches of Dog.

CLASSIC F⚽️OTBALL SHIRTS.CO.UK

THE MOST EXTENSIVE RANGE OF ORIGINAL SHIRTS ONLINE
HUGE CLEARANCE SECTION FULL OF 1000's OF BARGAIN ITEMS

GETAFE	FC YOUNG BOYS	LYON TECHFIT	MARSEILLE TECHFIT	VALENCIA
£11.99	£19.99	£34.99	£22.99	£19.99

STOKE CROUCH   **NAPOLI CAVANI**   **NAPOLI HAMSIK**
£29.99   £49.99   £44.99   **SHORTS, SOCKS, BAGS, JACKETS ETC**